IDEOLOGY AND THE HISTORIANS

IDEOLOGY
AND THE
HISTORIANS

Edited by
CIARAN BRADY

HISTORICAL STUDIES XVII

Papers read before the Irish Conference of Historians,
held at Trinity College, Dublin
8-10 June 1989

Ivan Berend
Aidan Clarke
Stefan Collini
Bernadette Cunningham
David Fitzpatrick
Luke Gibbons
Ian Green
John Lukacs
W.J. Mc Cormack
Eamon O'Flaherty
Dorinda Outram
Bertram Wyatt-Brown

THE LILLIPUT PRESS
1991

First published in 1991 by
THE LILLIPUT PRESS LTD
4 Rosemount Terrace, Arbour Hill,
Dublin 7, Ireland

A CIP record for this
title is available from
The British Library.

ISBN 0 946640 72 6

Jacket design by Jarlath Hayes
Set in 11 on 12 Elegant Garamond by
Phototype-Set of Drumcondra
and printed in Dublin by
Colour Books of Baldoyle

CONTENTS

Preface vii

Previous Volumes in the Series viii

Contributors ix

Introduction 1

Part One

ONE The Culture and Ideology of Irish Franciscan Historians at Louvain 1607-1650
Bernadette Cunningham 11

TWO The Theatre of Diversity: Historical Criticism and Religious Controversy in Seventeenth-Century France
Eamon O'Flaherty 31

THREE Honour and American Republicanism: A Neglected Corollary
Bertram Wyatt-Brown 49

FOUR 'Rousseau's Stutter': The French Revolution, Philosophy and the History of the Future
Dorinda Outram 66

FIVE The Tedium of History: An Approach to Maria Edgeworth's *Patronage* (1814)
W.J. Mc Cormack 77

SIX 'A Shadowy Narrator': History, Art and Romantic Nationalism in Ireland 1750-1850
Luke Gibbons 99

SEVEN Genealogies of Englishness: Literary History and Cultural Criticism in Modern Britain
Stefan Collini 128

EIGHT 'Repulsives vs Wromantics': Rival Views of the English Civil War
Ian Green 146

NINE The Futility of History: A Failed Experiment in Irish Education
David Fitzpatrick 168

Part Two

TEN History as a Scholarly Discipline and *Magistra Vitae*
Ivan Berend 187

ELEVEN Polite Letters and Clio's Fashions
John Lukacs 199

TWELVE A Commentary on John Lukacs's 'Polite Letters'
Aidan Clarke 211

Notes 221

Index 265

PREFACE

The Irish Committee of Historical Sciences inaugurated a series of biennial conferences of historians in 1953, and since 1955 papers presented to each one have been published under the title or subtitle *Historical Studies*. Since 1975 the conferences have been organized around a single theme, and that held in Trinity College, Dublin on 8-10 June 1989 maintained the practice. The Irish Committee of Historical Sciences expresses its gratitude to Trinity College for its generous provision of services and facilities. As conference organizer and editor of its proceedings, I have incurred a great many debts to individuals and institutions which I can acknowledge only briefly here. I thank the President and members of the Royal Irish Academy for permitting one of the papers to be delivered jointly as an Academy Discourse, and meeting the expenses of the speaker, and for the hospitality extended to the conference members on that occasion. I wish to acknowledge also the generous support given towards the costs of the conference by the United States Information Services, The British Council and the Hungarian Academy of Sciences; towards the costs of publication by the Faculty of Arts (Humanities) and the Grace Lawless Lee Benefaction Fund of Trinity College, Dublin; and towards the costs of illustrations by Dublin City University. Among the squads of individuals whose talents, tolerance and generosity I have been compelled to exploit, I should like in particular to thank Aidan Clarke, Peter Connell, Aidan Duggan, Eddie Hyland, Joseph Holt, Keith Jefferey, Joe Johnson, Vivien Jenkins, Patrick Kelly, Colm Lennon, Brid McGrath, Helen McGrail, Alice Tunney and Trevor West, and, *en masse*, the editorial committee of The Lilliput Press. Above all I am happy to express my indebtedness to the contributors to this volume, who have borne patiently, if not always silently, with the waywardness of the editor.

C.B.

PREVIOUS VOLUMES IN THE SERIES

T.D. Williams (ed.), *Historical Studies I* (London: Bowes and Bowes 1958)

M. Roberts (ed.), *Historical Studies II* (London: Bowes and Bowes 1959)

J. Hogan (ed.), *Historical Studies III* (London: Bowes and Bowes 1961)

G.A. Hayes-McCoy (ed.), *Historical Studies IV* (London: Bowes and Bowes 1963)

J.L. McCracken (ed.), *Historical Studies V* (London: Bowes and Bowes 1965)

T.W. Moody (ed.), *Historical Studies VI* (London: Routledge & Kegan Paul 1968)

J.C. Beckett (ed.), *Historical Studies VII* (London: Routledge & Kegan Paul 1969)

T.D. Williams (ed.), *Historical Studies VIII* (Dublin: Gill & Macmillan 1971)

J.G. Barry (ed.), *Historical Studies IX* (Belfast: Blackstaff Press 1974)

G.A. Hayes-McCoy (ed.), *Historical Studies X* (Dublin: ICHS 1976)

T.W. Moody (ed.), *Nationality and the Pursuit of National Independence*: *Historical Studies XI* (Belfast: Appletree Press 1978)

A.C. Hepburn (ed.), *Minorities in History*: *Historical Studies XII* (London: Edward Arnold 1978)

D.W. Harkness & M. O'Dowd (eds), *The Town in Ireland*: *Historical Studies XIII* (Belfast: Appletree Press 1981)

J.I. McGuire & A. Cosgrove (eds), *Parliament and Community*: *Historical Studies XIV* (Belfast: Appletree Press 1985)

P.J. Corish (ed.), *Radicals, Rebels and Establishments*: *Historical Studies XV* (Belfast: Appletree Press 1985)

Tom Dunne (ed.), *The Writer as Witness: Literature as Historical Evidence*: *Historical Studies XVI* (Cork: Cork University Press 1987)

CONTRIBUTORS

Ivan Berend, President, Hungarian Academy of Sciences 1985-9

Ciaran Brady, Lecturer in Modern History, Trinity College, Dublin

Aidan Clarke, Professor of Modern History, Trinity College, Dublin

Stefan Collini, University Lecturer in English, Cambridge University

Bernadette Cunningham, Librarian, Dublin Diocesan Library

David Fitzpatrick, Lecturer in Modern History, Trinity College, Dublin

Luke Gibbons, Lecturer in Communications, Dublin City University

Ian Green, Senior Lecturer in History, Queen's University, Belfast

John Lukacs, Professor of History, Chestnut Hill, Pennsylvania

W.J. Mc Cormack, free-lance author

Eamon O'Flaherty, Lecturer in Modern History, University College, Dublin

Dorinda Outram, Lecturer in History, University College, Cork

Bertram Wyatt-Brown, Richard J. Milbauer, Professor of History, University of Florida

INTRODUCTION

This collection of essays attempts to pursue, specifically in regard to the composition of history, some of the themes raised in the previous volume in this series.[1] In *The Writer as Witness* several contributors drew attention to the inadequate manner in which literary texts had been interpreted and used by historians in the past, and offered some alternative methods, suggested by developments in literary history and theory, by which these texts might be brought to perform a different or greater role in the explanation of historical change. It seemed appropriate, therefore, to inquire to what extent these perspectives might throw light on the question as to how history itself, either as a written text or as memory, symbol or myth, functioned as an ideological force underlying the social process.

The following papers are in their different ways all concerned with the degree to which the re-creation of the past as history – in written and other forms – has served, either deliberately or inadvertently, ideological purposes, and with the problem which this inevitable permeation of their work by known or implicit ideological influence presents to historians. Together their discussions raise a critical epistemological issue concerning the historian's claims to any form of objectivity – even of a purely methodological kind – and concerning indeed the intellectual status of the discipline as a whole. It cannot be contended that such major problems have been resolved in the pages below, or even that the issue has been identified or addressed in the same way by all of the contributors. But sufficient has been done to bring to light one pressing if awkward question: to what extent have the considerable advances made by historians, in their understanding of the complex ways in which the surviving sources of the past have been shaped and infused by hidden ideological influence, made necessary a fundamental re-examination of the assumptions underlying the very discipline within which these advances were made?

The multiple ways in which the representation of the past has been influenced by contemporary ideological forces is the subject of the series of case studies presented in Part One. At the beginning Bernadette Cunningham's investigation of the grand historical project undertaken by the Irish Franciscans at Louvain provides an instance of a relatively straightforward attempt to provide a contemporary ideological framework for the evidence of the ancient past which their researches had uncovered. The concept of the kingdom of Ireland which they employed was profoundly ambiguous. Yet, as Cunningham shows, it served a variety of functions both in relation to Ireland and to the larger world of Counter-Reformation politics which were more than enough to compensate for evidential discrepancy and internal contradiction.

The persistent desire to reshape our past in the interest of ideological convenience is further evidenced in David Fitzpatrick's ironic review of what he sees as the futile attempts of nineteenth- and early-twentieth-century educationalists to enforce rival versions of Irish history in school text-books. But this compulsion is by no means exclusively Irish. Stefan Collini's uncovering of a deep, self-congratulatory nationalism not only in English accounts of literary history, but in their very formulation of the central concepts around which such accounts were organized, reveals just how pervasive the impulse is. And in a similar fashion Ian Green's survey of a subject that has become a literary sub-culture in itself – the historiography of the English Civil War – details the degree to which shifting interpretations can be related to the changing ideological preoccupations of twentieth-century Britain.

Green's discussion also suggests an important question concerning the extent to which such influences were responsible for the initiation and development of new methods of research and analysis. His conclusions in this regard are tentative: he is inclined to the view that contemporary debates are at best responsible for forcing the pace of methodological innovations which would have occurred in a slower or slightly different manner in other circumstances. But the issue is more directly confronted in Eamon O'Flaherty's analysis of the dispute between Pierre Bayle and Père Maimbourg over the history of Calvinism. It was, O'Flaherty argues, Bayle's primary concern with the defence of religious toleration that compelled him to develop, in his critique of Maimbourg's methods, an early statement of the ground rules of historical methodology which are still at the core of the discipline.

O'Flaherty's argument will prompt some reflection on what may be seen in effect as the polemical origins of the historian's pretensions to an objective methodology. But more importantly, it points up a contrast between the understanding of the purpose and method of historical writing which most trained historians share, and an older, less critical view of history's relations to the past which is widely if silently adopted by those who have never written history. It is this unformulated but deeply rooted idea of history that informs Bertram Wyatt-Brown's critique of what is now the orthodox view of the role of ideology in the American Revolution. The views of early-eighteenth-century English political thinkers, for all their emphasis upon the supreme importance of cultivating republican civic virtue, could never have fuelled the massive force of outrage and moral indignation which powered the upsurge of revolution. It was rather the under-articulated but intrinsic sense of the individual's hereditary honour that supplied the energy behind violent collective action. Virtue, after all, was merely something to which one might aspire; honour was parcel of an individual's inheritance to be defended at all costs.

The importance of coming to terms with such implicit but deeply ingrained impulses in human conduct is also stressed in Dorinda Outram's critique of older Marxist and more recent anti-Marxist interpretations of the French Revolution. Because of their polemical engagement, both sides have failed to address a crucial alteration in human perception and conduct which, though not so readily apparent, can still be uncovered from the political, social and intellectual sources which they have used. This alteration in the perception of the body politic and of the individual's relation to action in the public domain was a central consequence of the Revolution to which these rival but equally neglectful schools are themselves the heirs.

Outram's call for a more critical investigation of such significant absences in the historical record, for the recovery of what has been repressed not by the accidents of the past but by the selectivity of history itself, is taken up by Luke Gibbons. In his strikingly original examination of the work of the painter James Barry, Gibbons demonstrates how a theoretically difficult but ideologically crucial fusion between Enlightenment republicanism and the romantic nationalism of nineteenth-century Ireland was achieved, not by abstract argument, but by the multi-layered symbolism permitted by Barry's exploitation of the genre of history painting. By such means a critical disjunction in Irish political development was transcended, and a tradition of resistance saved from incipient dissolution.

A related problem – the apparent gap between the progressive internationalism of Enlightenment republicanism and the brutal repression and religious sectarianism to which it gave place – is explored in W. J. Mc Cormack's analysis of some of the writings of Maria Edgeworth. Though the traumas of Ireland in the 1790s do not feature in Edgeworth's fictions, they are, Mc Cormack shows, repeatedly suggested by implication, and their recurrent appearance and disappearance in this manner is the author's way of registering their status as the unresolved problematic of her time.

The recovery of those repressed experiences which lie deep in 'the political unconscious' poses a methodological challenge to the historian which many of the papers here have attempted to meet. Collini's exhilarating exercise in counter-factual history provides an entertaining way of exploding unstated preconceptions. Gibbons's use of the techniques of art-criticism and art-history offers an important means of supplementing and compensating for the limitations of the historian's written sources. And Mc Cormack's deployment of critical theory to develop such useful analytic concepts as 'the place of interpretation' (which uses one stated location to elicit an opposite and ominously absent one) enables us to peer beneath the surface of a literary text to discover creative forces that were buried even at the point of its composition. Yet the implications of such innovative ways of interpreting the ideological function of history in the past for the analysis of what historians themselves do today have yet to be fully considered: and the task seems from the outset to be fraught with difficulty.

Certainly the three historians in Part Two, who have written on the relationship of their own work to external or inherited ideological influence, remain unperturbed by any epistemological doubts affecting their craft. In this, though they differ in much else, they are each firmly representative of the vast majority of practising historians. In his wide-ranging survey of the development of European historiography over the past three centuries, Ivan Berend confronts the arguments raised by sceptics and relativists against the historians' claims to have established a progressive and socially useful branch of knowledge, but rests his case on an undeniable record of experience rather than on any theoretical principle.

Though there have been biases, errors and misconceptions aplenty, the discipline, Berend affirms, has produced a vast body of knowledge and an increasingly sophisticated set of tools for manipulating it which has been of inestimable importance for the improvement of society.

John Lukacs also has no doubts about the social utility of history, yet for him it lies in an area far removed from that of his compatriot. Dismissing as fatuous the ambitions of the *Annales* school and all attempts to provide a comprehensive, objective account of major movements in the past, he contends that history, not as it is conventionally understood, but more generally 'as a form of thought', is best placed in our times to provide a critical understanding of the complex social and ideological forces that have overtaken us. In reply, Aidan Clarke is as sceptical of the idea of 'total history' as he is of Lukacs's contention that history can provide a general hermeneutic for understanding the modern world. Instead he advances a position that is at once modest and assured in its claim that history enjoys rules for the recovery, assessment and presentation of evidence which are sufficiently objective and coherent to withstand all challenges to its integrity as a form of knowledge.

Such unresolved differences about the value and purpose of history are as familiar to historians as they are unsettling to outsiders. For historians, as Clarke observes, have been notoriously dismissive of philosophies of history. Full-dress philosophical analyses of historical procedures such as those of Maurice Mandelbaum, William Walsh or Arthur Danto have exerted very little influence over the work of historians;[2] and when a trained historian like David Hackett Fischer attempted to apply some logico-philosophical techniques to the reasoning of his fellows, the reception which his work received was cool.[3] Confronted with some theoretical contradiction in their practices, they have been happy to ignore it or to resort either with embarrassment or with enthusiasm to the tough-minded pragmatism of Geoffrey Elton and Jack Hexter and their no-nonsense defence of the business of 'doing history'.[4]

Though it is doubtless due in part to some ugly empirical reflex in the historian's cast of mind, the reasons for this suspicion of theory lie deeper. The typical *modus operandi* of analytical philosophers, their pursuit of logical structures, of chains of causation, and their attempt to reduce historical discourse to discrete propositions, even to simple sentences, has never succeeded in producing, for historians at least, an adequate account of the way in which history is conceived and written. Unlike Monsieur Jourdain, historians know they are speaking prose, and they know it is not the prose which philosophers have prescribed for them.

On the other hand, historians have remained equally cautious of the alternative tradition of historical philosophy. However awe-inspiring Hegel's conception of world-history might have been, little guidance could be found concerning the significance of specific historical enquiry from a philosopher for whom any instance of the dialectical adventures of Mind would have served his metaphysical purposes as well as any other. Such relativism has reached its most extreme position in the deconstructionists' claim that historians' pretensions to recount the past in any more than a wholly fictive manner is both impossible and ideologically repressive.[5] Arguments of this kind have proved quite naturally unacceptable to working historians, who continue to believe that, whatever their epistemological muddles, something 'real' has intruded upon their imaginations, that events actually occurred in the past for which there is palpable, if all too fragmentary, evidence extant.

It is no accident then that Marxism, which has taken the historian's materialist point of departure as a fundamental principle, has proved to be the only complete philosophical system to which some historians have been willing to subscribe as a guiding influence. But outside of those countries in which it has been perverted into a doctrine of state, the historian's commitment to Marxism has generally been critical and conditional. And while for many it provided a key methodology for understanding the dynamics of change, for uncovering lost or repressed social processes, or for exploding ideological legitimations, few would cite Marx or any Marxist theoretician as having provided a definitive account of any particular historical event or theme.

This gap between the theoretical prescriptions of dominant traditions in western philosophy and the practical experience of working historians has led so many of them to discount theory and to content themselves with what Hayden White has termed (a little contemptuously) 'the *doxa*' of the profession as laid down by men like Elton and Hexter.[6] In so far as it has equipped them to get on with their doings, such practical formulations have proffered a powerful riposte to the disabling qualms of fastidious theorists. But though it has worked well enough over the past century or so, such a working consensus on the aims and practices of history was never wholly consolidated and it is now in many areas under serious threat.

There is much that historians continue to agree upon as a matter of convention. But where it has arisen, historical dispute has proven to be in large measure inconclusive.[7] Historical writing is always conducted by means of synecdoche, in the sense that one set of details is selected from the mass of evidence to represent the whole of the phenomenon described. But because such a selection can never be replicated, and because one synecdoche cannot refute another, historical argument can never be 'falsified' in scientific terms. Thus, with the exception of those instances where historians have been shown to have misconstrued, misdated or faked their evidence, historical controversies have generally displayed strikingly closed formal patterns. The arguments advanced have been exclusive – of the 'if I were he I wouldn't have started from there' variety – and, as Ian Green's survey of English Civil War debates shows, highly circular, as old orthodoxies are debunked and rehabilitated again in a more modern guise. In regard also to their content, arguments have displayed a similar tendency toward closure, as differences in interpreting the evidence are ultimately reduced to untestable, rival assertions: matters of temperament in Green's case-study, or in more heated exchanges with which we in Ireland have become all too familiar, charges of lack of professionalism, partisan bias, lack of imagination, lack of empathy.[8]

At best such sterile wranglings are wasteful of time, intellectual energy and resources that could well be used more profitably elsewhere. More seriously, the perception of the discipline as merely another form of public debate has persuaded many undergraduates to the view that all that is required to do well in the subject is 'simply to have a good argument', and confirmed cynical non-historians in the belief that, like shady lawyers and politicians, historians will always find the evidence that suits their case. With such corrosive anti-intellectualism abroad, the failure of academic history to alter ideas of the past in the primary and secondary schools which David Fitzpatrick has recounted may yet await the discipline as a whole. But most seriously of all the inability of the discipline to find the conceptual tools appropriate not for the resolution, but for the analysis, refinement and better comprehension of such disputes is now threatening the very integrity of the craft, as in many areas it becomes fragmented into warring ideological and methodological camps between whom dialogue has become increasingly impossible.[9]

This makes more pressing than ever Tom Dunne's call for the appropriation of the work of those philosophers and critics, like Paul Ricoeur and Hayden White, who have at once accepted the ideologically infused nature of historical composition and yet striven to supply a defence of its operations as a distinct and coherent body of knowledge.[10] Historians will remain troubled by Ricoeur's abstraction, and by the difficulty of applying his conceptual categories to the routines of their practice. They will baulk at some of Hayden White's more extreme – and clearly polemical – *dicta* concerning the essential unity of history writing and fiction.[11] And they may question the relevance of his critique of a distinctively nineteenth-century style of historiography to their own work.[12] But such thinkers have offered a set of strategies for the analysis of historical thought and writing which transcends the convenient yet increasingly untenable distinction between the business of research and the art of writing it up to which historians have for long resorted, and goes beyond Hexter's slightly more advanced but unformulated injunction that we should pay more attention to 'the rhetoric of history'.[13] The recognition of the essentially allegorical nature of historical discourse, the formal analysis of the tropes which historians use to develop their allegories and of the plots which they employ to sustain them, will not end historiographical debate. For historians will continue to assert that their plots, and the modes in which they are expounded, have reference to some external phenomenon of the past which can privilege one account of its occurrence over another. But in place of untestable or simply abusive allegations of error, such recognition will provide a more objective means of comprehending the nature of each historian's engagement, of assessing the internal integrity of each account, and of measuring the distance between one historian's perspective and another's. It may thereby extend an understanding of ourselves and of others – which was, after all, the whole point of the enterprise in the first place.

CIARAN BRADY,
Trinity College, Dublin

Part One

ONE

THE CULTURE AND IDEOLOGY OF IRISH FRANCISCAN HISTORIANS AT LOUVAIN 1607-1650

Bernadette Cunningham

I

The use of history as a political tool was commonplace in early modern Europe. Ecclesiastical history, in particular, had a special significance in the age of the Reformation and the Counter Reformation as Catholics and Protestants presented claim and counter-claim for the historical justification of current theological and political positions. In Ireland, James Ussher, Church of Ireland archbishop of Armagh, was leading the way by claiming that the Irish Church in the early days of Christianity had been independent of Roman influences and was thus free from corruption. His *Discourse of the Religion Anciently Professed by the British and Irish*, published in 1631, argued that the religion of the Irish, like that of the British, differed substantially from that of the corrupt Roman Church.[1] A further study of the Irish Church from the sixth to the twelfth century illlustrated the flourishing nature of Irish Christianity in those centuries when it was independent of Rome – his version of the island of saints and scholars.[2] The twelfth-century reform of the Irish Church was presented by Ussher as the beginning of Roman corruption, a trend which needed to be counteracted. In this way, the Reformation policies implemented under Henry VIII and Elizabeth I were legitimized in terms acceptable to the state Church. It was difficult for Ussher, a man with an Old English cultural background, to explain exactly how the coming of the Normans, his own ancestors, had been beneficial, while simultaneously arguing that the corruption of the Church stemmed from this time. And it is little wonder that Ussher did not pursue his argument beyond the twelfth century in any detail.[3]

The version of events proposed by historians emanating from the Irish Counter-Reformation tradition was rather different. The Catholic view was illustrated by the writings of secular clergy including Peter Lombard in *De Regno Hiberniae Sanctorum Insula Commentarius*, and Geoffrey Keating in *Foras Feasa ar Éirinn*. Most comprehensive was the research and writing embarked on by Irish Franciscans in Paris, Rome, and especially in Louvain. The Old English and Gaelic Irish Catholics had slightly different views of the history of the Irish Church. Lombard, with an eye to impressing the pope, for whom his work was intended, stressed the Roman element of the twelfth-century reform spearheaded by St Malachy. He claimed that Malachy had prophesied the pontificate of Clement VIII during which the darkness of heresy and schism, which had oppressed Ireland at the hands of English governors for sixty years, would at last be dispelled.[4] Lombard wrote polemic and not scholarly history, and a more appropriate comparison with the writings of Ussher is Geoffrey Keating's major historical work, the *Foras Feasa ar Éirinn*.[5] Written by an Old English continentally educated secular priest, this presented a view of Irish ecclesiastical history acceptable to Old English Catholics in the 1630s. Like Ussher, an Old English Protestant, Keating, an Old English Catholic, ended his history with the Normans. Keating's portrayal of the Old Irish before the coming of the Normans as a civilized, Christian people was a fundamental element of his argument that the Irish Church had never deviated from the true faith.

Keating presented the twelfth-century reform as the key element in remodelling the Church in Ireland. The diocesan hierarchical structure, based on the archdioceses of Armagh, Dublin, Cashel and Tuam, ratified by the Synod of Kells in 1152, was emphasized, thereby giving historical sanction to the parochial and diocesan structure favoured by the secular clergy in the seventeenth century. This was more a blueprint than an actual structure in the twelfth century, and was still a matter of major controversy in the 1630s. Implicit in Keating's version was the view that the twelfth-century

Church had not subsequently become corrupt, but that its structures had survived intact down to his own day. This argument, and indeed the entire *Foras Feasa ar Éirinn*, had the dual objective of supporting the position of the secular clergy, and of fitting the Old English Catholic group into a new Counter-Reformation version of the history of Ireland.[6]

In the mid-1640s a Louvain-based Irish Franciscan, John Colgan, sketched the outline of a third version of Irish ecclesiastical history, beginning with Patrick, from the native Irish point of view. There had been, he asserted, 'four hundred good years when the holy island of Ireland had flourished in piety and literary studies, both sacred and secular'. Then followed a period of two hundred years when Ireland suffered the incursions of the Danes and Norsemen with consequent civil discord and disruption to the Roman Catholic Church. However, Colgan argued, by the zeal of saints Celsius, Malachy and Lawrence, holiness was restored in the twelfth century, and the practices of the Church improved. There is no mention in Colgan's version of the diocesan reorganization of the Church which accompanied the twelfth-century reform. This Franciscan interpretation concentrated instead on spiritual reform. Colgan continued his summary account by relating that, at the time of the Anglican schism, heresy prevailing in England meant that all study was prohibited in Ireland. The heretical administrators were responsible for the destruction of the possessions of monasteries and sacred antiquities and the appointment of heretical bishops and pastors. But again, as after previous disruption, Colgan recorded that due to the efforts of holy men some of the sacred antiquities were saved, and these were the sources Colgan was using for his lives of the saints.[7]

Colgan's neat summary of Irish ecclesiastical history, both in what it omitted and in what it mentioned, was the essence of the ideological underpinning of the Counter-Reformation mission embarked on by the Irish Franciscans. Using a line of argument not available to Irish writers of Anglo-Norman descent, past imperfections were accounted for as resulting from external influences which were ironed out by the efforts of saints. The Henrician and Elizabethan Reformation was presented as having temporarily disrupted this idyllic island of saints and scholars but, he continued, even despite the war of the 1640s on behalf of the faith, the continuity of learning and scholarship was being promoted from Belgium, using sources rescued from destruction. Not only had Ireland been an island of saints and scholars in the past, there was an unbroken continuity with the early holy men of the Irish Church, disrupted, but not destroyed, by external events in the middle ages and again in the sixteenth century.

Colgan's version of the Irish past was published as a preface to the first of a projected multi-volume work entitled *Acta Sanctorum Hiberniae* in 1645. The publication of this, together with a second large folio volume on the three 'national' saints, Patrick, Brigid and Columcille, which appeared in 1647, was the high point of a programme of scholarship initiated some twenty or thirty years earlier by Hugh Ward and his compatriots at the College of St Anthony at Louvain.[8] The research relating to Ireland which was undertaken by the Louvain Franciscans commenced with researches in continental libraries for material on the lives of Irish saints, particularly those who had worked in Europe in the middle ages. The historians soon realized that much of the source material for the projected history of Ireland was still dispersed in various parts of Ireland, and so they despatched scholars to collect and transcribe what original material could be found on the history of Ireland and its saints. Contact was made with the hereditary families of historians in Ireland and with other scholars who could assist.[9] Among the works compiled in Ireland arising from this initiative were a genealogy of saints, genealogies of kings, a new version of the *Book of Invasions*, and – the major work – the *Annals of the Kingdom of Ireland*. This was a compilation of Irish history assembled from a wide variety of earlier annals and other documents, covering the history of Ireland from earliest times down to the death of Hugh O'Neill in 1616.[10]

The material collected and transcribed in Ireland was used as the source material for the central work of the research programme, the lives of the Irish saints, and it was parts of the hagiographical studies, rather than the histories and genealogies, which were published by the Franciscans on the Continent in the 1640s. Yet the compilation of saints' lives was not an end in itself, even though the schedule of publications indicates that hagiography was the priority of the Franciscans or their sponsors. It may be useful to see these lives of Irish saints as the link between the historical and devotional writings of the Louvain school. The distinction between theology and history was then a very fine one, and the early modern preoccupation with ecclesiastical history was inspired in large part by theological controversies over the origins and continuity of the 'one true Church'. History was at the core of the theological debate.

Thus the research programme of the Louvain Franciscans, inspired by Hugh Ward, Florence Conry and Bonaventure Ó hEodhasa, and carried on in the 1630s and 1640s by Micheál Ó Cléirigh and John

Colgan, was directly related to the objectives of the seminary which Ward and Conry had founded in 1607 at Louvain to direct and support an Irish mission to promote the Counter Reformation in Ireland. Within this cultural context, hagiography, catechetics and history blended together so that none developed in isolation from the others.[11]

II

The Irish Franciscan community based at Louvain from the early years of the seventeenth century was particularly well equipped to embark on an enterprise to produce a 'New History of Ireland'. Some were from learned families, some had trained as professional bardic poets. The Conrys and Ó Cléirighs, for example, were hereditary historians; the Ó hEodhasa family were hereditary poets to the Maguires of Fermanagh.[12] Others were connected with the élite of Gaelic society, and particularly with the dominant O'Neill and O'Donnell lordships in Ulster. Some of the Irish Franciscans at Louvain in the 1610s had earlier been involved in the Nine Years' War, which had culminated in military defeat for combined Ulster Irish and Spanish forces at Kinsale in 1601. Prominent among these was Florence Conry, who was at Kinsale in the company of the Spaniards, having come with them from Spain. He left Ireland for Spain again early in 1602 with Red Hugh O'Donnell. Later, in 1607, when the earls of Tyrone and Tyrconnell and their allies left Ireland, it was the same Florence Conry, founder of the Irish Franciscan College at Louvain, who met the exiles at Douai, accompanied them to Louvain, and thence to Rome.[13] Other early members of the college such as Robert Chamberlain and Hugh Ward had similar networks of contacts in Ireland and abroad.[14] Hugh Mac Caughwell (Aodh Mac Aingil) was chaplain to Irish regiments in the Spanish Netherlands, a connection which continued between the guardian of the College of St Anthony and the military community throughout the seventeenth century.[15]

The presence of a community of Irish Franciscans in the south Netherlands in the early seventeenth century was not surprising. Irish students had long gone abroad for their university education and from the 1570s the continental mainland had replaced Oxford and Cambridge as the destination for Roman Catholics. Although difficult to quantify since the Louvain University registers are incomplete for the late sixteenth century, the numbers going to the Continent were sufficient to attract notice from Lord Deputy

Sidney in Ireland. In 1577 he reported to Elizabeth that 'there be some principal gentlemen that have their sons in Louvain, Douai, Rome and other places where your Majesty is hated rather than honoured'.[16]

By the early seventeenth century, papal support for the University of Louvain and its related religious orders, together with government support as expressed through the financial involvement of the Archduke Albert and Isabella, worked to create an environment in which the University and its associated colleges (including the Irish Franciscan college) prospered. Theologians from Louvain had won papal support by having been at the forefront of the discussions of the Council of Trent in the 1560s. The reorganization of the Church in the Netherlands in the reign of Philip II of Spain had resulted in a favourable environment for Catholic-Reformation activities there. The concerns of Trent included improved supervision of seminaries; and the Irish Franciscan seminary at Louvain, established to train clergy for the Irish mission, operated under the supervision of the archbishop of Malines, in whose diocese it was situated.[17]

The college had nominal financial support from the Spanish crown, although payments were not always readily forthcoming. In addition, those who served as chaplains to the Irish regiments had personal financial rewards from the Spanish crown for these duties. The college was by no means a wealthy institution but by 1619, although still fund-raising for the final phase of building, it had its own premises and comprised a community of forty to fifty men, living under a vow of poverty.[18] Their principal concern was the education of priests for the Irish and Scottish mission, and this they achieved with reasonable success. It has been estimated that between 1590 and 1615 the colleges of Douai and Louvain together produced approximately 300 priests for the Irish mission. Numbers continued to grow and the Franciscan college at Rome was established in 1625 to help cope with the large numbers of students at Louvain.[19]

That the Irish Franciscans should have embarked on Irish research while at the centre of the European Counter Reformation at Louvain was not coincidental. The Irish at St Anthony's did not exist in a political or social vacuum. Rather, they were one of the main channels for news between Ireland and Europe, and the Louvain college became a focal point for the Irish on the Continent.[20] This is not to say that their culture and ideology was identical with that of their fellow Irishmen at home in Ireland. Rather, the Irish developed their own sense of community in Spanish Flanders, influenced by the Louvain environment of reform. Their sense of identity and their views on Ireland, as revealed not only in their historical and hagiographical writings, but also in their catechetical works prepared with Irish audiences in mind, were moulded by their continental Counter-Reformation experience as well as by their Irish origins.

This is evident from the major historical text produced by the Louvain Franciscans, the *Annals of the Four Masters*. A blending of Gaelic tradition with Counter-Reformation ideas, the annals were intended to present Ireland in a respectable light to Catholic Europe. The authors' claim that the compilation was undertaken to save the record of the Irish past from oblivion should not obscure the fact that this history, like all history, was also interpreting that past for the contemporary generation. It was possible to do so in many subtle ways without necessarily being obviously innovative.[21] Yet the compilers certainly found themselves constrained by a necessity to adhere to traditional and accepted forms and terms of reference. Traditionalist constraints, as well as the nature of the sources, prompted the annalistic format used.[22] It followed the model used in Irish monasteries for many generations and consisted for the most part of obituaries arranged in chronological order. Even the alternative of prose narrative adopted in the 1630s by Geoffrey Keating, while innovative in language and style, was equally traditional in adhering to the standard chronological and ideological framework of the *Book of Invasions*. This saw Ireland's past in terms of a series of settlements, with each successive group of newcomers being integrated into the society. A history of Ireland which did not fit these frameworks could not have secured the approval of the heads of the schools of history, whose endorsements were apparently still considered essential. Although the *Annals of the Four Masters* were traditional in format, they were innovative in scope. The sixteenth-century annals, such as those of Loch Cé, Connacht, or Ulster, were local works, dealing with the past from the perspective of the local monastery or historical school. The *Annals of the Four Masters* differed in perspective in that they encompassed the whole island of Ireland in concept if not always in content.[23]

These writers were also constrained, as historians usually are, by the nature of their source material. The Irish historians who had a continental training appreciated the value of primary sources. Keating, presenting his work as a refutation of the uncomplimentary claims made by English writers on Ireland, boasted that he had read the Irish sources, which the English writers, such as Camden, could not have understood. Micheál Ó Cléirigh, chief of the Four Masters, was equally familiar with the primary source material, which he spent many years collecting. However, he repeatedly expressed a desire to be more critical in his use of the available material than the instructions of his Louvain-based superiors allowed. He had been dispatched to Ireland to assemble, not to distill, and thus included material which he was convinced was not historical.[24]

Even when meticulously based on primary sources, and presented in accepted formats, the subject-matter of the Counter-Reformation Irish historians acquired a new slant. In Geoffrey Keating's history, for example, that Christian attributes were sometimes assigned to pre-Christian personages is only to be expected. While the available sources for any particular year largely determined the text of the *Annals of the Four Masters*, the ordering of events within the year gives a hint of the compilers' priorities. In the majority of instances obituaries of bishops or abbots were given first, followed by other persons of note. This structuring of entries illustrates that their concern was with ecclesiastical rather than secular history. Although the earlier extant annals had usually been composed in or were associated with monasteries, they were less predominantly concerned with ecclesiastical personages than were the *Annals of the Four Masters*. Even where the source depicted an excessively warlike chief, the Franciscan annalists consistently described the Christian death, after repentance, of the nobles they recorded. Following the obituaries and notable deeds of bishops, abbots, and others, minor events considered by the annalists to be worth recording, are relegated to the end of the entry for the year. In such subtle ways did Counter-Reformation values become superimposed on the version of the Irish past inspired by the Louvain historians. Though fully authenticated by representatives of traditional schools of history, the *Annals of the Four Masters* were nothing less than a Counter-Reformation version of the Irish past.

A clear example of the 'revisionism' of the Four Masters is their treatment of the events of the late 1530s. The sixteenth-century *Annals of Connacht* and the *Annals of Loch Cé* both contain an almost identical entry for the year 1538 in which they note the destruction of

> the miraculous image of Mary at Trim which had been venerated for ages by all the Irish, which used to heal the blind and the deaf and the lame and all other sufferers, and the Staff of Jesus which was in Dublin, where it worked miracles and wonders renowned in Ireland from the time of Patrick to this time, which was in Christ's own hand when he was among men and in the hand of Moses son of Amram at the drying up of the Red

Sea before the children of Israel, these were burnt by the English . . . nor was there one of the seven orders which their power could reach in Ireland that they did not destroy.[25]

The *Annals of Ulster* presented these events as part of a military expedition by Lord Leonard Gray into Ulster, destroying the monastery of Down and burning relics of Saints Patrick, Brigid and Columcille and carrying off the image of St Catherine with them.[26] The Four Masters told of the events of the late 1530s in a different way. The context of religious controversy which gave rise to the destruction of images and monasteries was provided. Thus, in the vocabulary of the Counter Reformation,

a heresy and new error in England arose through pride, vain glory, avarice, and lust, and through many strange sciences, so that the men of England went into opposition to the Pope and to Rome . . . They destroyed the orders to whom worldly possessions were allowed, (namely the Monks, Canons, Nuns, Brethren of the Cross,) and the four poor orders: (the orders of the Minors, Preachers, Carmelites and Augustinians,) and the lordships and livings of all these were taken up for the king. They broke down the monasteries, and sold their roofs and bells, so that from Aran of the Saints to the Iccian sea [English Channel] there was not one monastery that was not broken and shattered with the exception of a few in Ireland, of which the English took no notice or heed. They afterwards burned the images, shrines, and relics . . . They also appointed archbishops and sub bishops for themselves and though great was the persecution of the Roman emperors against the church, scarcely had there ever come so great a persecution as this, so that it is impossible to narrate or tell its description, unless it should be narrated by one who saw it.[27]

The narrative retained references to the destruction of famous images, but added detail on the fate of the religious orders not found in earlier accounts. Unusually for an entry in the annals, events were presented as affecting both Ireland and England (e.g. from the Aran Islands to the English Channel) and the explanation for events was not that it was just another military expedition (as in the *Annals of Ulster*). Rather the particular narrative was set within a wider Reformation context, the local events of Irish history presented as the result of a heresy which had arisen in England. The word for heresy, *eithriceacht*, was an innovation in the Irish language at this point. The Four Masters presented the consequences of heresy as various acts of destruction and expropriation of property, acts which were in turn depicted as a persecution – another Counter-Reformation concept – equivalent to the persecution suffered by the early Christians in Rome.[28]

From the perspective of the Continent in the 1630s with the benefit of hindsight, the events of the 1530s were unquestioningly portrayed as persecution by heretics. The impact of late-sixteenth-century Reformation legislation was seen to have had effect not just in Ireland. The geographical unit alluded to as having been affected by heresy from England was the British Isles. The mission territory which was the responsibility of the Louvain Franciscans included Scotland as well as Ireland. Opposition to the 'heretic' was not a question of opposition to England, and reaction to religious persecution as expressed by the Franciscan writers was not focused on ethnic or nationalistic lines.

This was not unbiased history. The fundamental conflict between king and pope was clearly outlined, but the claim that the events of 1538 constituted persecution on the scale of that suffered by the early Christians, given the annalists' admission that most Irish monasteries survived, was a highly misleading conflation of events from the Elizabethan and Stuart eras. The annalists had a specific Counter-Reformation objective in mind. They were doing rather more than preserving the Gaelic past: they were remoulding that past in accordance with their own values.

Breandán Ó Buachalla has recently argued that despite the fact that the annalists hinted at a 'now or never' motivation for their work, it was not written as an epilogue to the history of a defeated Gaelic Ireland. Rather the work was intended as a prologue for what was to come. It was intended to be the basic source-book of the emerging Irish Catholic nation.[29] Ó Buachalla has also drawn attention to the Irish concept of kingdom – the idea of seventeenth-century Ireland as a distinct kingdom with James (and later Charles I) as the legitimate king.[30] Loyalty to the English crown in secular matters was not questioned. For example, when reporting the death of the son of the earl of Desmond in 1582 the annalists noted: 'were it not that he was opposed to the crown of England, the loss of this good man would have been lamentable on account of his liberality in bestowing jewels and riches, and his valour in the field of conflict.'[31] Writing in the 1850s, John O'Donovan argued that such royalist views must have reflected the views of Ó Cléirigh's patron, Feargal Ó Gadhra, rather than the Four Masters themselves.[32] But the same unquestioning acceptance of Ireland as a kingdom, with a Stuart monarch, is evident in all the works of Micheál Ó Cléirigh, not just those sponsored by Ó Gadhra. The *Genealogies of Saints and Kings* was dated the '5th year of the reign of King Charles.'[33] And of course the annals themselves were officially entitled the *Annals of the*

Kingdom of Ireland. It was not so much an 'island of saints and scholars' which was being promoted through recording their history in the annals, rather it was a 'kingdom of saints and scholars'. It is likely that the constitutional position of the Stuart king was not given serious consideration by the annalists. Even if it was a multiplicity of minor kingdoms rather than one, the story they recorded was the story of an illustrious nation, a fitting background and setting for Counter-Reformation-style saints and virtuous men, whose cause they sought to promote.

III

The *Annals of the Four Masters* provided an orthodox historical underpinning for a version of the Irish past which conformed to the ideals of the Counter Reformation. In so far as a battle for the minds and hearts of the Irish people was necessary in the ecclesiastical controversies of the seventeenth century one could hardly have asked for more solid documentation to support the views promoted by the Franciscans. But the programme of the Franciscans did not stop with the historical model of a Catholic Ireland. The work extended to a comprehensive presentation of the lives of the saints of Ireland on similar lines. The cult of the saints appears to have been traditionally strong in Ireland, and the devotional element of saints' lives was in all probability enthusiastically harnessed by the Catholic-Reformation preachers.[34] Certainly, the Louvain scholars prepared the ground in a methodical way. Their motives, as described by Micheál Ó Cléirigh, come as no surprise:

> Upon its having been observed by certain members of the dutiful order of St. Francis that the holiness and righteousness of their nurse and mother, Éire, had diminished, because the lives wonders and miracles of her saints were not disseminated within herself nor within other countries, the counsel they decided upon was to send a poor Friar Minor of their order, the Observantives, Micheál Ó Cléirigh, a chronicler by descent and education, to Ireland, that he might gather to one place all the books he could find having any account of the sanctity of her saints or of their descents or pedigrees.[35]

The Franciscan interest in saints is understandable enough in a Counter-Reformation context, and indeed it has been shown that throughout Europe the religious orders enjoyed a decided monopoly in Counter-Reformation saints. However, the Irish Franciscans do not appear to have devoted any attention to promoting the cause of new saints at Rome.[36] Instead, they publicized those Irish saints who were already well known and for whom there was abundant documentation. In the Reformation controversy, antiquity implied significance, and continuity with the tradition of an 'island of saints and scholars' was the point at issue.

The genealogy of Irish saints compiled by Micheál Ó Cléirigh and his assistants in Ireland was accompanied by a list of kings because, the compilers argued, 'it was impossible to trace the descent of the saints directly to their origins without first setting down the descent of the kings, for it is from those that the saints sprung'.[37] Irish saints were no peasants. The Ireland whose past was being analysed by the Franciscans was seen as a kingdom with an illustrious past, and the saints were likewise regal in their origins. The clear delineation of their descent was important for other reasons also. The work of documenting the lives of Irish saints had been commissioned on the Continent, where Thomas Dempster and his fellow Scottish historians were being accused of stealing Irish saints as their own, thus enhancing Scotland's standing in the eyes of Europe, at the expense of Ireland's reputation. The Irish hagiographical project must have been partly designed to counteract such claims.[38]

Concerns of nationality and of royal descent were only part of the story. These genealogies of saints and kings were being transcribed in Ireland in 1630, a year when the rivalry between the seculars, or diocesan clergy, and the regulars, members of religious orders, was at its height. This dispute was primarily a manifestation of deep-seated rivalries between the Old English Catholics, whose clergy were primarily advocates of the diocesan structure, and the Gaelic Irish, whose clergy for reasons of traditional family connections tended to be members of religious orders, particularly the Franciscans.[39] It was probably not entirely by chance that the nuncio of Flanders pointed out in 1631 that the civility of the native Irish could be proven

> inasmuch as all the saints of Ireland as well ancient as modern who are venerated by the Church are sprung from the Old Irish whereas from the Anglo Irish no man of special sanctity as yet is known to have sprung.[40]

But it may not have been only for reasons of ethnic or political rivalry that the Franciscans researched the genealogies of the Irish saints. Their second stated motive for so doing was in order that

> the reverence and devotion of the nobility for their saints, comharbs and churches might be increased by knowledge of their connection and kinship with their holy patrons and with the tribal saints of the stock to

which each family belonged, and by knowledge of the number of saints connected with each family.[41]

This shows that their work was intended as the basic text for the Irish Catholic nation they were creating in men's minds. This reconstruction of the evidence of the past in accordance with the ideology of the Counter Reformation was the vibrant response of a living community, not the death knell of a civilization whose time had passed.

The Franciscans, imbued with such values, would have genuinely sought to promote devotion to the saints as part of their attempt to promote the values of the Counter-Reformation in Ireland. Throughout Europe, cults of individual saints were used by local monasteries to promote their particular interests in their rivalries with neighbouring monasteries.[42] The local nature of the medieval cults of various well-known Irish saints was revealed all too clearly by the comprehensive researches of the Franciscans. When the first volume of his *Lives of Irish Saints* was published at Louvain in 1645, John Colgan drew attention to the problem of a multiplicity of saints of the same name. There were, for example, he observed, twelve St Brigids, each with distinct birthplaces and family connections, fourteen St Brendans and all of one hundred and twenty St Colmans.[43] Clearly the cult of saints in the medieval Gaelic world had operated on a very localized or fragmented basis, and individual monasteries had promoted the cult of particular saints as best suited local circumstances, inventing local connections where convenient.

This proliferation was paralleled on a larger scale in the controversy as to whether many of the saints were Irish or Scottish. The evidence gathered by Counter-Reformation scholars from Scotland and Ireland served to highlight anomalies in the hagiographical traditions of both areas which laid claim to many of the same saints. Though Thomas Dempster's arguments were attacked by Fleming, Lombard, and Fitzsimon, and later more systematically refuted by the Franciscans, the problem of confusion over the Irishness or Scottishness of saints had probably arisen through the multiplication of earlier localized cult traditions of saints whose origins were shrouded in the mists of time.

Just as individual Gaelic monasteries and the lordships they served needed their own personalized saints in the medieval period so, in an early modern European context, did Ireland come to need nationally representative saints. The Franciscan effort to promote Ireland as the land of Patrick, Brigid and Columcille, as part of their presentation of Ireland as the island of saints and scholars, received documentary underpinning in Colgan's second major work, the *Triadis Thaumaturgae*, published at Louvain in 1647. A large folio volume of sources for the lives of Saints Patrick, Brigid and Columcille, it was intended as a comprehensive compilation of references to Ireland's three most famous saints, arranged in chronological sequence. Given the constraints under which the edition was prepared, the results were impressive. Further sources have come to light since Colgan's day, particularly on Patrick, but Colgan's compilation on both Brigid and Columcille, together with his own notes and commentaries have not yet been entirely superseded. His treatment was a major scholarly achievement transcending the parochialism of the Scottish/Irish debate.[44]

These published works were intended primarily for a European academic audience and also for a select Irish one. In the case of the historical annals, Fearfeasa Ó Maolchonaire, an assistant to Micheál Ó Cléirigh, described their intended Irish audience as being made up of 'persons of understanding either of the church, the nobility or the arts, persons by descent informed in the interpretation and setting down of the history of the Gael'.[45] For the most part, the minutiae of the *Lives* or of the *Annals of the Kingdom of Ireland* were not relevant to the activities and teachings of the Franciscans at home on the Irish mission. This research which flourished in the learned environment at Louvain was primarily a weapon of scholarly propaganda, needed not so much for its intrinsic value but because every one else was doing it.[46] The availability of source material for the history of Ireland and its saints, the academic background of some participants, and perhaps particularly the example of other 'national' efforts, all contributed to the scholarly endeavours of the Irish Franciscans, of which Colgan's *Acta Sanctorum Hiberniae* and Ó Cléirigh's *Annals of the Kingdom of Ireland* are the prime examples.

IV

The Irish Franciscan college of St Anthony at Louvain had been established as a seminary charged with the education of clergy for the Irish mission. Returning to Ireland, the preacher had to leave behind his scholarly volumes, apart perhaps from a small catechism. The Franciscans had been producing catechisms in Irish conveying the essence of Counter-Reformation doctrine from the 1590s at least.[47] The first to be printed, that by Bonaventure Ó hEodhasa, appeared in 1611, and was reprinted twice.[48] This catechism, and its successors, were the Franciscan response to the perceived need to render Counter-Reformation values in the vernacular for a general Irish audience, adapting not just the language but the message also.

The printed word could be effective only if the target population were literate, and so it was not surprising that Aodh Mac Aingil regarded the printed catechism as a poor alternative to preaching in person. According to Mac Aingil, Ó hEodhasa had

> planned to write much that would have been to the good of the souls and honour of the nation if he had lived. But God's anger at the community of sinners cut short his life when his work was only beginning to be printed and before he could teach us the mother tongue, so that we could write something for the good of souls since we cannot, because of persecution, do anything by word of mouth.[49]

In this reading the catechist echoed the motto of the compilers of the *Annals of the Four Masters* – Do chum Glóire Dé agus Onóra na hÉireann.

Ó hEodhasa's catechism was principally a translation from a Latin Tridentine text. The emphasis was on dogma: the creed, commandments and sacraments, at the expense of spirituality. The text was partly in prose and partly in verse, the latter being intended as a means of imparting the essentials of doctrine within the context of an oral culture. That these sections captured the interest of the audience is suggested by the evidence of the later manuscript tradition.[50]

The approbation from the archbishop of Malines presented the work as protecting the Irish from heresy.[51] While it was probably not necesssary for Ó hEodhasa to counter heresy at the level of theological argument, he considered it necessary to stress the unacceptability of the heretics, particularly as represented by Luther and Calvin. He did this in a peculiarly Irish manner, adapting the Roman catechism.[52] While outlining the characteristics of the Catholic Church as expressed in the apostles' creed – 'one, holy, catholic and apostolic' – Ó hEodhasa introduced both Irish and Franciscan examples of holiness, citing Saints Patrick, Brigid, Columcille and Ciaran, together with St Francis, as personifications of holiness. Their pious lives were then contrasted with the immoral behaviour of Calvin and with Luther's sinfulness in leaving his order to live with a nun.[53] Apart from this short section most of the text was non-confrontational, and was designed more to combat ignorance of basic doctrine than to counteract heresy. Yet the very existence of this catechism was viewed as confrontational by Protestant commentators. One hostile writer noted that the Antwerp printing was in use among Irish soldiers on the Continent, having been 'set forth by the friars of Louvain confirming their own religion, and to the contrary infirming and refusing that of the Protestants, in such sort that infinite readers and hearers of the Irish will presently believe the contents thereof to be true'.[54]

Other Franciscan authors were more outspoken than Ó hEodhasa about the aims of their works. Aodh Mac Aingil, for example, in *Scathán Shacramuinte na hAithridhe* [A mirror to the sacrament of penance], stated that he undertook the work because 'every other Catholic nation has a book like this and it is essential for our nation especially since it is without masters, without prelates, without preachers apart from a few in hiding for fear of death or imprisonment as the apostles were after the death of Christ for fear of the Jews'.[55] Here the political context in which the catechetical aims of the author were to be achieved was left in no doubt. The message imparted directly through the printed word, or through the preacher as intermediary, was one in which the teaching of Counter-Reformation doctrine went hand in hand with resistance to persecution on religious grounds in Ireland. Mac Aingil appealed to his readers to support the returned missionaries working in dangerous circumstances:

> It is for your benefit that the lord has drawn so many of the young abroad and given their hearts to accept the yoke of holiness and to study theology so that they can return to you to cure your troubles and free you from the sermons of the heretics.[56]

Overall, the Franciscan writers were more preoccupied with the threat of persecution which prevented them carrying out their catechetical and preaching functions than with a concern to counteract heresy. There was little need for the niceties of apologetics. The perceived need, which the catechisms and devotional works were designed to meet, was to educate Irish-speaking people, now facing the political reality of a life of recusancy, in the basics of Tridentine doctrine. The need for catechisms was explicitly stated at various diocesan synods. The synod of Armagh in 1616 stipulated that clergy should equip themselves with the Roman Catechism, that of Peter Canisius, or one compiled by some other approved authority; recommendations which were repeated at the synod of Tuam in 1631 and 1660, and the synod of Ossory in 1672.[57] Ó hEodhasa's 1611 Irish-language catechism would have served this need where it could be made available, and the fact that it was reprinted indicates that it was in demand.

In terms of existing social and devotional practices, the catechisms and devotional writings stressed changes where necessary. But in so far as possible the Franciscans were attempting to superimpose Counter-Reformation teachings on traditional Gaelic systems, structures and ideologies, by stressing continuity rather than change. The Tridentine teaching on marriage, for example, set down in the 1563 decree *Tametsi* and clearly spelt out in the first Franciscan catechism, was certainly an innovation in an Irish context. Yet the 1611 catechism made no reference to existing practices which would have indicated that the catechism was innovative.[58] The teaching presented marriage as an indissoluble sacrament, to be conducted publicly before a parish priest or his appointee, together with two witnesses, and for which the Church reserved the right to define the impediments to a valid sacrament. There is ample evidence that such was not yet the norm in Ireland.[59]

Attendance at mass and the sacraments would appear to have been the norm, however, since the texts tended to concern themselves more with stipulating proper behaviour when attending mass, or going to confession, rather than exhorting people to attend in the first place. Talking, coughing, or sleeping in church seem to have been of more concern to the friars than was non-attendance.[60] The main thrust of the various texts was directed towards the fundamentals of Christian doctrine: faith, hope, and love. Florence Conry's translation of *Desiderius* included many sections not contained in the original Spanish text, and one of the lengthier additions dealt with the Christian teaching of loving one's enemies. This section did not specify what 'enemies' the author had in mind, but elsewhere in the text Conry discussed the issue of suffering persecution, insults and injury at the hands of those previously considered to have been friends.[61] These Franciscan religious texts were tailor-made for an Irish audience by Irish men who had come strongly under the influence of Counter-Reformation ideology in Europe. They aimed to meet the immediate need of the clergy returning to the Irish mission, but did so under the ideological cloud of 'persecution'.[62]

V

The programme of history, genealogy, saints' lives, devotional works and catechisms had an intellectual coherence. The catechetical works were directly relevant to the primary Franciscan purpose of conducting an Irish mission, on Tridentine lines. They represented the best attempts contemporaries could make to adapt the European Counter Reformation for an Irish audience. They documented the ideas of men who wished to promote a new brand of Catholicism among their own people. Their initial success was probably very limited. Commenting in 1639 Theobald Stapleton indicated that the Irish laity could, at best, recite some prayers in Latin, but could not understand them.[63] Later Franciscan catechisms, particularly the popular *Parrthas an Anama* by Anthony Gearnon (1645), simplified the basic doctrines even further, this time in question and answer form, which suggests that the earlier catechisms had not achieved their target.[64] The slow rate of progress was not something peculiarly Irish. The influence of seminaries on the Tridentine model was almost unnoticeable in most Catholic countries until the late seventeenth century.[65]

The works of history and hagiography were primarily produced for propaganda reasons on the Continent, not just in response to the Scots, but as part of a comprehensive portrayal of Ireland in a manner acceptable to the authorities in Spain and in Rome. They represent primarily the values of Irishmen in Europe, but not necessarily those of Irishmen in Ireland. It may have been necessary for the Louvain Franciscans to believe in the idea of an Ireland where learning and piety had always flourished, to sustain them in their work. Their status as exiles from Ireland provided added motivation. Much the same could have been done at home but was not done. This was not because the funding was absent. Almost all the Louvain publishing projects were sponsored from within Ireland. Feargal Ó Gadhra sponsored the *Annals*. Turlough MacCoghlan paid the costs of research for the *Genealogies of Saints and Kings*. Hugh O'Reilly, archbishop of Armagh, funded Colgan's *Acta Sanctorum* for which there was also a levy on all Franciscan convents in Ireland, and the expenses of the *Triadis Thaumaturgae* were borne by Thomas Fleming, archbishop of Dublin.[66] Yet it was not just that the material had to be printed abroad; the entire project was conceived and for the most part implemented abroad. Why Louvain and not Dublin? The constraint of 'persecution' is only a partial answer. Indeed it may well have been overemphasized and scholars from the Protestant community were even acknowledged as having assisted Franciscan historians. Thomas Strange reported to Luke Wadding in 1631 regarding a further projected history of Ireland being planned from Rome:

[Sir James Ware] can give us more help toward this history than all the kingdom besides. I am concerned at the slight zeal that I mark in our own people for these matters: they would like to see them done, but are not disposed to take the trouble to search out in writing what they find, in short we are an indolent folk in what concerns the public weal, but very active in regard of our particular interests.[67]

It took the impetus of exile and the example of other continental scholars to spur the Irish into action. But the image they portrayed did not accord with the reality. The sort of Catholic Ireland encountered by Rinuccini, the papal nuncio in the mid-1640s, was not the sort of island of saints and scholars the authorities in Rome had been led to believe existed.[68] Yet, in spite of Rinuccini's charge that the Franciscans had a vested interest in prolonging a state of unrest in the 1640s so that they could perpetuate their peculiarly personal type of pastoral service, their method of operating had its justification.[69] Their effectiveness is best illustrated in the way Ireland became the only country in western Europe in which the Counter Reformation succeeded against the will of the head of state.[70]

This pastoral success was achieved at a considerable social and political price. The Franciscans, and their fellow Irish clergy who had been educated in continental seminaries, imported into Ireland not just the Catholic spirituality of the European Counter Reformation, nor merely the Tridentine theology of the mass and the sacraments: they imported also a theology of persecution. This continental concept of persecution on the grounds of religion was not originally conceived of in relation to English activities in Ireland, but was subsequently adapted to this context. Like the religious teachings of the Counter Reformation, such sentiments were only gradually adopted by the Irish at home, but were gaining ground as the seventeenth century progressed.

In so far as the literature examined here can be taken as evidence of Franciscan influence in creating in Ireland a 'Catholic nation', any success must be attributed not so much to formulations about national identity or the nature of the kingdom revealed in the historical works, but rather to the mundane renderings of Counter-Reformation teachings, within an Irish social and political framework, to be found in the catechisms and devotional works. It is these ostensibly theological works which come closest to illustrating the political and social implications of Counter-Reformation ideology in Ireland in the seventeenth century.

The whole corpus of Louvain Franciscan scholarship emphasized the continuity of the faith in a way which contributed to a new sense of the Irish past and subsequently to the development of a sense of national consciousness.[71] The continuity of the Catholic faith was a central tenet of the Counter-Reformation movement, and the sense of Irish national identity which developed gradually in the centuries after the Louvain scholars had been active was one which focused on this European theme of the continuity of Catholicism and the Catholic community. It featured a sense of unquestioning loyalty to the pope, and was defined by a sense of grievance against persecution on the grounds of religion. The culture and ideology of the Irish Franciscan scholars at Louvain inspired a corpus of writing, of which the catechisms and theological tracts reached the widest Irish audience, which reflected many aspects of the idea that Catholicism, even in the face of persecution, was 'the fact that makes an Irishman'.[72]

TWO

THE THEATRE OF DIVERSITY: HISTORICAL CRITICISM AND RELIGIOUS CONTROVERSY IN SEVENTEENTH-CENTURY FRANCE

Eamon O'Flaherty

The growth of criticism in seventeenth-century Europe, and particularly in Francophone culture, was accompanied by a simultaneous development of sceptical and eclectic writings which exposed critical and philosophical problems to a different, rather more public, light. Scholars like Joseph Scaliger, Isaac Casaubon and their successors in the seventeenth century, brought a powerful scholarly apparatus to bear on subjects such as the age of the world and the authenticity of classical texts.[1] The writing of history also benefited from the development of an international scholarly culture in this period, but history, and especially modern history, posed considerable philosophical problems for academic and learned criticism well into the late seventeenth century. In part this was a tribute to the perceived importance of history within a classical, rhetorical tradition inherited from the Renaissance. In France, the writing of official history still owed a great deal to the Renaissance model which saw historical writing as a means of inculcating civic principles. The idea that history was a work of art devalued its importance as a repository of knowledge for some philosophical writers on the subject. The French Pyrrhonist La Mothe Le Vayer stressed the uncertainty of historical writing in a number of works, including *Du peu de certitude qu'il y a dans l'histoire*, where the rhetorical definitions of history writing were reiterated. The writing of Reformation history was still a highly controversial subject in the late seventeenth century and, as in the case of earlier theological controversy, was an appropriate arena for displays of historical scepticism. This paper considers one such discussion about the truth of history at an important moment in the development of seventeenth-century French thought.[2]

Between 1682 and 1687, Pierre Bayle produced a series of philosophical treatises on the related themes of providence in human history, the possibility of historical knowledge, and the particularly topical issue of religious toleration. Although ostensibly addressed to different subjects, there is a thematic and chronological unity about Bayle's writings in this period which makes it appropriate to consider them as a unity. The work in which Bayle most directly addressed the subject of historical scepticism was the *Critique générale de l'histoire du Calvinisme de M. Maimbourg*, published in 1682. In this, Bayle cast fundamental philosophical doubts on the truth of history, and based his criticism of Maimbourg on historical pyrrhonism and on a distinction between history and learned criticism.[3] This distinction was of great importance in a period when the practice of critical history was developing in the Republic of Letters in contradistinction to the public, official histories which were produced by royal historiographers like Maimbourg.[4] Bayle's criticism of history, however, is not based on an unmitigated scepticism. The treatises of the 1680s, taken together, define an important period in the development of Bayle's historical thought arising out of his preoccupation with the subjects of divine providence and religious toleration. His approach to both these subjects, of which the *Critique* of Maimbourg forms a part, involved a rejection of schematic providential interpretations of history, and also of the application of rational, as opposed to critical, methods of historical analysis. Bayle's scepticism, while ostensibly founded on pyrrhonian doubt that history could produce any claim to truth, integrated the relativist and probabilistic traditions of French thought of the preceding decades into an argument which sought to transform historical thought rather than reject the possibility of historical knowledge.

The divisive effects of the Reformation were felt in France with particular acuteness in the sixteenth and seventeenth centuries. The long period of civil war in the sixteenth century, and the tensions between the Huguenot minority and central government in the seventeenth century, had important consequences for intellectual, as opposed to purely confessional, elements in French thought in the early modern period. In intellectual terms, the divisiveness of confessional disputes in the period of the Reformation and Counter

Reformation obscured, but did not quite remove, the impact of philosophical, ideological and historiographical movements deriving from the recovery of classical learning in the Renaissance. The intellectual culture of the Renaissance and of the Reformation and Baroque periods was pervaded by a respect for classical antiquity which almost balanced their respect for sacred texts. A perfunctory and sequential periodization can hardly accommodate the overlapping effects of religious conflict and of the deliberate revival of classical antiquity in the sixteenth century. In addition, European thought was also exposed to the cumulative impact of older heterodoxies during the seventeenth and eighteenth centuries, and to the development of ancient philosophies, such as scepticism, which had far-reaching implications for the status of both confessional and historical arguments. Religious polemic 'made arrows of all wood', as one Calvinist cosmographer wrote in the 1590s.[5]

Religious controversy in the sixteenth and seventeenth centuries had made use of powerfully destructive arguments in the service of confessional invective. From Erasmus's use of scepticism in his work on free will in 1519 to the sceptical prefaces of Pierre-Daniel Huet in his *Demonstratio Evangelica* in 1678, religious writers had made extensive use of the destructive potential of scepticism.[6] The epistemologically destructive content of religious controversy derived from the rediscovery of classical scepticism in the course of the sixteenth century – from the works of Cicero, Gianfrancesco Pico Della Mirandola and Henri Estienne's translations of Sextus Empiricus, which circulated in France at the height of the Wars of Religion. As Richard Popkin argued nearly thirty years ago, one of the cumulative effects of sceptical arguments on both sides of religious controversy in the sixteenth and early seventeenth centuries was to undermine the status of belief on each side and to force philosophers into a re-examination of the grounds of faith and knowledge alike.[7] 'Conservative' Calvinism in the sixteenth and early seventeenth centuries developed particularly effective techniques for demolishing Catholic doctrines, based on the marshalling of long lists of concrete examples demonstrating the absurdity of the Catholic position.[8]

Historical writing in France was also influenced by the history of religious and philosophical debate. More significantly for the development of historical writing, however, the French monarchy had institutionalized historical writing in the course of the seventeenth century to the extent that official history, which existed within an increasingly bureaucratized system of royal patronage, reflected the exclusion of dissident groups and schools of thought from French intellectual culture under Louis XIV. The tight organization of official patronage under Louis reinforced the political function of the historian, placing great emphasis on the glorification of the dynasty and, in the case of the royal historiographers, on the role of eloquence rather than learning in the writing of history.[9] The Bayle-Maimbourg controversy involved a clash between the imperatives of royal historiography and those of the dissident groups in Ludovician France – in this case the Huguenots. On a more profound level, however, it involved a clash between two distinct philosophies of history in which Bayle abandoned the sectional imperatives of confessional historiography in a far-reaching philosophical critique of historical knowledge and argument and a reassessment of the role of divine providence in history.

As a Protestant intellectual, Bayle, in deciding to embroil himself in historiographical debate on the history of the Wars of Religion, was faithfully reflecting his own background and coming to terms with the crisis of allegiance and of their place in history which faced the French Huguenots in the first half of the 1680s. As a Huguenot scholar – professor at the Sedan academy – who had been forced into exile by its closure in 1681, Bayle witnessed the steady dismantling of the rights of the French Protestants from the safety of Rotterdam.[10] From the vantage point of a religious exile, of a scholar immersed in traditional erudition, a *journaliste* who began the systematic criticism of texts as they appeared in print, and a member of an essentially francophone culture, Bayle was very well placed to reflect on the historical and philosophical consequences of the destruction of French Protestant rights under Louis XIV. Bayle's critique of Maimbourg was, in part, a rejection of the processes of marginalization which had come to define the position of the Huguenots in seventeenth-century France.

One of the consequences of marginalization was a perceptible change in Calvinist history-writing, in which the confident, almost triumphant, notes of the reforming period had been obscured. Yet such attitudes were deeply rooted in French Protestantism. The poetry of du Bartas associated the Reformation with divine providence. The unorthodox southern Protestant Jean de Frégeville, writing in the late sixteenth century, combined religious and secular chronology in a messianic vision of the ultimate victory of his own brand of judaizing Protestantism.[11] Jean Perrin, from Lyon, published books in 1618 and 1619 which traced the antecedents of the

French Reformation in his *Histoire des Chrétiens Albigeois* and *Histoire des Vaudois*, which were translated into English and published in London in 1629 under the title *Luther's Forerunners; or a Cloud of Witnesses Deposing for the Protestant Faith*. In much French Protestant history written in the first decades of the seventeenth century, history was a table of evidence of the perseverance of the true religion and of signs of the reign of Antichrist.[12] The decline of the political and public fortunes of the Huguenots was reflected, from the 1630s, in an increasingly defensive historiography which sought to minimize, or condemn, the military and political excesses of the wars of religion[13] and to reinforce the official toleration of the French Protestants by demonstrating their essential loyalty. This 'intellectual disarmament', to paraphrase Elizabeth Labrousse,[14] did not apply to official, Catholic historiography in the same period. A *politique* tradition, represented by Du Thou, was always supplemented by a vigorous condemnation of the principles and historical behaviour of the Huguenots. Counterpart to the earlier Protestant themes of the sign of Antichrist were Catholic arguments such as those of Florimond de Raemond's *Birth, Progress and Decline of Heresy in this Age* (1605), where Calvin's horoscope is drawn as one of the proofs of his malign influence in this world.

Under Louis XIV, official history was only partly inspired by confessional imperatives. The development of the office of royal historiographer as intellectual pensionary of the state was determined by the demands of the monarchy and was, as Ranum has convincingly argued, inspired by a Budean model in which eloquence and the inculcation of civic principles were at least as important as learning.[15] Central to the demands of the crown, however, from the late 1660s at least, was the objective of religious uniformity as part of the developing ideology of royal power. The Protestants were only one element in the religious life of France in the second half of the century. The very intensity of the French Counter Reformation, when superimposed on earlier traditions of theological and ecclesiastical liberty, posed a greater threat to centralizing uniformity. Jansenism threatened the unity of the Church in the reign of Louis XIV in a way in which the Huguenots could not. Indeed, Protestant intellectuals, when divorced from their roots in the south of France, developed a false sense of security owing to the good behaviour of Protestants generally in the great crisis of 1648-52: a time when the lower clergy of the Gallican Church were infected with Jansenism and opposition to Mazarin.

The target of Bayle's historical critique in the 1680s, the Jesuit historian Louis Maimbourg, is important as an apologist in print for many of the intellectual positions of the monarchy. In his initial reviews of Maimbourg's work on the history of the Catholic league in the *Nouvelles de la République des lettres*, Bayle noted his popularity: 'He has found the secret of giving history the atmosphere of a novel, and giving the novel the atmosphere of history.'[16] In the earlier stages of his *Critique* of Maimbourg's history of Calvinism, Bayle supplied a further and more detailed picture of the Jesuit historian. What emerged from Bayle's analysis was an assessment of Maimbourg's work which was situated in the context of the literary politics of the clergy and the court. Bayle was also provided with a basis from which to criticize the religious policy of Louis XIV towards the Huguenots and, more specifically, to denounce Maimbourg's lack of historical objectivity and his failure to distinguish between personal ambition and the imperatives of his political position, on the one hand, and the historical subject-matter of his works on the other. In addition to this, Bayle moved beyond the limits of an academic or historical *querelle* to engage in a philosophical criticism of the historiography of religious controversy, and to develop themes which lay at the centre of his philosophical and religious position as a product of scepticism and scholarly criticism, as much as of his religious background. The *Critique* also occupies a middle place between two of Bayle's most sustained philosophical works – the *Pensées diverses sur la comête*, published in 1682 and the *Commentaire philosophique* on the biblical injunction 'compel them to come in', published in 1686. The three texts can be read as an internally consistent series, belonging to a distinct period in Bayle's career. The paradox which emerges from them is that Bayle's critique of Maimbourg involves a reappraisal of history which, while demonstrating the invincibility of scepticism as a means of undermining accepted views of the relationship between providence and human history, nevertheless validates a critical approach to historical truth which sought to rescue history from being a mirror to the commonplace.

Maimbourg, a Jesuit, had been involved in controversy with the Jansenists in 1667, attacking the Mons translation of the New Testament and accusing the Jansenists of Calvinist leanings. His historical works, which he began to write in the 1670s, and which proved him to be an adept stylist, carried on the anti-Jansenist theme by concentrating on the subject of heresy in works such as the *Histoire de l'arianisme* (1673).[17] In his critique of Maimbourg's work, Bayle was engaging an entire approach to historical writing:

Bayle's interest was not in a point-by-point refutation of the details of Maimbourg's histories – he admitted that he had spent only a fortnight on the work and hoped that someone else would undertake a detailed refutation[18] – but was an attack on the defects of the kind of history which Maimbourg wrote, and a defence of the critical and erudite approach to historical writing as opposed to the rhetorical approach adopted by Maimbourg.[19]

Maimbourg did present a disturbing challenge to a Protestant critic on the eve of the revocation of the Edict of Nantes. His *History of Calvinism* provided, among other things, a vigorous denunciation of the horrors of the St Bartholomew's Day massacre and an admission of the complicity of the court. Yet two principal themes emerge in Bayle's criticism of Maimbourg, in addition to a basic fear of a Jesuit bearing gifts of even-handedness. The first is that Maimbourg's even-handedness is deceptive, since it rests on a sustained bias against the French Reformation which continually distorts the position of the Protestants. The second, more immediate point is that the book purports to be a history, but actually conceals a political message – that religious division is harmful to the state and that the sovereign has the right, and duty, to extirpate heresy both for the defence of true religion and for the good of the state. Although he took issue with Maimbourg on many points of fact and interpretation concerning the history of the Reformation, Bayle's principal concern was not to trade historical blows with his opponent in an extension of traditional controversy, but to raise fundamental doubts about the validity of Maimbourg's enterprise and to take issue with the contemporary arguments, disguised as history, which his work contains.

Bayle depicts Maimbourg as a failed preacher and failed scourge of Jansenism who discovered in the writing of history a viable arena for his literary talents and ambitions. He analyses Maimbourg's historical writings as a series of metaphors for the political causes which he took up in the 1670s and 1680s. The extent to which Bayle's attack on the author of the *History of Calvinism* is as important as his refutation of the book's contents derives from the fact that the *Critique* is as much an attack on the state of historical writing, and on the possibility of historical truth emerging from the rhetorical imperatives of contemporary historiography, as it is an attempt to validate one version of events against another. Maimbourg's *History of Calvinism* is seen as typifying the uncertainties which abound in the writing of history and which, in Bayle's terms, pose radical doubts about the possibility of writing any history. 'Nothing is more difficult', Bayle wrote in the preface, 'than to apprehend, from specious appearances, the true cause . . . of man's actions.'[20] This statement is central both to Bayle's attitude to the motives of historians and to his more general argument in favour of religious toleration, based on the difficulty of judging the validity of any act of religious conformity. The attack on history which Bayle presents in the *Critique* is essentially an attack on historical judgment rather than on the facts of history. The certainty of history can be pursued to a certain level of detail, when all sides agree. There is even the possibility of a limited amount of evaluation which results from 'examining the relations of a number of facts, considering the nature of the actors and, by weighing all the circumstances and comparing what various authors have written, one can illuminate many things, and discover many impostures'.[21] Set against this limited statement of the possibilities of history is, however, a clear sense that there are enormous obstacles to historical certainty. To some degree this is so because of the partiality of historians – and here the history of the Reformation is a prime example. Beyond the attitudes of the historians, however, Bayle argues that there are severe problems with the materials of history. The history of the Punic Wars can never be known from the other side – we are left, forever, with a one-sided account. Modern history, which on the surface supplies us with both sides of the case, is, in fact, baffling in the extent of its contradictions. Our knowledge of events is distorted by the partisan nature of the accounts provided by interested parties, and by the fact that these accounts – specifically the fugitive journals which proliferate around every conflict, as in the Dutch War – are destined to provide ammunition for future partisan histories.

Bayle's arguments against history do not partake of an absolute scepticism, but they nevertheless form part of the legacy of radical philosophical doubt which was part of French pyrrhonism in the seventeenth century. Several commentators on Bayle's thought have convincingly argued that in Bayle's case the argument against historical certainty was not absolute to the extent that he denied the possibility of any knowledge.[22] Bayle's remarks on history constitute rather a mitigated, but nonetheless damaging, argument against the possibility of determining the truth or falsehood of a given historical statement. Certain propositions, such as the existence of Julius Caesar, or of the Roman Republic, are sufficiently probable that their status as historical facts is virtually certain – they do not require an act of faith or a belief in their moral certainty.[23] On the other hand, beyond this level of scientific certainty there are grades of probability which undermine the status of historical facts, and when the problem of interpretation is introduced, human intervention can ensure that the same facts, arranged in a different way, can turn a eulogy into a satire.[24]

When stated in this way, Bayle's historical Pyrrhonism has much in common with the debate conducted among German jurists and philosophers of the late seventeenth century on *fides historica*. References in his works, particularly to the Pyrrhonian philosopher and writer on history François La Mothe Le Vayer, and, indeed, the consequences which he draws from his historical scepticism, lead us back to the sceptical tradition within French thought and to the development of an important body of statements about the nature and function of beliefs in human societies contained in that tradition.

A whole tradition of positivist historiography up to the 1940s, and even beyond, focused on the search for intellectual forerunners in the early modern period. Perhaps derived from an Enlightenment concern to trace the history of those who had taken part in the gradual emancipation of the human mind from the shackles of superstition, much effort has gone into tracing the clandestine history of atheism in the renaissance and seventeenth century. Pintard's great work on the *libertins érudits* devoted much of its exhaustive scholarship to proving the existence of a secret network of unbelievers in France in the first half of the seventeenth century.[25] The question of the private religious belief or lack of religious beliefs of seventeenth-century sceptics has long ceased to be the primary focus of interest, and the search for a proto-history of European atheism has come in for some serious criticism.[26] On the other hand, much of the discussion of the religious beliefs of sceptical authors – and particularly of earlier French Pyrrhonists such as Michel de Montaigne and La Mothe Le Vayer – obscures the importance in the sceptical tradition of a sustained discussion on the nature of belief. This discussion of belief stemmed from an extension of some of the basic elements of classical scepticism and from the application of these ideas to available problems of belief, and awareness of the diversity of beliefs, in the world of seventeenth-century Europe. The most widely known summary of sceptical arguments against knowledge, and the source of many seventeenth-century sceptical arguments in the tradition of Montaigne, were the ten tropes, or kinds of argument, contained in the *Outlines of Pyrrhonism* by Sextus Empiricus. The eighth trope argues against the possibility of certainty on the grounds of relativity: 'implying, firstly, relation to that thing which judges (for the external object which is judged appears in relation to that thing) and, in a second sense, relation to the accompanying percepts'.[27]

A famous instance in Montaigne's *Essays* in this respect is his wondering whether he is playing with his cat or she is playing with him.[28] But this mode of argument is carried further into the realm of human society in the tenth trope which focuses on ethics, 'rules of conduct, laws, legendary beliefs and dogmatic conceptions'. As a mode of argument, the tenth trope is the one which is most dependent on history and comparative cultural evidence for its effect. The elaboration of the kinds of argument used in these tropes forms an important – and perhaps underestimated – element in French Pyrrhonist ideas on history and society.[29]

If the source of sceptical ideas is traceable without too much difficulty, and if the history of scepticism as part of the history of philosophy proper can also be readily appreciated[30] – the same cannot be said about the assimilation of these ideas into discussions about the nature of history and human societies. The sixteenth and seventeenth centuries were forced to assimilate a greater evidence of human variety than had hitherto been known to exist. Religious controversy was one area where opposite varieties of obstinacy, or *opiniâtreté*, seemed to be locked in perpetual and irreconcilable conflict. By the time Bayle was composing his philosophical works in the 1680s hopes for a reconciliation between divided Christian churches were virtually dead. But other evidence of apparently invincible diversity was not lacking. The discoveries of new worlds in America and Asia confronted Europeans with cultures and religions radically different from their own. Perhaps the most famous text in this respect is Montaigne's essay 'Des Cannibales', in which it is argued, somewhat mischievously, that the practice of cannibalism as a ceremony of honour by the Brazilians is a social custom, to be understood in its own terms and not in terms of European morality.[31] Montaigne's essay is only one example of an awareness of radical differences in history, customs and beliefs which went far beyond the traditionally 'closed' image of the world. 'Des Cannibales' was itself based on a substantial cosmographic literature. From the 1630s, travel literature emerged as an important source for philosophical writing and, significantly, as a source of raw material for sceptical arguments based on the apparently limitless diversity of customs and beliefs which were described in the *relations de voyage* of missionaries and travellers. La Mothe Le Vayer, whose *Discours de l'histoire* (1638) and shorter work, *Du peu de certitude qu'il y a dans l'histoire* (1668), were sources for Bayle's historical pyrrhonism in the *Critique*, made extensive use of evidence from the new literature on non-European peoples in his pyrrhonian dialogues on *Divinité* and *Opiniâtreté*, first published in 1634.[32] La Mothe's 'amplification of the tenth trope', as Joseph Beaude has called it,[33] consisted of juxtaposing the immense varieties of religious worship to reinforce Pyrrhonian arguments against religious certainty. It was not just that human religion and ethical standards showed such a bewildering diversity that the philosopher could not choose between them, but that there even existed societies without religion.[34]

The refuge for religious belief in this context was a resort to fideism in the face of the impossibility of providing a rational justification for religion.[35] Other works informed by travel literature, or what might be called a rudimentary exercise in comparative religion, were not as overtly sceptical in orientation as La Mothe Le Vayer's dialogues. But the writings of François Bernier, a physician, friend of La Mothe Le Vayer and of Cyrano de Bergerac, and author of a French abridgement of the works of the sceptical philosopher Gassendi, showed a similar interest in cultural comparison as a philosophical exercise.[36] From another direction, Jesuit missionary activity in China in the seventeenth century drew attention to the existence of a religious and philosophical system of such complexity and antiquity that it provided an explicit challenge to Christian and European attitudes towards paganism. These strands in the history of French scepticism provide an important background for Bayle's construction of a philosophical approach to history which went beyond the elaboration of a simple recitation of the difficulties involved in describing historical events. Indeed, as will be argued below, they provided him with a philosophical framework from which to reject the rhetorical and political imperatives informing official histories like that of Maimbourg and to construct an argument in favour of religious toleration.

Cultural and religious diversity offered one challenge to the possibility of constructing a history which was seen as possessing meaning as part of a larger providential pattern, along the lines of Bossuet's *Discours de l'histoire universelle* of 1681, which restated the standard providentialist schema of world history in a magisterial way. Historical and textual criticism provided another such challenge – indeed, the two together constituted a formidable battery of arguments when marshalled in the service of a single argument. Renaissance historiography had managed to reconcile learned respect and admiration for classical antiquity by incorporating ancient religion, and much of ancient philosophy, into a providentialist *schema*. An important element of this was the growth of the belief that there were elements of truth in ancient theology and philosophy which could have derived only from a providential source, and that the wisdom of antiquity was partly the product of divine revelation.[37] Yet increasingly, from the beginning of the seventeenth century, the basis for belief in a valid ancient theology was undermined by waves of erudite textual scholarship which demonstrated either that the Christian elements in the ancient theology actually dated from the Christian era and not from antiquity, or that the discovery of Christian elements in texts which were of genuinely pagan origin – for example, Virgil's fourth eclogue – was the result of excessive willingness on the part of credulous Christian interpreters such as Isaac Vossius to read meanings into the texts which could not be sustained. The truth of history as a repository of meaning was thus challenged in a number of ways, leading to the progressive dismantling of grand providentialist schema which had offered the possibility of reconciling profane and Christian learning, and even pagan and Christian religion. The progress of learning undermined certainty to the point where, ultimately, historical events themselves might be without meaning; and values, ethical standards and religions might be arbitrary, almost random, phenomena.

Bayle can be seen as the heir to this critical tradition in philosophical and historiographical thought. His negative comments on the truth of history in the *Critique* of Maimbourg can best be understood in the context of his discussion of history in his *Pensées diverses sur la comête* of 1682. Ostensibly a work written to prove that comets are natural phenomena and that a belief in their portentous nature was groundless superstition (and also ostensibly written by a Catholic), the *Pensées diverses* in fact operates partly as an attack on Catholicism and partly as an exploration of the radical disjunction between divine providence and human history.[38] As in the *Critique*, Bayle opened his argument on the comet by elaborating on the fallibility of history. Historians, like poets, deal in the marvellous, and in doing so 'the majority of them show such a great desire to report all the miracles and visions authorized by the credulity of peoples, that it would not be prudent to believe everything they relate in these matters'.[39]

A key problem here is that of causation. Whereas historians 'who have worked in the archives and in secret documents and explored the pure sources of the truth of facts' can be accurate, they are frequently mistaken in assigning causes to events.[40] The power of tradition and of transmitted beliefs also obscures the historical record, and nothing is so dangerous, in this respect, as argument from consensus, the danger of believing in opinions largely founded on the large numbers of people who held them.[41] In part, Bayle's purpose in attacking the belief in the *consensus gentium* as a proof of the truth of an idea is related to the overriding theme which unites the treatises of the 1680s – the provision of a coherent defence for the religious rights of the French Protestants against persecution at the hands of a Catholic majority. In the *Pensées diverses* he linked this theme with a profound re-evaluation of the function of providence in history, drawing on the historical and cultural relativism of French Pyrrhonism and expounding it in a far more coherent form than had previously been attempted. It is clear from the outset of his argument that Bayle sees the ostensible question as to whether or not comets cause or presage disasters to be simply an introduction to the more important question of the role of superstition and belief in society.

Despite his castigation of historians, Bayle's arguments are essentially historical. The argument of the book is not based on physics, but on what he calls 'experience'. The central part of the argument is an attack on the idea that there is a direct link between divine providence and human history. Recalling Augustine's defence of Christianity against the accusation that it was responsible for the fall of the Roman Empire, Bayle argues that divine providence in history is characterized by infinite diversity: 'God punishes peoples in their turn, but it does not follow that those by whom he punishes are better than those who are punished. These punishments have no regular order.'[42] To believe in a regular, or even in a comprehensible, pattern to the operation of divine providence in history is a notion which Bayle compares to the 'puerilities' of 'those who think that they can detect a regular change in states after a given number of years and who tell us about who knows how many revolutions which take place every five hundred years'.[43]

In surveying successive states of paganism – or idolatry as Bayle significantly terms it throughout his work, making an implicit comparison with Catholicism – two key points are made to disprove any automatic connection between true religion and civil history. The first point is that ethical behaviour is a function of civil society and of individual temperament rather than divine grace. The second, related point is that the vicissitudes of civil history are the result of processes which have little or nothing to do with the truth or falsehood of the religions professed. Bayle's Augustinian pessimism about the depravity of human nature extended well beyond the coming of Christianity. Belief in itself, without the operation of divine grace, has no effect on ethical conduct. Thus religion cannot destroy vice without the aid of the civil law. In a manner reminiscent of Machiavelli and the Machiavellian tradition in French libertine thought in the seventeenth century, Bayle argued that religion, in pagan societies, generally tended to conserve the state rather than discourage vice and that ethical conduct was enforced by the civil power rather than by religion. Throughout the work, Bayle, posing as a Catholic, is careful to confine his judgments to pagans/idolaters and atheists, but it is not difficult, as he condemns Catholic good works and immorality in the same breath as the vices of the pagans, to see that the argument applies to contemporary society also. 'Short of a continuous miracle,' he writes when considering the state's role in ethical conduct, 'I am sure that a city like Paris would be reduced to the most miserable condition possible within a fortnight if it relied on the preachers and confessors as its sole remedy against vice.'[44] Thus ideas of honour, coercion or fear of public opinion are more effective than religion in governing human conduct. 'One can say . . . that human justice commands the virtue of the greater part of the world, because once it relaxes the bridle on a given sin, few people abstain from it.'[45] The relativity of moral standards between various societies in history constitutes a further proof that social behaviour and conceptions of good and bad conduct are human or social creations.[46]

The best-known and most controversial part of Bayle's *Pensées diverses* was his conjecture on the possibility of a society of virtuous atheists. Yet, despite its ability to shock contemporaries and its apparent affinities to the heterodox and libertine traditions in 'French free thought', Bayle's counter-factual exploration of an atheist society as one which would be no worse and probably better than a society of idolaters is a logical, if far-reaching conclusion of his rejection of any axiomatic link between divine providence and human social behaviour. In the last analysis, an upright and virtuous action not inspired by divine grace cannot be meritorious in the religious sense. The workings of providence are as ineffable, in Bayle's view, as the inner workings of individual conscience; both can only be known to God and neither can be ascertained by human means. The corollary, perhaps, is that Protestants need not feel deserted by God despite the fact that the state has begun to persecute them and that Catholic apologists for religious uniformity in the state cannot reasonably draw any historical parallels between the establishment of true religion in the state and the degree of virtue exhibited by its citizens.

Two rather different but not unrelated consequences emerge from these arguments. In historical terms, Bayle produced an account of human society which assimilated much of the accumulated weight of philosophical scepticism and critical learning of the preceding generation of sceptical and critical writers – albeit a more powerfully constructed and integrated argument. The schematic providentialism of redemption history, as restated and expounded by Bossuet in 1682 was increasingly difficult to defend by the second half of the seventeenth century. Under the successive assaults and quibbles of scientific chronologers, textual scholars, primitive anthropologists and historical pyrrhonists, providential history was an unwieldy and creaking explanatory mechanism which raised more doubts about the truth of history – and possibly also religion – than it could solve. Against this was the blank historical scepticism of a writer like La Mothe Le Vayer, or a Machiavellian political historian like Gabriel Naudé,[47] in which history dissolved into a series of processes or events which were either random, or were explicable solely in terms of civil prudence. In Bayle's view of history, the diversity and contingency of historical events was itself a guarantee of the maintenance of civil society and a record, however ineffable and perplexing, of the obscure workings of divine providence. Some of Bayle's strongest statements of this position are to be found in the continuation of his *Critique* of Maimbourg, the *Suite de la critique générale.* 'The world', he wrote:

> is only preserved in its present state because men are filled with a thousand unreasonable passions; and if philosophy succeeded in making men act according to clear and distinct ideas, one can be very well assured that the human race would perish very soon. Error, passions, prejudices and a hundred similar faults are a sort of necessary evil in the world. Men would be worth nothing if they were cured of them.[48]

And further:

> who can see without some amazement, that unregulated passions, unreasonable prejudices are necessary to the world so that it can be the theatre of this immense diversity of events which causes providence to be admired.[49]

It does not seem to stretch the point to suggest that Bayle saw in the vicissitudes of human history, the contingent but nevertheless human and social processes of conduct and public behaviour, an inner dynamic of history operating at a sort of Rankean distance from infinity. In arguing the contingency of historical processes and their irreducibility to 'clear and distinct ideas' Bayle seems to posit a recognition of another, historical level of human behaviour which was not amenable to an abstract, Cartesian analysis any more than it was amenable to simple providentialism. Implicit in the Cartesian project was a dismissal of all such erudition as was merely probable in favour of a few, abstract sciences on which a foundation of knowledge could be built.[50] The merely probable truths of history, and of the kind of critical and historical erudition to which Bayle was to devote the remainder of his life after the 'philosophical treatises' of the 1680s considered here, could not provide any validation of the clear and distinct ideas. Nor, indeed, could history be seen as a mirror of providence. In rejecting both rational and providential explanations of the historical 'theatre of diversity', Bayle was attempting, on one level perhaps, to reconcile the fundamental pessimism implicit in the notion of an ineffable providence acting in ways which seem to be bizarre or unjust, with a faith in the validity of his own religious position and in some unseen divine purpose. On a simpler level of historical explanation, however, Bayle's separation of divine providence from the processes of human history seems to validate these processes, though they are frequently baffling from the Christian or the moral point of view. This is not to say that the processes of history are irreducible to explanation – at many points in the treatises the explanations offered point to a radically Augustinian separation of civil society and religious truth – but merely to acknowledge that they operate differently from the dictates of the clear and distinct ideas of reason. Bayle's action in this respect seems to have a Copernican simplicity in rescuing the phenomena of historical knowledge from an unwieldy and unworkable systematization.

Bayle's approach to history in the treatises grew, of course, out of a real context in the history of French Protestantism in a period of increasing persecution under Louis XIV (culminating in the revocation of the Edict of Nantes) as much as it derived from the development of seventeenth-century historical and critical learning. The concern with the problem of evil which Labrousse identifies in Bayle's work was related, as remarked earlier, to the progressive destruction of the rights of French Protestants in the 1680s. Bayle's rejection of the notion that human history was a direct or easily legible reflection of divine providence, and his emphasis on the civil rather than the divine origins of social morality is closely linked, both in the *Pensées diverses* and the *Critique* of Maimbourg's *History of Calvinism*, to a denunciation of the practice of forcible conversion, the doctrine that religious belief can or should be enforced by the state and the doctrine that useful social purposes are served by religious uniformity. Bayle's arguments against these policies were not unique to Protestants, and even at the higher levels of the French Catholic Church there were many who opposed the policy of forcible conversion in order to avoid the religious and political evils that might flow from the forcible conversion *en masse* of the entire Protestant population.[51] In Bayle's work on this subject there is also a process of sustained contemplation of the inscrutable providential design which has brought about the division of Christianity and the shipwreck of his own people. The culmination of this process of thought is Bayle's majestic *Philosophical Commentary* on the words of the gospel, 'Compel them to come in.'

The theme of opposition to the forcible conversion of the Huguenots was signalled in the *Pensées diverses* as part of an argument showing that the alliance of political power and Christianity was damaging to the Church, and its existence in the early centuries of Christianity was responsible for the introduction of pagan (or idolatrous) beliefs and practices into the Church.[52] The theme was further developed in the *Critique*, where Bayle employed the additional argument that, whether conviction is based on truth or error, it is no less binding on the individual conscience, given that it is sincerely held.[53] Bayle had already, in 1682, argued that the individual conscience, like the operation of providence in history, was unknowable. The relativity of beliefs, which is such an important part of Bayle's view of the civil basis of ethical behaviour in history, is an important element in his argument for toleration.

> Everyone knows, or ought to know [he wrote] that evidency [*évidence*] is a relative quality . . . the evidency which we find in certain objects can derive from the way in which we see them, or from the proportion between our senses and those things, or from education or habit, or some other causes, thus . . . another man will not see things in the same way as we do, not having been brought up in the same way, and so on.[54]

Again and again, Bayle applies the Pyrrhonian relativism which informs his view of human society to the question of individual conviction and private belief. On the social level, there is an explicit extension of the historical ideas about religion and the state found in the *Pensées diverses* to the question of toleration as it is discussed in the *Commentaire philosophique*. The Jewish state was justified in punishing idolaters, not because of an eternal divine sanction, but because of the specific political conditions of its existence:

> Since the basic and fundamental law of that state was to have no other God than he who led them from the land of Egypt; since this was the first convention entered into with God, I say, considered not simply as the creator of all men, but as the Lord and temporal ruler of the Judaic commonwealth, it is clear that every idolater was worthy of death and that every man who preached that it was necessary to serve strange gods and to follow the religion of neighbouring peoples, merited execution as much as someone who, at the present time, exhorted the people of London to take an oath of fidelity and obedience to the king of France, or the king of Spain.[55]

With the single exception of the Jewish state, an exception nuanced by a recognition that the Jewish religion was a political covenant which Christianity, by implication, was not, there are no conceivable grounds for persecution and no certain distinctions can be made between what can and cannot be tolerated. Religious belief is seen, as in the *Pensées diverses*, as a function of environment, education and history. Just as in history the operation of divine providence is obscure and unknowable, so in the realm of conscience man, corrupt by nature, cannot presume to usurp divine functions. The philosophical and chronological parallels between the treatises of the 1680s reveal the closeness of Bayle's ideas about historical diversity and religious conscience. They also demonstrate the degree to which there are substantial positive elements in his historical thinking. In rejecting the notion that human history was a mirror to an all-determining providence, Bayle provided himself with an important area of freedom to speculate in what were, for many of his critics, unthinkable terms about the nature of human society and the place of religious belief in history. The product of this freedom was not a synthetic philosophy of history but the subsequent construction of the massive critical edifice, the *Dictionnaire historique et critique* of 1696.

THREE

HONOUR AND AMERICAN REPUBLICANISM: A NEGLECTED COROLLARY

Bertram Wyatt-Brown

In 1767, nearly a decade before the outbreak of the American Revolution, Josiah Quincy, a young attorney of Boston, warned the readers of the *Boston Gazette* that ministerial powers in England were about to snuff out the lantern of liberty and enslave the white population of America. In graphic terms he depicted the scenes that would quickly ensue: how the 'rank adulterer [the Tory neighbor] riots in thy incestuous bed, a brutal ravisher deflowers thy only daughter, a barbarous villain now lifts his murtherous hand and stabs the tender infant to the heart . . .'. On the basis of such popular notions of danger, despotism, and ministerial conspiracy, American revolutionaries hoped to unite the colonies against the degradation of tyranny.[1]

Historians of the American Revolution, however, seem rather uncomfortable with the bloodthirsty rhetoric to be found in the hundreds of revolutionary pamphlets, reports of political rallies and riots, and correspondence of the founding fathers. As Gordon Wood noted some years ago, scholars have been preoccupied with the Revolution as a purely intellectual movement – with somewhat mixed results.[2] We know much about the evolution of republican theory but have missed the ardour that gripped the revolutionary soul. We should remember that, unlike the mid-nineteenth-century sectional conflict, the Revolution was both a civil and a foreign war. The violence of the 1770s included proportionately more horrors than occurred in the carnage of the 1860s – the shooting of prisoners and civilians, vigilante executions, torture, and looting.[3] In the pre-revolutionary tumult, both sides, Tory and Patriot, used 'inflammatory words so forcefully' that they stir the blood even in this violent age.[4] As Quincy's words indicate, the fervid expression of liberty and virtue on the one hand and base subjection and villainy on the other, would seem, as colonial historian Jack Greene and others put it, 'exaggerated'.[5] According to Bernard Bailyn, the leading authority on the subject, such impassioned expression arose from 'real fears, real anxieties, a sense of real danger . . .'. They accompanied a conviction, Bailyn says, that the powers in London had engaged in a secret plot to steal American birth-rights to justice and autonomy.[6] But Bailyn is surprisingly incurious to know why fears of diabolical designs and impending doom arose.

In contrast to Bailyn's diffidence on this score, Robert Middlekauff, another major scholar of the era, takes a direct but unfortunately unconvincing line. After a few remarks on Oedipal factors, he dismisses psychological explanations. Instead, he contends that the causes of eighteenth-century American 'discontent – or aggression' are too remote to be reconstructed now. Instead he seeks an answer to the mystery in the familiar, intellectualized solution: the notion that late-seventeenth-century radical Whigs like John Trenchard, Thomas Gordon, and Bishop Hoadley inspired American enthusiasms. But that proposition does not address causes; it merely describes some reading activity.[7] Besides, study of English tracts in America was scarcely widespread enough to inflame a substantial portion of the country to war. The average man in the street or behind the plough had not studied Thomas Gordon's *Cato's Letters*. Most likely he never heard of it.

Nor can we simply claim that Americans were responding to British oppression. Admittedly, American grievances were considerable. Great Britain had abruptly changed imperial policies in 1763. There were new taxes to pay for the war with France just ended. Even before the close of the Seven Years' War, royal authorities were aware that the colonists might rebel if trade restrictions and other regulations were imposed. But, the reasoning went, the insolent Americans needed firm handling, particularly since their illicit trading with neutrals and enemies during the war had been so shameless.[8] With the French and Spanish presence removed from the Atlantic seaboard, the English government at last had the opportunity to force its will upon the wayward colonists. As a result, new rules appeared to regularize the colonial bureaucracy. New patronage posts ripe for nepotism and corruption had been created. Moreover, leaders in Parliament were prepared to enact harsh penalties to repress dissent. These and other aggravating decisions came as a shock. After 150 years of relative neglect, the colonists were used to running their own affairs.[9] The upsurge of pro-British patriotism which common cause against the ancient rivals had engendered during the war quickly turned to disillusionment.[10]

Yet compared with the tragic history of Ireland, for instance, the colonists had very little about which to complain. For one thing, white Americans were largely freeholders. In Ireland, 90 per cent of the land was held by British landlords. Although a virtual wilderness, America was rich, Ireland 'desperately poor'. As Gordon Wood has concluded, 'The objective social reality scarcely seemed capable of explaining a revolution.'[12] Moreover, despite varied levels of oppression from colony to colony, anti-English reactions were remarkably uniform throughout the whole.[13] Something more dynamic, more basic in the nature of man, had emerged in the decade prior to armed rebellion. The neglected element was the ethic of honour. That ancient code of conduct and social perception helps to explain American resentment of English authority. The Age of Reason was also the Age of Honour.

In a world of chronic mistrust and instability, particularly in face-to-face, localized societies where personality, ritual and appearance more than institutions and abstraction or law dominate, honour and shame become the twin poles of the social gyroscope. Although historians have neglected this aspect of revolutionary and even counter-revolutionary rhetoric and action, the honour-shame code forms the structure by which emotions, not just the mind alone, find an ethical outlet. An upsurge of anger is no less likely to be channelled into ritual forms of expression and symbolic actions than is rational discourse. American scholars of republicanism seem to disagree with our proposition. Yet power, it seems, must lie at the heart of any revolution, even a conservative one like the American. The rhetoric denoting a claim to power is its chief enabling force beyond the use of arms itself.[14] Examining stylized forms of speech and ritual actions in their emotional context is no less relevant to understanding the American Revolution than tabulating those economic and political grievances that gave them rise. The ethic described here filled that mission.

As anthropologist Julian Pitt-Rivers explains, honour requires a sense of self-mastery, independence. Shame implies inability to exercise will and power, a failure that involves deep opprobrium. Under these conditions, honour, among other things, is a personal or collective claim for public approval. When favourably rendered, that signal of respect and moral standing is incorporated into one's sense of selfhood or group identity. But the opposite is also true. To be shamed tends to diminish one's own self-image. The honour-shame ethos is deeply conservative and defensive. It relies upon familial connections and attitudes so that the individual identifies with his lineage and his posterity. Kinlessness and solitude are the twin dangers to be avoided at all costs. Such a posture was well suited to a people certain that liberties already won were being assaulted and eroded by forces alien to the corporate body in which the individual finds protection. Powerlessness, argued the patriot Aedanus Burke, degrades 'men in their own opinion' of themselves. Unless quickly redressed, he continued, they soon manifest 'timid, cringing habits' and become 'fit tools for the ambitious designs, and arbitrary dispositions of haughty aspiring superiors'.[15] This aspect of honour will guide the remarks to follow: the interrelationship between personal and communal hopes for glory and dread of shame in the political arena.

Before proceeding further, however, one should acknowledge that the patriots had no monopoly on the concept of honour. Instead it was the *lingua franca* of all factions and groups in the transatlantic world. Certainly monarchists could even lay greater stress on the ethic than could the restive American Whigs. After all, submission to the crown seemed to many the sole means for the maintenance of what order could be obtained in that age of fragile institutions. The image of the happy family, over which the patriarchal monarch reigned, accompanied American Tory appeals for submission to the homeland across the ocean. Thomas Chandler, a New York loyalist, in 1775 urged men to defy the insurrectionary Continental Congress because 'You must know, that singularity in right conduct will be an honour to you, and a shame only to them that act otherwise.' In once more appealing 'decently' and 'humbly' to 'King, Lords, and Commons of Great Britain', we must assure them, the Tory continued, 'that we dread the very thoughts of an absolute independency; and that we see no prospect of security or happiness but under the powerful protection and mild superintendency of the mother country'.[16] In similar fashion, James Chalmers replied to Thomas Paine's *Common Sense* that 'Independence and Slavery are synonymous terms.' His premise was one that American patriots naturally would take as the very negation of honour.[17] In his many pamphlets, John J. Zubly of Savannah, a dissenting clergyman, stressed the theme of colonial gratitude to a generous, fatherly monarch. After the repeal of the Stamp Act in 1765, he recommended 'a still greater degree of attachment' to the 'illustrious house' of Hanover 'in return for this royal condescension and favour'. In 1780, after suffering persecution at the hands of Georgia Whigs, he wrote, 'Great Britain's condescension will do honour to them as a nation, and bring a blessing on the King's arms . . .'.[18]

As these examples demonstrate, like any other ethical mode, honour permitted a variety of interpretations about the nature of exemplary or shameful behaviour. Clearly principles of hierarchy and largesse collided with the republican imperative: personal and collective independence, another priority in the exercise of honour. But to expect consistency in any ethical system would be mistaken. Ambiguities, even tragedies, about the preservation of one's own honour in opposition to the superiority of another's claim for obedience were always part of the competitive system, as the classic works of Homer, Shakespeare and Calderón attest.[19] Differences of this kind, however, by no means negated the utility of the ethic as a fountain of language and action.

Our concern, however, is the patriots' appropriation of honour to justify republican revolution and experimentation. Three ways in which this form of honour figured were these: first, as the basic language of freedom from external, metropolitan authority. In reaction to specific, unpopular imperial measures, that discourse rejected any sense of obligation to an unreliable mother country. The second was the colonial determination to obtain a status of parity with the enemy by creating a new environment in which Americans could gain pre-eminence as gentlemen, warriors, or statesmen serving the cause of nation-building. Third, the colonists sought honour as a repudiation of its opposite polarity of servitude. That despised condition involved, they thought, dependency, unmanly passivity, and moral degradation. Rejection of bondage to England, as it was presumed to be, was a matter of considerable weight in a nation half-slave and half-free at the conclusion of the revolutionary era.

With reference to the first proposition, American revolutionary pamphlets employed the grammar and style of honour with a regularity that suggests its importance in everyday colonial life and habit. Sentiments regarding Christian faith, republicanism and liberty were also evident, as historians have long recognized.[20] But self-expression in terms of the ethic must also be taken very seriously. As linguists would say, the rhetoric employed was 'conative' or 'performative'. The purpose was to arouse the readers and listeners to action. To meet that objective a writer or orator had to find common ground by which to move the audience addressed.[21] The foundation of patriot polemics was simple, indeed primitive. Tract writers sought to arouse the manly instincts by portrayals of Tory or neutral citizens as craven cowards. Charlestonian John McKenzie raged that Britain had 'insulted – bullied' and generally treated Americans as 'emasculated eunuchs'.[22] Thomas Paine spoke similarly in *Common Sense*, 'Are your wife and children destitute . . .? Have you lost a parent or a child by their hand . . . if you have, and can still shake hands with the murderers, then you are unworthy of the name of husband, father, friend or lover, and whatever may be your rank or title in life, you have the heart of a coward, and the spirit of a sycophant.'[23]

When asserting their complaints, the patriots constantly spoke in polarities: glory and purity against villainy and disgrace, liberty and craven abasement.[24] A committee of the Continental Congress resolved: 'We are reduced to the alternative of chusing an unconditional submission to the tyranny of irritated ministers, or resistance by force. Honour, justice, and humanity, forbid us tamely to surrender that freedom which we received from our gallant ancestors, and which our innocent posterity have a right to receive from us. We cannot endure the infamy and guilt of resigning future generations to that wretchedness which inevitably awaits them, if we basely entail hereditary bondage upon them.'[25] A communication from the Massachusetts legislature neatly condensed the major themes of the Revolution in its declaration that patriots should enlist for military service in response to 'the dread of slavery, the sensations of honour and humanity, and the dictates of religion'.[26]

In stating the case for independence, the slave and free colonies adopted somewhat different language. The old ethic underlay both sectional self-justifications. The peculiarities of southern polemics will be treated later, but pious New Englanders, more than southern patriots, tended to couple honour with scriptural reference. They found the Old Testament especially appropriate, as well they might. The ancient Hebrew nation, like the modern Middle East, was well versed in the dictates of honour.[27] The irascible John Allen, a Baptist minister of Boston in 1773, took Micah, 7:3, for his text. He expounded on the right of a chosen people to protest and even overthrow the tyranny of evil rulers. Allen concluded menacingly: 'Has not the voice of your father's blood cry'd yet loud enough in your ears, in your hearts? "ye sons of America scorn to be slaves." Have you not heard the voice of blood in your streets, louder than that which reached to Heaven, that cry'd for vengeance, that was, said the Lord to Cain, the voice of thy brother's blood.'[28] Peter Thacher of Malden, Massachusetts, however, became so overwrought that he forgot the formality of providing an opening text. At once he plunged into the heart of the matter, urging his flock to 'spring to action, let us gird on the sword of the Lord and of Gideon, and determine to conquer or die! . . . Do not us hear of any of you who behave like cowards.' Only as he summed up did he recover the text – 2 Samuel 10:12 – but it was quite appropriate: 'Be of good courage, and let us play the men for our people.'[29]

New England laymen also rhapsodized on God's pleasure in righteous display of manly feelings. John Hancock, a leading politician of Boston, declared, 'I conjure you by all that is dear, by all that is honourable, by all that is sacred, not only that you pray, but that you act . . . Break in sunder, with noble disdain, the bonds with which the Philistines have bound you.'[30]

Such biblical phraseology, however, was mild compared with the angry extremities that arose among those men like Josiah Quincy quoted at the outset, who thought their sense of honour personally violated. Thomas Paine, Moses Mather, Samuel Adams, and many others in the northern states employed a rhetoric designed to rouse the passions by posing the direst calamities imaginable as the outcome of continued British rule: towns sacked, friends slaughtered, estates forfeited, houses burnt, wives and children made destitute, and daughters raped. Terms like infamy, villainy, demonic, fiendish, and shameless filled the printed pages and the ears of listeners at political assemblies. As early as 1770, Dr Joseph Warren, for instance, defied verisimilitude in conjuring up the image of the 'murdered husband gasping on the ground', whose 'infant babes' had to step on slippery stones 'bespattered with your father's brains'. Such scenes, he concluded, were the handiwork of 'Britain that inflicts the wound'.[31]

References to a familial paradigm suggest the conservative character of American republicanism. Separation from the 'mother country' was as necessary, the patriots believed, as the departure of youth from the parental hearthside. In drawing upon this familiar metaphor, Richard Wells declared in separating from England, 'we look to manhood'. But the departure was by no means amicable in light of the mother country's alleged betrayal and unnatural feelings of hostility toward her subjects abroad. As Samuel Landgon put it, the colonists were no longer satisfied to be the dependents of a parent ready to 'wage cruel war with its own children in these colonies, only to gratify the lust of power, and the demands of extravagance!' In his study of this rhetorical construction, Melvin Yazawa observes: 'The logic of the parent-child analogy thus had a compelling simplicity for the Revolutionaries: "if they are not considered as children, their Treatment is that of Slaves, and therefore, if oppressed, they must unite," as Nicholas Ray put it.'[32] The benignity of the familial image sharply contrasts with the extreme hyperbole of the language employed. Such 'mob-high eloquence', as Governor Thomas Hutchinson called it, suggested that the English nation was clearly bent on mass abuse and butchery of its colonial offspring.[33] The heightening of the rhetorical stakes went far beyond the exigencies of the case.

Behind these outbursts, of course, there were just complaints, most especially outrage over three topics, each to be discussed separately: unfair taxes; official corruption; and unjust parliamentary reprisals against the restive colonies. To treat the first: taxation and honour have always been incompatible. Coerced payment signifies abject disgrace. From the dawn of history, defeated enemies and inferior people had to forfeit property as tribute or tax. Free peoples, however, contributed to the king's treasury in terms of subsidy. In earliest times, revenue for the head of state was more or less a matter of gift exchange, albeit an unequal reciprocation. The revenues furnished were traded, as it were, for the benefits of leadership and responsibility vested in the king. So it had been understood by the Parliament, for instance, at the time of the Ship Money crisis in the reign of Charles I. The outcry against British taxation without American representation and voice in the process arose from this concept. It was based on the honour of grant or subsidy and the mortification of taxation. Oft-times polemicists turned to ancient history for precedent in developing this argument. James Otis, for instance, pointed out that in Periclean Greece, colonists were obliged only 'to pay a kind of deference and dutiful submission to the mother commonwealth'. But, he insisted, nothing more demeaning than that was required of them.[34]

As historians have long known, the parliamentary exactions on Americans to help reduce British indebtedness for the Seven Years' War were remarkably light by contemporary standards.[35] Colonists smarted under the affront of taxation with no means to bargain, modify, or persuade the parliamentary parties through colonial representation. In the Virginia resolutions to Lord North in 1775,

Thomas Jefferson argued that 'Whereas, we have right to give our money, as the Parliament does theirs, without coercion, from time to time, as public exigencies may require, we conceive that we are alone the judges . . . Because at the very time of requiring from us grants of Money they are (planning war against us) which is a stile of asking gifts not reconcileable [*sic*] to our freedom.' Likewise, the Congress's resolutions of 31 July 1775, spoke of taxes as 'gifts' not to be 'wasted among the venal and corrupt for the purpose of undermining the civil rights of the givers'.[36]

The category of tax and taxpayer entailed reduced social and political status. Such exactions lessened one's own and family's independence, that is, freedom from the control of or obligation to another. Machiavelli had long before warned that unwise rulers overtaxed their subjects at great peril, 'for men forget more easily the death of their father than the loss of their patrimony'.[37] In fact, by custom those who gained the most glory and authority from either military victories or office-holding were expected to pay for such honorifics. They should not burden marginal folk. Taxing Americans, however, had become popular in the home country, argued one pamphleteer, because the British had drained themselves while Ireland had been 'impoverished to almost the last farthing'.[33] Even Ireland, which, in James Otis's opinion, had fallen into English hands as 'a conquered country', deserved 'the same right to be free under a conqueror as the rest of his [majesty's] subjects'. How much more worthy then, he asked, should America be when at no time was it a defeated province, but one created by 'emigrant subjects'?[39]

The second grievance, problems of official venality, aroused almost equal fury. They violated the code in two specific ways. Nepotism and favouritism in office-seeking made even more uncertain than ever the advancement of Americans when competing for titles and posts against placemen with contacts at Whitehall unavailable to the distant colonists. Second, on a more uplifting plane, corruption of this kind reinforced the sense of impotence that men of honour felt in the handling of political affairs. Their anger stemmed from the implied dependency and alienation from authority that the indignity of open corruption flaunted in their faces. After all, the British were masters in the art of condescension and arrogance. No wonder Americans were vexed. The Rev. William Gordon of Roxbury, Massachusetts, summed up American reaction with a quotation from Proverbs: 'A brother offended is harder to be won than a strong city, and their contentions are like the bars of a castle.'[40] In thunderous response to the Stamp Act crisis, the Rev. Enoch Huntington of Massachusetts preached: 'Already do the avaricious courtiers of Great Britain, with the numerous train of their . . . hangers-on, with the whole tribe of dissolute spendthrifts, and idle deboshees, feast themselves' upon 'the spoils of our future earnings'. John Adams of Boston echoed the sentiment: 'When luxury, effeminacy, and venality' have reached 'a shocking pitch in England, when both electors and elected are become one mass of corruption; when the nation is oppressed to death with debts and taxes . . . what will be your condition under such a parliament? You would not only be slaves, but the most abject sort of slaves, to the worst sort of masters!' [41]

The third objection intimately connected with honour was the outcry against standing armies. Not only were they potential instruments of lawless tyranny, their presence signified mistrust of the local élite and the populace. The use of professional forces set at conflict the members of a locale against military inquisitors into their exclusive affairs. Such an opposition has been traced to the late-seventeenth-century Commonwealthman John Trenchard and earlier to James Harrington.[42] Suspicions of occupying armies, however, long pre-date that era. Clearly they violated the sense of local independence, the honour of the community. To the American colonists, the imposition of permanent forces, especially when quartered in civilian billets instead of barracks, signified humiliation, naked despotism.[43]

In sum, the language of protest and the source of the anger grew out of emotions for vengeance and self-vindication. Given a choice, men will not allow themselves to be treated as children or beasts; British indifference to the Americans' welfare reflected a sense of hauteur and disrespect that had to be challenged with violent words, violent deeds. Sometimes the form of protest was rather pacific: such as the movement against imported British goods. Yet the rationale was still linked to honour and its opposite. A Philadelphia editorial warned the city that '[There is] no Benefit in Wearing English woollens, but dishonor.'[44] Or, more grimly, the patriots' activities involved mobs and mass rallies. The various charivari or tarring and feathering to mock and enfeeble the loyalists signified the adoption of old popular European shaming rituals.[45] Like their cousins overseas, colonial Americans believed in a corporate ideal whereby a community, in the name of consensus, 'might join together and riot to purge itself of deviants or to protect itself from outside intrusions', as historian Paul Gilje has noted. In New York City, for instance, a lowly Tory shoemaker named Tweedy fell victim to a mob, endured an application of tar and feathers for denouncing the patriot cause, and had to beg mercy on his knees by ritualistically 'praying for Success to General Washington, and the American Arms, and Destruction to General Gage and his Crew of Traitors'.[46] Claiming 'Motives of Honour and Virtue', the magistrates of Westmoreland County, Virginia, refused to collect the Stamp Act revenues – after mobs had forced them to reconsider their plans.[47] Along with crowd destruction of statues of George III and other symbols of the hated régime, these protests weakened the sense of legitimacy that the English crown had previously enjoyed in America. The cross-Atlantic tie was no longer based on the idea of submission in exchange for 'that protection which the King affords his subjects', as the Whig Blackstone had defined allegiance in his *Commentaries*. The king had lost his royal mystique.[48]

With regard to the second issue – the question of self-regard in a worthy cause – one can discern the significance of another and higher form of honour: the stoic mode of gentility. Of course, English radical Whiggery – Gordon, Hoadley, Bolingbroke, and others – supplied revolutionary pamphleteers with ideas, precedents, and useful citations. But Americans were also influenced by such writers as Joseph Addison. His essays and especially his sententious play, *Cato*, in dramatic form sketched the struggle between tyranny and liberty.[49] As historian Forrest McDonald points out, the eighteenth-century gentleman cherished his 'character' or public reputation above all else. Addison's *Cato* was largely designed to demonstrate illustrious reputation. The playwright had not sought to serve partisan purposes. The tragedy's American popularity, however, arose from its current pertinence: the role that heroes could play in the war against despotism.[50]

Defence of reputation became a matter of acute significance in the pre-revolutionary years because of a growing awareness of British culture. As America had become more 'anglicized' and sophisticated as a result of increased contact with the English during the Seven Years' War, the more self-conscious they became of their own status in the eyes of the Old World. One manifestation was the adoption of the duel as a signal of gentlemanly status and values. Being a martial code, the ethic was evident in the regularizing of personal violence in the upper classes during the war with England. The custom of duelling, which those styling themselves gentlemen adopted from French and English military example, replaced the older and more haphazard modes – fistfights, cart-whippings and tavern brawls. Thereafter gentlemen, especially southerners, were more likely to meet on the field of honour than to brawl indiscriminately as they once had done. Penalties were light enough to serve as no deterrent.[51] The phenomenon coincided with the rise of duelling throughout the empire, including Dublin, where the reformer Henry Grattan exchanged shots with Isaac Corry, Chancellor of the Exchequer, and the Phoenix Park became a danger to passers-by owing to the stray bullets fired.[52] In fact, the appearance of so many Irish in America during the century may have helped to reinforce the principles of honour that required men to vindicate their reputations by such lethal means. In more general terms, the Irish presence had much more to do with the antipathy toward the crown than we have been led to believe.[53] If the Irish herdsmen brought their special economic and social patterns, particularly evident in the southern back-country, they also contributed to the concepts of honour beyond ritual duelling. The ethic relied upon a sturdy social and political localism such as that to be found in the Irish and Ulster heritage.[54]

In any event, the duties of honour were not confined to the upper classes alone. Ordinary young men who entered military service used appropriately martial language for self-inspiration. In writing home on the first Fourth of July, a young revolutionary recruit declared, 'Our own and our country's honor all calls upon us for a vigorous and manly exertion, & if we now shamefully fail, we shall become infamous to the whole world.'[55]

Nonetheless, the officer corps was particularly inspired by the pursuit of glory, one that brought out the touchy competitiveness with which honour has always been associated. General Robert Howe, hoping to assume command of American forces in South Carolina, wrote to patriot Henry Laurens, 'I have been long on the Brigadiers list and pant to get higher.'[56] An appropriate military title always enhanced one's status as a gentleman, especially throughout the slaveholding south.

In a country where there was relatively little distance among whites between high and low and where advanced education was rare, the task of fashioning a gentlemanly officer class was only partially successful.[57] Feeling injured by an order from the Continental Congress, General Nathanael Greene wrote to George Washington in 1776 that he feared an attempt 'to degrade me in Publick estimation. [A measure] of that sort would sink me in my own estimation and render me spiritless and uneasy in my situation and consequently unfit for the service.'[58]

By the rubrics of the code, a desire for fame was virtuous so long as ambition was limited by deference to the judgment of those whose good opinion warranted respect.[59] Uncontrolled yearnings for power, like avarice, led directly to corruption under the honour-shame code of gentlemen. Nonetheless, self-restraint in this regard was hard to achieve. Although democratic ideals were emerging, the European code of honour which dignified leaders with appropriate marks of distinction still applied. Douglass Adair, historian of the Revolution, once remarked that he had discovered in the founding fathers 'a sort of pathology of the "love of fame"' that accompanied the pursuit of liberty.[60] One might expect that so secular an ideal would animate men in the deistical south more than in the evangelical north. Yet even in New England, the classical view of honour had such strong advocates that one is tempted to say that the ethic was itself a factor that helped to bind north and south at this time. With Addison's drama in mind, at the funeral for General Enoch Poor, military chaplain Israel Evans of New Hampshire, in 1781 likened the dead hero to Cato. Like the ancient Roman, he said, General Poor 'chose to be virtuous rather than appear so; he preferred that self-approbation which arises from meritorious actions, to the changeable and tumultuous acclamations of the fickle multitude'.[61] New England clergymen could preach the virtues of manliness as well as any host of army colonels. Samuel Sherwood rejoiced that the 'main body' of Americans 'know they are men, and have the spirits of men; and not an inferior species of animals, made to be beasts of burden to a lawless, corrupt administration'.[62]

Whether northern or southern, revolutionary leaders entertained hopes for eternal remembrance for their deeds during the crisis. From their reading, especially of Plutarch and Machiavelli, patriots knew that builders of empires and republics stood next highest to founders of religion in the annals of history.[63] Alexander Hamilton, the leading New York patriot, espoused 'that love of fame which is the ruling passion of the noblest minds'.[64] What they sought was 'the esteem of wise and good men'. That aim might be called the political side of stoic, Christian gentility, a refined, class-based concept.[65] To be true to others first, and thereby earned the respect and deference of the virtuous was the means for reinforcing one's own sense of identity and self-worth. Such pursuers of honour, as Forrest McDonald argues, reversed the advice that Shakespeare put in the mouth of Polonius. Truth to others came first; after that one could be true to oneself.[66] So phrased, the maxim fits the nature of honour. The ethic relies upon external appearances of bravery, magnanimity, self-regard, and other stalwart virtues, but not upon the inner life, an area usually unselfexamined.

To amplify the point, one can do no better than turn to General Washington. In his own day, as well as throughout the nineteenth century, he seemed the model of Horatian self-sacrifice, prudence, courage, dignity, and self-discipline, the classical, stoic virtues most admired at home and in the British Isles. Yet Washington practised all the licit male vices – gambling, wenching, money-grubbing, and he was 'a most horrid swearer and blasphemer'.[67] Such vices took nothing from his status. Oft-times, such displays were greeted as welcome signs of virility. Under these conditions, to press forward for the sake of glory offered two advantages to the patriot-hero – honour for himself and the creation of a nation prepared to revere him in gratitude for generations to come.

These feelings were not simply personal in character. The desirability of fashioning a corps of leaders for the republic included the notion that honour was an indispensable element in republican education. It found its way into the curriculum of the new nation. As John Adams pointed out approvingly some years after the Revolution, 'Knowledge will forever be a natural cause of aristocracy.'[68] The classics were culled for examples of honourable behaviour, for heroes exemplifying the appropriate marks of Ciceronian patriotism, judgment, tough-mindedness, and proper ambition for glorious remembrance in ages to come. One revolutionary preacher declaimed over the bier of General Montgomery in early 1776 that, 'according to the ancient Romans, in pedagogy, honour is a more powerful incentive than fear'. Men were seldom punished severely for 'cowardice or neglect of duty but by what was accounted worse, a life decreed to ignominious expulsion and degradation from Roman privileges'.[69] In keeping with frequent reference to pagan forms of virtue, John Adams and most other founding fathers believed that mankind was forever governed by the same motives, both good and bad. Therefore by reading ancient history the best precepts of government could be ascertained as well as the surest means of restraint against perfidy and disorder.[70] Americans did not study the ancients in the original or through English literature of the 'Augustan Age' simply to ponder the nature of republics, their pristine origins and subsequent degeneracy and fall. In addition, they sought to inculcate the essentials of pagan morality.[71] At late-eighteenth-century Dickinson

College in Pennsylvania, for instance, the professor of Latin, Robert Davidson, taught grammar by demonstrating the relation of ambition to slavery in this fashion: 'Rome was enslaved. Caesar was ambitious. Connect them by the conjunction because and then it will be Rome was enslaved because Caesar was ambitious.'[72] The purpose of such exercises was not just to instill a love of liberty but to quicken awareness of an exemplary honour by imitating the excellencies of superiors and peers and rejecting the vices and disgrace of inferiors.[73]

My final theme is how honour was a factor in the relationship between liberty and what the Rev. James Emerson of New England called 'vile ignominious slavery'.[74] It has long puzzled American historians that the founding fathers seemed blind to the contradiction between ownership of slaves and the insistence upon universal freedom, as expressed in the Declaration of Independence. Among other meanings attributable to the phrase 'all men are created equal' is the notion that claims to honour are open to all members of the white fraternity upon an equal footing. So it was later understood in the antebellum south. According to the hierarchy which the ethic upheld, slavery, on the other hand, represented the most disgraceful, humiliating, and pitiable condition known to man. As Orlando Patterson has observed, human bondage is a form of 'social death'. The victim is rendered nameless, kinless, penniless, defenceless and hopeless, except by the mercy, convenience or whim of the master. In the eighteenth century, slavery was the most extreme form of social alienation. But other types of involuntary subordination – indentured servants, redemptioners, apprentices, landless labourers – were well-entrenched parts of the social structure. As a result, the notion of freedom implied some minimal social standing as one capable of self-provision or freedom from subordination under another. Hence the constant message of revolutionary propaganda was to protest all signs of what Josiah Quincy called 'the chains of vassalage'.[75]

Even if there had been no slaves in the colonies, the patriot whites would have referred to slavery as the opposite of liberty. The presence of black bondspeople, however, did add a note of immediacy and example. The American Whigs took for granted black isolation. Slaves simply did not belong except as dependents. Thus, when criticized for hypocrisy, American polemicists argued not on grounds of universal rights but on matters of treatment as if asked about the way planters handled their horses. When challenged, most of the American spokesmen considered the slaveholders as men of honourable intention and deportment. Pride and interest combined, it was thought, to assure kindness and forbearance of their black menials.[76]

The rhetoric involved should be understood within the context of an assumed connection between liberty and honour, slavery and shame. Said Thomas Gordon in *Cato's Letters*, 'Oh Liberty! Oh Servitude! how amiable, how detestable, are the different Sounds! Liberty is Salvation in Politicks, as Slavery is Reprobation.'[77] The conflation made possible the seeming paradox of slaveholders demanding freedom for themselves even as they implicitly denied it to a whole race. By the ethic of honour, such a discrepancy involved no paradox. It simply reflected a proper division of labour. The fitting analogy was the assurance, by usage and common law, that men held proprietary rights in their wives and children, on the basis of natural, God-given ascriptive hierarchy.[78] As if to underline the point, the Rev. Jonathan Mayhew of Boston observed that colonial slaves shared their masters' opinions about British tyranny. They knew, he said, that 'it would be more ignominious and wretched to be the servant of servants, than of free-men'. We should not, however, readily accept the New England clergyman's judgment about the reaction of slaves.[79]

In the south the connection between the honour of whites and the presumed dishonour of blacks was naturally more intensely felt. The white populace was well aware of the dangers that emancipation or insurrection might visit upon the social order. Furthermore, racial levelling would threaten community and personal honour. In the low country of South Carolina, for instance, attorney Timothy Ford declared, 'The instant a citizen is oppressed below par . . . in point of freedom, he approaches to the condition of his own slave, his spirit is at once aroused, and he necessarily recoils to his former standing.'[80] Upon that basis, the classes of the south were united. No one could countenance slave uprising. It threatened the status of honour of all whites. For that reason, punishment for slave insurrection, which often included capital punishment, had universal approval. Heads were placed on poles as warning to would-be conspirators. The barbarism suggests just how insecure and fearful the whites were in contemplating a racial levelling.

Whether the danger came from below or from English authorities abroad, the revolutionary response was quick and potentially violent. Christopher Gadsden of Charleston urged that citizens be prepared 'to avert by every means in our Power the abject Slavery intended for us and our Posterity; for my part I would rather see my family reduced to the utmost Extremity and half cut to pieces than to submit to their damned Machinations'.[81] To show any sign of weakness was to lose face entirely. As George Washington put it, 'we must assert our rights or submit to every imposition . . . till custom and use shall make us as tame and abject slaves as the blacks we rule over with such arbitrary sway'.[82] He intended no irony.

This approach to the American Revolution by no means serves as the ultimate solution to problems of causality. Certainly there had to be basic economic and political conflicts at the heart of the matter. Nonetheless, anger, a sense of insult and outrage against arbitrary and arrogant behaviour had to play a major role in the first great revolution of modern times. Whereas other scholars have stressed the role of republican idealism, homegrown and imported, this interpretation has sought to explain why those ideals accompanied a language and set of actions of a deeply conservative but inspiring character.

During the revolutionary era, love of honour and fear of shame drew the north and south together in common antipathy for British overlords. Tragically, that once-unified paradigm of ethical and political values – faith in a rational republicanism and a continued devotion to honour for the defence of selfhood and vindication of repute – was not to last beyond the middle years of the next century. Southerners continued to admire the revolutionary rhetoric with its primal overtones that glorified ascriptions of power and race. Meantime, however, northerners had developed a different ethic. It was based upon evangelical and secular principles of individualistic redemption and material advance. Only a second and still bloodier test of arms would provide a grander, more humanitarian, but still imperfect meaning to both liberty and to the concept of honour.

FOUR

'ROUSSEAU'S STUTTER': THE FRENCH REVOLUTION, PHILOSOPHY AND THE HISTORY OF THE FUTURE

Dorinda Outram

Someone is posted missing. The favourite stalking-horse of historians of all epochs, 'the middle class', a class which has held centre-stage in French revolutionary historiography since time immemorial, seems to be now strangely absent from the events of 1789, currently being celebrated with such lavish outpourings of ceremonial celebration and rapid historical writing. I want to argue that this current, and currently modish, position is doing no good to our understanding either of the French Revolution, or of our investment in the Revolution, whether as historians or as members of late-twentieth-century western society.

But how has this situation come about? After all, from the outset the Revolution has normally, even compulsively, attracted totalizing interpretations, and interpretations which placed the middle class or their stand-ins, 'spirit' or 'reason', at centre-stage. Hegel and Marx are only the two greatest exponents of this view. In other words, the history of the Revolution and the history of the future have traditionally been wrapped up in each other. But since the 1970s we have been able to watch the collapse of Marxist paradigms: and, further, we have also seen the establishment of a unique position, one whose emergence should be impossible under Kuhnian laws of paradigm change, in which the field has shed the immensely strong paradigm granted to it by Marx, and has received instead an infinitely weaker one from François Furet's 1978 *Penser la Révolution*.[1] Furet's objective was to contest the Marxist hold on the interpretation of the Revolution which he perceived as dominant in France. According to him, the political, intellectual and institutional dominance of such figures as Albert Soboul, had led to an interpretation of the Revolution which compulsively linked it to the Russian Revolution of October 1917, and which made its main conceptual referent Marx's theories of the historical succession of the forms of economic organization.

Furet's view attempts to return the Revolution to its definition as a political event, and furthermore a distinct kind of political event, which he calls a 'revolutionary phenomenon'. According to Furet, it is a 'phenomenon' characterized by the use of a particular political discourse, that of the Jacobin language of 1792-4. Furet alleges that the polarized, abstract quality of this discourse, with its inability to mediate between opposed interests, idealization of the general will and of individual political virtue, provided the essential motor of revolutionary politics, characterized by the use of violence and terror and the rapid turn-over of dominant factions.[2] Terror, in fact, gave a political economy to that General Will which Rousseau had declared unrepresentable. Where Rousseau had stuttered, the Revolution clenched its teeth.

Yet, while Furet's work did valuable service in returning the French Revolution to the political universe, it also poses more problems than it solves. Firstly his account not only detaches the Revolution from the history of the future; it also has little to say about its relations to the past. His account does little to answer the repeated pleas of Enlightenment historians, such as Keith Baker, for an account of the tie-up between Enlightenment, political culture and the explosion of events post-1789. [3] It is also true that the history of the French Revolution has yet to absorb the new history of power and intelligence associated with Foucault. In that sense, Furet's work operates as an anti-paradigm, appearing to explain less rather than more: and, leaving the reader with (in spite of Furet's verbal virtuosity) a feeling of why should we care? Why, in this year of 1989, should we be sinking such huge resources into the bicentennial of 1789?

Some apprehension may also be felt on the grounds of the implicitly conservative orientation of Furet's argument. Not only does his account carry much unacknowledged philosophical freight about 'discourse' and its analysis – but, secondly, the account, which gives 'discourse' a crucial place, is also gender-blind. 'Discourse' is seen as a catch-all category, ignoring the extent to which male and female experiences of, use of and reception of language is, as we well know, strongly differentiated.[4] This is particularly important point when the revolutionary discourse itself hinged on the concept of virtue, a concept which is hardly univalent in respect of gender. Even more significant is what Furet leaves out.

Concepts crucial to his theme, such as 'the political' are left totally unexamined – a major feat in the post-Foucault era. As well, Furet leaves out the social class analysis beloved of his forebears. Not only the middle class disappears but the sans-culottes too. Concepts like 'behaviour', 'ideology' and 'public realm' are also conspicuous by their absence: thus Furet's account denies itself crucial bridges by which he might translate from the 'political phenomenon' which is the Revolution to the significance of that cacophony of events, words, prescriptions, theatres and categories.

I am going to stop here in my analysis of the strange defects of Furet's account. Not because I have exhausted the topic, but because to devote more time to it would carry the impression of frivolous nit-picking and churlish ingratitude towards Furet's very considerable achievement. It is also far more interesting to put forward positive suggestions as to how this field of French revolutionary history might be reinfused with the driving vigour which it once contained.

The most crucial intellectual move here is to take on Furet's wish to detach the history of the French Revolution from its automatic referent in Marxist theory and Marxist-Leninist praxis. Furet fails to consider the idea that there might be ways in which the history of the Revolution could be reuniversalized, reinscribed with meaning, which are yet not connected to a Marxist paradigm, and which also allow us to differentiate ourselves from a definition of the 'revolutionary phenomenon' restricted to 'discourse' and a narrow version of 'the political'.

Long ago, Ferdinand de Saussure remarked that an account of discourse is meaningless without an account of the behaviour which accompanies the words. And behaviour is what gets left out of Furet's account. To restore both specificity and meaning to the Revolution we have to face up to the fact that the behaviour produced by the Revolution was often of a kind which rationalist historians, who think that they have described an event when they have described speech acts which have accompanied the event, find difficult to tolerate. The mouthings about reason, virtue, and the republic, about the general will and the rights of man were of course accompanied by events which historians of the Revolution in the twentieth century have preferred to pass over, and seem happy to see consigned to popular histories, to films, television and the French equivalents of *History Today*. The group suicides and assassinations, the strange theatricality with which members of the Convention dress up as Albanians and Romans, the mob dismemberment of corpses, the mass executions, the prison massacres and the mechanization of death through the guillotine, the atrocities of civil war, the crowds waving Féraud's head in the Convention during the *prairial* days, seem to be somehow routinely ignored in the modern academic vision of the Revolution; or are they simply too threatening for a profession still mesmerized by what has been called the phantom of objectivity?[5] Few historians have heeded Linda Orr's recent calls for a 'retraumatization' of the Revolution.[6] The blood, fear and dismemberment are best left, one might gather from many a modern account, to ideologically engaged historians of the nineteenth-century right, such as Taine or Thiers. But it seems to me that in thus sanitizing the French Revolution we were dangerously likely to misperceive quite vital features of it – in fact to destroy our entire perception of it as a syndrome of events which taken together are capable of being invested with meaning and life.

In ignoring what happened to bodies in the Revolution revolutionary historians are ignoring an area where contemporary sensibilities and their immediate, nineteenth-century heirs invested huge historical weight: the men and women of the 1790s and the historians of the 1820s onwards are obsessional in their willingness to relate stories about the body, its theatrical uses, its dire fates. Why have we largely abandoned this insight? Might it not be because that most historians of the Revolution in England lack the conceptual baggage to make sense of the body in history, while French historians of the Revolution are still prisoners of the fact that the modern history of the Revolution was created in the 1890s not only in the light of a new socialist and Marxist slant, but also in the light of new claims by the profession – and its leading edge, the historians of the Revolution – to be acting as professionals, in a nineteenth-century neo-positivist way based on 'objective' assessment of facts – who were therefore deeply fearful of too close an encounter with both the irrational and the natural.

It was precisely this which attracted me, in my most recent book, *The Body and the French Revolution*, to the idea that it might be possible to use the history of the body to give body once more to the Revolution. Partly because of the suspicious nature – which Richard Cobb has called the historians' tendency to snoop – which is or should be part and parcel of the historians' equipment, that instinct which immediately leads one to suspect something amiss when the dog doesn't bark in the night, when something is not talked about. That which is absent is often the most important. The body is capable of acting as a conceptual focus in a way which may allow us to produce once more an idea of the Revolution as capable of focusing meaning.[7] Far be it from me to appear to emulate at this point the messianism of some recent historians, particularly that which has focused on the idea of historical return in the context of Jewish history.[8] What I am proposing though is an approach to the history of the Revolution which would have been characterized as Jewish by many fascist ideologues of the 1930s, in so far as they identified irony, especially irony in attitudes towards the state, as a particularly Jewish stance.[9] It seems to me that the particular history of the body and the Revolution which I am about to propose fulfils this purpose. My own view of the encultured body is of that of a prism: a unique place of concentration of both ineluctably individual subjectivity and of social needs and readings. Like a prism, the body concentrates rays of light from many different originating points in our knowledge of society, and sends out those rays differently coloured and broken up through our knowledge of their interaction. This conception of the body also allows us to restore a place to the subjectivity of historical actors, to see them as actors choosing from among the options present in what Habermas would call the life-world, to make their own relationship with the systems in the society around them.

This means that my own idea of what I mean by a history of the body is rather different from that contained in some recently fashionable versions and notably to that of Michel Foucault. How does my own version of the history of the body differ from that produced by Foucault? Mainly in that, in spite of his many statements to the contrary, Foucault's 'death of the historical actor' has in fact led him to leave individual subjectivity experienced through and by the body out of the count. His subjects do not create their own bodies through their awareness, their choices, their acts, their speech, their narrative; rather, their bodies are inscribed upon the state with its changing rationale of power and authority.[10] In this sense Foucault's account of the state and the bodies of individuals is itself as coercive as the relations he describes. There is little room for the ironic approach of the history that works in the gap between what is and what should be, which is in a profound sense the grateful heir of two other radical category shifts of the Enlightenment: Hume's division between Is and Ought, and Kant's between Ends and Means.

This is also an important point to make because the late Enlightenment faced individual men and women with the gap between what is and what should be in very acute forms. As corporate identities broke down as the end of the Old Régime approached, prescriptions for the achievement of individual authenticity multiplied, to such an extent that the same individual might feel called upon to act out the roles of ancient Roman Stoic, man of feeling in effusions of tears over the fate of Pamela, Clarissa or La Nouvelle Héloïse, and man of the world, masking his true feelings behind a barrage of conventionalized gestures, speech and language. Whether to be Cato, Julie or Grandison, Wolmar (or even Melmoth) was a problem which faced the late-eighteenth-century person in a continuous way: because the question of who controlled real personal authenticity, who could personify virtue, was fast becoming, even before the Revolution, the key to the question of who could control and define public space.

This was happening because the traditional definition of authority as respect for monarchy, and the traditional definition of the public realm as co-terminous with the mystical entity, 'the king's body', was breaking down in Enlightenment Europe. The political and financial pressures of international competition had forced the monarchs to compromise their historic bases of support in society, the nobility and the old agrarian order. This had set off the increased series of challenges to monarchies all over Europe which Robert Palmer long ago christened the 'Age of the Democratic Revolution'.[11] At the same time, the reform programmes of the monarchies had validated in society the Enlightenment values of rationality and ordered progress, and set these values into circulation well beyond the middle classes where they had originally found a lodging. By the end of the Old Régime, the increasing discrepancy between the traditional values in society and Enlightenment rationales was becoming painfully apparent.

Reforms and government advisers alike began to realize that if their programmes and rational values generally were to be kept alive then they would have to look for support beyond the shifting personal will of the monarch. They would have to create a third political force, that of 'public opinion', to create stable support for the projects of the Enlightenment.[12] How was their appeal to public opinion justified, in a world where politics was still – nominally at least – something that focused on the sacred figure of the monarch? The justification came through the appeal to superior virtue and rationality. The creation of the archetype of the virtuous man – self-controlled, austere, seeking public good – was in spite of its classical and Renaissance antecedents one of the major projects of the eighteenth century, and it is arguably the project which underlies the cacophony which accompanied the Enlightenment. It was also what permitted the intrusion of a self-consciously middle-class self-image onto the public sphere as an alternative validating force, in the light of which the aristocracy could be portrayed as an opposite force – dedicated to power through display, to ostentation, to extravagance, to an outward-looking, self-spending, image which had nothing to do with the self-retentivity of the enlightened middle class. It was this development also which made embodiment, the filling of the body with the referrents of the universal virtue, such a central issue to the politics both of the late Enlightenment and to the Revolution itself. To embody virtue was to be able to make legitimate demands to exercise power and command deference. As Mme Roland's friend Sophie Grandchamp said of the arch-virtuous Roland: 'the stamp of virtue on his features made me long to obtain his approval'.[13]

Norbert Elias, in a theory of the body which more successfully pulls together subjectivity and the state, has argued that the end of the eighteenth century saw the consummation of a process of increasing self-control in society, a process whereby the externally imposed restraint of violent emotions and their accompanying physical expression from the late middle ages on had by the 1780s produced an internalized feeling in many individuals of a radical separation, an invisible wall between themselves and others, of being locked inside themselves. This figure Elias has labelled *homo clausus*: it was this man who became the archetype of virtue in the late Enlightenment and Revolution: who carried with him the idea of knowledge as objectivity, the separation of the self from the object of knowledge, and with whose legacy of alienation we are still dealing.[14] The apparently bizarre nature of much political behaviour in the Revolution itself, the suicides, the claims to be Cato or Brutus comes down to this anxiety about embodiment, this anxiety to validate the seizure of power from the king's body by the physical embodiment of the countervailing magic of virtue in Everyman. It was on this fact that Rousseau prophetically stuttered that the General Will could not be represented. It was this, rather than a 'discourse', which was the precondition for revolutionary terror.

After the destruction of the monarchy, it did become vital to locate that general will: what was to be done with the vast reserves of sovereignty which the monarchy had possessed? How to justify its redistribution and the sacrilege that had preceded it? The answer to that was to make the figure of the virtuous man take on the shape of the public realm, make the state and individual virtue one and the same thing, just as before 1792, the king's body and the public realm had also been the same thing. It is only in this sense that it becomes impossible to understand the French Revolution as an affair of words; it was a world where the intersection between individual self-consciousness, the embodiment of virtue, and the shape of the public realm were inextricably linked.

Thus, to think about the Revolution in terms of bodies and of behaviours, to revitalize the problem of embodiment, is also to help to fill the Revolution itself with significance which is yet not compulsively linked to a Marxist and socialist view of the past and future. It is because of the absence of a history of embodiment that the account of middle-class seizure of dominance presented by Marx should also have failed to bring to bring to consciousness the whole problem of the definition of the political and the public sphere. This has also happened because the Revolution has been presented from the close of the nineteenth century by a highly professionalized 'scientific' history, part of the claim by middle-class knowledge-professionals to control the past, and by doing so contribute to the constitution of the middle class in their own times. It is not an insignificant fact that both the nineteenth- and twentieth-century Marxists and Furet himself, their declared adversary, should have found difficulty in confronting what should surely be the central task of any revolutionary historian, the delineation of the public realm. To bring into historical being that realm is also to start to situate the middle class, and by implication the author himself, in relation to the state, to make manifest the relationships of political power which in fact operate on the so-called objective or scholarly text and thus potentially open the way for a questioning of middle-class legitimation. No wonder Roland Barthes once remarked that the bourgeoisie was a class that dared not speak its name.

This is especially the case at the moment, when the relationship of the public realm, state and society is problematic as never before, except possibly in the era of the Revolution itself. Many of the problems we face today are not only the direct products of the twentieth century, but are also the legacy of the Revolution itself. In particular, the image of the validated public actor, that of the autonomous individual, *homo clausus*, endowed with 'rights', has come under repeated attack without being meaningfully replaced, both from the twentieth-century state, and also for very different reasons from groups in society, particularly women, whom it has excluded from validated public representation. The twentieth century has seen many other groups excluded from the public realm, or even from legal existence, on the basis of their physical constitution: the power of embodiment is denied them. Many works on the currently fashionable topic of republicanism have raised this issue but very few, if any, have explicitly connected it with the problem of embodiment, or the idea that the body has become a major site of crisis in modern public culture.[15]

It is also significant that one of the few works to treat the interaction of the French Revolution and the public realm, that by Joan Landes, *Women and the Public Sphere*, should have come from a historian who herself is not only a member of one of the groups excluded from public legitimacy in the supposedly universalistic revolution of 1789, but is also ready to use that exclusion as the basis for her analysis of the public realm.[16] But it is therefore doubly unfortunate that this pioneering analysis, the first one which has broken the collusive, mystificatory relationship between middle-class historians and the history of the coming to power of the middle class, should have relied on Habermassian concepts of the public sphere. For Habermas's theory itself cuts across the lines of gender in society, and does not really come to terms with how the appropriation of the public realm by the middle class was itself performed through the manipulation of a gendered rendering of the public realm and the public man. If the republic was one of virtue, it had to be so because only the claim to virtue could exorcize the claims of divine-right kingship, and redistribute its attributes over the totality of virtuous men; only the claim to male virtue as well could justify the destruction of the monarchy defined as a corrupt and corrupting form of government due to the influence of women over it from the queen down.[17] So if the republic was one constructed on male virtue, it was also crucially constructed on a sexualized definition of female virtue which meant the enforcement of separate spheres and the repression of female sexuality as the price of public stability.

In doing so, it also constructed, far more I think than Landes will in fact allow, what the Frankfurt school in its critique of Enlightenment defined as the unstable and dialectical nature of middle-class public culture and hence of the middle-class triumph over the public realm.[18] Increasing challenge, which destabilized politics and the ideological justifications of the male definition of the public sphere, came throughout the nineteenth and twentieth centuries from those excluded from participation on the grounds of the alleged consequences of their physical construction. It can surely be read as a mark of the continuing mystificatory element of the relationship between the middle class and the definition of the public realm that even works ostensibly devoted to the 'future' created by the Revolution, e.g. the collection of essays edited by Geoffrey Best, *The Permanent Revolution*, contains not a single female author and possesses no entry for woman in its index.[19]

The revolutionary triumph of embodiment was also inseparable from the massive changes in the structures of western thought. It was in this period that science became the characteristic mental form of the bourgeoisie. Chief among these was the unravelling of the nexus of nature, divine intention and hierarchies of power which had formed the conceptual bases of divine right monarchy. Without this disaggregation, republican government is not thinkable. The abolition of the monarchy, on 23 September 1792, ostensibly liberated Is from Ought, set science free to stake its own claims as the dominant form of bourgeois instrumental rationality, enshrining the principle of objectivity and capable of producing the partitioning of the intellectual realm into distinct disciplines open for colonization by competing fractions of the middle class.[20] In doing so, it not only became an immensely more powerful weapon for asserting man's control over nature; it also formed one of the major ways that the middle class, by internalizing the objectivity principle, could reinforce the figure of *homo clausus* and mystify their political relationship with the public realm. After all, as Peter Brown's studies of the holy men of the the early Church have repeatedly shown, there is no more powerful way to place leverage on the public world than the making of claims to virtue, rationality, objectivity and disinterestedness.

In conclusion, I am arguing for a genuinely total history, a history where bodies, language, inter-subjectivity and the public realm would genuinely converge. From such a prismatic approach, a new enlightenment would result, which would throw light forward onto the present and the future. History, as I have said before, works in the space between Is and Ought where facts and values face each other. To have the right to work in that space at all, we should be consciously thinking of our vocation not as antiquarians but as inhabiters of Is, and enlargers of Ought. It is for this reason that a reworking of the relations of history with philosophy is a vital agenda for the profession to face.[21] The putting together of the Revolution and the body, natural and political, enables us to exert pressure on the modern crisis of the body which, tortured, trivialized, consumerized or coerced, lies at the basis of many current problems of political culture. The future of the body is not identical with any single history, whether it be a history of sexuality or a history of illness, or of discipline or confinement, nor is it a passive area where the state inscribes its meanings. The future of the history of the body in the formative period of the modern world lies in reminding us that the bodies of individuals were once repositories of power and dignity, and the whole crisis of the public realm since the Revolution has been precisely how to conserve that role and detach it from the totalizing ideologies which gave it birth. Neither divine right nor fascism on the one hand, nor depoliticization on the other, are alternatives: but then neither is the dimestore body of consumer culture.

FIVE

THE TEDIUM OF HISTORY: AN APPROACH TO MARIA EDGEWORTH'S *PATRONAGE* (1814)

W. J. Mc Cormack

INSURRECTIONARY TEDIUM

The events of 1798 interrogate Enlightenment and its legacy. But the Irish rebellion is not just an event in the calendar, it is a complexly constructed historiographical issue, to which novelists and poets have contributed in ways perhaps as yet unrecognized.

On 31 May 1798 Maria Edgeworth's father, Richard Lovell Edgeworth, married Frances Anne Beaufort as his fourth wife. Coming home from the ceremony the couple saw the body of a hanged man slung between upturned cart-shafts.[1] Edgeworth had entered the Irish House of Commons in February, and in the late summer the family were driven from their house as much by fear of the aroused Orange yeomanry as by the advance of an invading French army. The fate of the independent Irish parliament was virtually sealed, and proposals for a legislative union between Britain and Ireland sprang directly from the rebellion. Such proposals had been heard earlier of course, but the final Act of 1800 was ratified in the light of its dying embers. And these embers flared briefly again in 1803.

With the rebellion and invasion over, the family – including Maria Edgeworth – returned to find Edgeworthstown House largely undisturbed. A few weeks later Mrs Edgeworth, writing to Beaufort on 1 November 1798, reported fears of renewed insurrection, and mentioned a French fleet off the west coast. But in a household where attitudes to radicalism were as complex as those of the Edgeworths, the response to rumour was analytical, even self-mocking:

When I began to write I intended my dear father [she continued] to have given you some account of my opinions about Hume, Robison etc. etc. but with regard to those sceptical gentry who, like Wieland, consider truth as an unstable, relative, individual term little connected with the active circumstances of this world, and all the nonsense they have with art & glowing language engrafted upon that stock of absurdity; and also of the apparent excess of credulity into which Robison seems to have gone . . . It is hard to conceive so much abominable iniquity as what is disclosed in the correspondence between Spartacas & his friends.[2]

The anxieties of an age are inscribed in short-hand here. The trajectory from the German novelist Christoph Martin Wieland (1733-1813) to the British writer on science and engineering John Robison (1739-1803) emblemizes a movement from thoroughgoing endorsement of Enlightenment attitudes in social and personal morality to frantic denunciation of masonic and other alleged conspiracies against order and authority.[3] Beyond individual cases of self-correction (Wordsworth for example), there lies a deeper ambiguity in the notion of Enlightenment itself, ambiguity which finds expression in the contradictory verdicts of historians on the issue of revolution – as a product or a travesty of Enlightenment. In local Irish terms, one might ask how long the process had been which culminated in those intellectual conditions surrounding the insurrection of 1798, and what were the consequences for literature.

In its subtitle, *Castle Rackrent* (1800) had ostentatiously insisted that its action lay wholly in an implied era with 1782 as its specific closure. But in terms of what we might now term high literature, one of the earliest reflections of the rebellion comes in 1809 with the first of Edgeworth's *Tales of Fashionable Life*. Doubtless, there are earlier instances but none which contains and displays the contradictions of the period as clearly as the tale *Ennui*, the twelfth chapter of which touches on incidents similar to those experienced by the author and her family in the late summer of 1798. It is not the plot of *Ennui* which intrigues, however, but certain textual gestures away from the apparent setting towards a larger interpretive place. Reflecting on his experiences of Irish rebellion, the narrator concludes:

I remember hearing, some years afterwards, a Frenchman, who had been in imminent danger of been [*sic*] guillotined by Robespierre and who at last was one of those who arrested the tyrant, declare, that when the bustle and horror of the revolution were over, he could hardly keep himself awake; and that he thought it very insipid to live in quiet with his wife and family. He further summed up the catalogue of Robespierre's crimes, by exclaiming, 'D'ailleurs c'etoit un grand philantrope!' I am not conscious of any disposition to cruelty, and I heard this man's speech with disgust; yet upon a candid self-examination, I must confess, that I have felt, though from different causes, some degree of what he described. Perhaps *ennui* may have had a share in creating revolutions.[4]

Elsewhere, Lord Glenthorn is embarrassed by his ignorance of French literature, and if he has not blushed at reporting this out-of-the-way detail, it may be because his narrative opens with an epigraph at once more obscure and more ironic. The source is Dieudonné Thiebauld's memoir of court-life under Frederick the Great: translated into English it reads:

'What do you do at Potsdam?' I asked Prince William one day. 'Sir,' he replied to me, 'we pass our lives all conjugating the same verb – "I ennui-ise myself, you ennui-ise yourself, he ennui-ises himself, we ennui-ise ourselves, you ennui-ise yourselves, they ennui-ise themselves, I have ennui-ised myself, I will ennui-ise myself . . .".'[5]

Revolution may have been in part a consequence of ennui, generally regarded as a slothful or, at best, splenetic condition leading to little of consequence in the way of action. In addition, however, the court of the philosopher-king himself, the embodiment of active Enlightenment principles, was given over to the recitation of its own complicity in that condition. These must seem unexpected depths in stories of regional or fashionable life. Nevertheless, the Longford/Potsdam axis is no mirage, even if the means of interpreting it remains obscure. One initiative might pursue Edgeworth's theme into the middle of the nineteenth century where it is familiarly associated with the poetry of Charles Baudelaire. Though ennui has been widely accepted as *une condition humaine* peculiarly French and characteristic of France after 1848, its story is stranger than citation of Baudelaire's name would indicate.

In 1719, the Abbé Du Bos opened his *Réflexions critiques sur la poésie et la peinture* by identifying escape from ennui as a negative motive force in the appreciation of art. The first section of the *Réflexions* introduces 'the necessity of being occupied so as to escape from ennui' and the work proceeds to lay down laws for the various arts considered as a means of release from imposed conditions.[6] As a participant in the 'querelle des ancients et des modernes' Du Bos also contributed to the growing literature which sought to instruct the young ruler on the principles by which he should govern an ideal, enlightened state. This theme, central to continental Enlightenment, illuminates the larger place of interpretation in which (I suggest) Edgeworth's fiction should be seen, with '98 as its unstated occasion.

For want of princes, the ideal prince's education never featured prominently in Anglophone literature. Instead, amelioration of society at large drew forth appeals, theories and invocations. In the relentless satire of Swift's *Modest Proposal* (1729) the existence of a prince overseas (to whom the destitute were thought passionately attached and the opulent hostile) was mockingly stressed as an extenuating circumstance. That poverty and luxury went hand in fist is not surprising, but the corrosion of culture induced by both exerted less evident pressures on religious belief. Free-thinking among the upper classes was the target of George Berkeley's concern in *Alciphron, or The Minute Philosopher* (1732), and in the second dialogue he has Crito declare:

> I can easily conceive that, when people of a certain turn are got together, they should prefer doing anything to the ennui of their own conversation: but it is not easy to conceive there is any great pleasure in this . . . I can easily comprehend that no man upon earth ought to prize anodynes for the spleen more than a man of fashion and pleasure.[7]

The general argument against luxury, and the specific intermittent Irish arguments in favour of sumptuary laws, accommodate the notion of ennui as a sort of dangerous vacuum into which Jacobitism, atheism and – in time Jacobinism – might indiscriminately rush. The paradox of ennui, that it should be a form of lethargy and of unbounded energy, is true to the antithetical shape of much eighteenth-century anxiety. Conspiracy partakes of the same kind of paradox, an alliance of a few radical aristocratic names and an anonymous dishevelled mob. And as a configuration in political and ideological debate, conspiracy may yet be found to have its analogue in the emergent distinctions of the literary genres, or rather, in the newly elevated status given to literature *per se* as the especial domain of Imagination. Edgeworth's fiction revels in the cryptic, as if to insist on the necessarily conspiratorial relations obtaining between text and reader.

The double allocation of blame for the recent rebellion – to a desperate, and insurgent lower estate and to an irresponsible, sophisticated, and infidel element in higher society – is a familiar response to 1798. Indeed, Edmund Burke anticipated such a theory when, in December 1796, he unfolded for the Catholic bishop of Waterford a twin image of Irish Jacobinism. There was, he conceded, 'the Jacobinism which arises from penury and irritation', but there is also 'that Jacobinism, which is Speculative in its Origin, and which arises from Wantoness and fullness of bread . . .'.[8] Yet this association of philosophical radicalism in aristocratic circles with inchoate material want is not new. A precursor form can be detected as a prime target of the *Modest Proposal*, where the imagery of eating and of bodily excess is neatly concentrated: 'I grant', says the projector, 'this Food will be somewhat dear, and therefore very *proper for Landlords*; who, as they have already devoured most of the Parents, seem to have the best title to the Children.'[9]

Edgeworth's relation to this long debate can be best appeciated as a engaged resistance to her father's intellectual inheritance. Born in 1744, a year before Swift's death, Richard Lovell Edgeworth came to maturity through the Lunar Society in the English midlands; that is, he had imbibed the ideas of the Scottish Enlightenment. Like John Robison, he experimented in mechanics and natural philosophy. He met Rousseau and the two men had parallel (if distinctive) interests in the theory of education. In 1772, he established a rather more substantial association with d'Alembert, together with several lesser luminaries in French intellectual life. In 1802 the ageing Edgeworth and his ever more renowned daughter spent a prolonged period in France during which contacts were renewed with survivors or relicts of such company.[10] Straddling the tumultuous events at the Bastille and at Waterloo (and the more intimate disturbances of '98), Edgeworth personified the *durée* of that movement of ideas and forces which climaxed in the late-eighteenth-century revolutions. His posthumously published *Memoirs* provide a characteristically split-level view of an Irish-landowner *cum* English-inventor, with digressions on Longford political chicanery and French theories of human behaviour.

From his upbringing in the Irish midlands, Edgeworth recalled a curious case of ennui in 'a very delicate lady of fashion' and the extraordinary treatment prescribed for her by a Catholic neighbour recently returned from exile in France. The lady was seized by four mutes dressed in white and taken to

> a distant chamber hung with black and lighted with green tapers. From the ceiling . . . a swing was suspended, in which she was placed by the mutes, so as to be seated at some distance from the ground. One of the mutes set the swing in motion; and as it approached one end of the room, she was opposed by a grim menacing figure armed with a huge rod of birch.[11]

'Disappointment produces ennui and ennui disease,' the memoirist declares, and the treatment might be described as the external representation of the complaint – exaggerated distance from the ordinary rooms of social activity and even from the ground itself, this effected by attendants lacking the ordinary powers of communication. If the patient has been a person of fashion, her medical superintendent has been quite otherwise, one of an attainted and banished tribe.

In this regard, Edgeworth's contribution to her father's *Memoirs* rearranges the historical background against which '98 should be read. After his death in 1817, she completed the *Memoirs,* and her post-revolutionary perspective on Enlightenment supersedes his more antiquarian one. Maria Edgeworth, commencing the second volume, begins with 1782, that is, at the point where (we are to believe) the action of *Castle Rackrent* ended. It would scarcely be possible to devise a more strategically placed *terminus a quo* for an Irish memoir: that year saw not only the return of the Edgeworths from England but also the declaration of legislative independence and the inauguration of that curious *mélange* of period and performance known as 'Grattan's Parliament'. A paradigmatic merger of private and public events inaugurates the new era:

> We landed in Dublin at the moment when the nation voted a parliamentary grant of fifty thousand pounds, as a testimony of their sense of the services of their great and successful orator and patriot Mr Grattan. My father was in the gallery of the Irish House of Commons, when that vote passed, and he saw and sympathised with the public enthusiasm.[12]

Thereafter, her build-up to 1798 proceeds through an honourable return to residential landlordism, improvements in estate management, moderation in politics, grief and happiness, technical inventiveness allied to a willingness to serve government. The events of 1798 are localized geographically within Longford, and the very grammar of the narrative, especially the intermission between its nominative ego in the first volume, and its accusative in the second establishes the rebellion as an intrusion upon liberal progressiveness.

HISTORY AND FICTION

Through its preface, *Castle Rackrent* announced that 'of the numbers who study, or at least who read history, how few derive any advantage from their labours!' And continued:

> The heroes of history are so decked out by the fine fancy of the professed historian; they talk in such measured prose, and act from such sublime or

such diabolical motives, that few have sufficient taste, wickedness, or heroism, to sympathise in their fate. Besides, there is much uncertainty even in the best authenticated ancient or modern histories; and that love of truth, which in some minds is innate and immutable, necessarily leads to a love of secret memoirs, and private anecdotes.[13]

The implications of this sly preference are remarkable, even if they were not taken up at the time. History tends towards a kind of anti-mimetic, because of the ethical qualifications with which it is conventionally encumbered. Fiction has a capacity to contain and display a consciousness of historical process. The unofficial, or scarcely approved, border crossing-point is the secret memoir, the story told in private. Edgeworth wrote this preface at a time when historical writing was undergoing a kind of galloping inflation, '98 and its aftermath having stimulated a vigorous pamphleteering that utilized narrative, memoir, court-report, ballad, etc. The highly coloured incompleteness of her characters does not simply reproduce a historic condition; it seeks to state an urgent political problem. The final sentence in the preface catches the interconnection of national and personal development:

When Ireland loses her identity by an union with Great Britain, she will look back with a smile of good-humoured complacency on the sir Kits and sir Condys of her former existence.[14]

The action of *Castle Rackrent* is ostentatiously set before 1782. But this timetable also charts a national history in that it seeks to exempt the years of Grattan's Parliament from the comic satire of the novel. *Ormond* (1817), the last of her Irish novels, is in a general sense set in the eighteenth century also, but if we seek a more precise date we must look to France rather than Ireland for an answer. We are told that the hero's visit to Paris took place 'in the latter years of the life of Louis XV'.[15] Taking the compound date 1782/1774 as one terminal of an excluded history, we find the other in various implied moments of a commencing contemporaneity in the *Tales of Fashionable Life*. The rebellion of *Ennui,* whether it's 1798 or 1803, is the most clearly recognizable of these. And of these, the second saw a slow commencement of the writing of the *Tales*.

There is a further, more extensive pattern. The *Tales* opt for fashionable, that is, contemporary life. But the past does not begin simply at some frontier just behind the contemporary, for more than a period (this decade or those sessions of parliament) is evacuated between history and the contemporary. A term closer to 'vector' is required to suggest *the intervention of an exclusion.* The vector intervening between the history invoked in *Castle Rackrent* and the fashion of the *Tales* has an ideological tendency: the period excluded is precisely that of accelerating conflict, is indeed the birth-season of the ideological in the most literal sense of that term's coinage. Ideology, dating from 1796, was somehow the science of ideas; more specifically it was the encapsulated philosophy of Condillac, Enlightenment philosopher and adviser on princely education.

In shaping Edgeworth's representation of history and the contemporary, the actual and the fictional, the vector renders these fully conceptual and differentiates them from the rule-of-thumb. We have then a body of work, together with the material forces of its production, gradually releasing some image of its conceptual figuration. 'Vector' serves for a moment; the Freudian term of repression might do as well in certain circumstances. But as a characterization embracing both, one may say that the intervention of an exclusion which relates history and fiction in Edgeworth's case, history in and out of fiction, may be named 'ennui'.

PATRONAGE

One of the self-obscuring features of literary tradition has been a relentless, if unconscious, classification of Edgeworth's fiction into mutually exclusive categories. Thus, there are 'the Irish novels' beyond which few Irish critics have bothered to direct their inquiries. 'The fiction for children' holds a fascination reserved, it seems, for educationalists. Further off are the 'English novels', too long unfavourably compared with the achievements of Jane Austen, but in recent years drawn revealingly into a discussion of the 'war of ideas' between novelists of a Jacobin and anti-Jacobin persuasion. Edgeworth's fiction offers a means of dissolving these encrusted partitions. More important, the argument against a cultural nationalist division of her work into English and Irish camps is recognizable as being applicable also to her own fictional strategy by which she circumvented, updated and reinscribed her father's Enlightenment inheritance. An appreciation of this dimension in the fiction, and in the criticism which fiction (cf. the preface to *Castle Rackrent*) incorporates, can be sought through specific features which are finely done in *Patronage*.

A neglected novel, dated 1814, *Patronage* was actually in circulation before the end of the previous year. The time of publication, adjusted according to Marilyn Butler's calculations, falls between the second series of *Tales of Fashionable Life* and the defeat of

Napoleon in April 1814.[16] Few commentators have attempted a synopsis of this large and discrete work, its official concern with the effects of patronage on the young being to some extent blurred by the very number of young people who populate it. Repeated on several occasions, the phrase 'patronage of fashion' suggests that the theme is broader than the simple relation between a protégé and a patron, indeed that it implicates an impersonal and pervasive ideological structure of which fashion (in clothes, behaviour, idiom, etc.) is representative.

Considered more generally, *Patronage* retains one's attention for its massively comprehensive account of cynicism. The early chapters present Lord Oldborough (whose patronage is sought) as a once-mighty intelligence engrossed now in the mechanical administration of a political system founded on manipulation, the realm of 'Old Corruption' locked into what amounted to a world war. This is not a psychological condition in Oldborough, whose very title is constructed of political elements. Personality is entirely functional, role determines behaviour, and insofar as ambition is condemned the reasons offered are practical.

Even the exemplary attitudes of the Percy family constitute a sort of benign cynicism involving the same denial of inner reservations of thought or feeling:

> 'Why should not we talk it over before the young people?' said Mr Percy. 'We always speak of every thing openly in this family,' continued he, turning to lady Jane; 'and I think that is one reason why we live so happily together. I let my children know all my views for them, all my affairs, and my opinions, I may say all my thoughts, or how could I expect them to trust me with theirs?'[17]

In the preceding chapter, the Percy girls have stumbled upon a secret which is generally regarded as unspeakable not only by the particular fictional character but by the novel form itself. At a nearby cottage, they meet a young woman and her illegitimate baby. The defaulting father, Buckhurst Falconer, had recently proposed marriage to Caroline Percy, and so the impact of illicit sexuality strikes very close to the heart of Percy enlightenment. What is crucial in Miss Percy's case is her having refused Falconer's renewed attentions *before* she discovers his bastard, and the narrative dwells on the happy fact that she was ignorant of his behaviour when she refused him. This emphasis on a positive quality in such ignorance may seem unimportant in itself. Yet such concealments, repressions and denials are pervasive in the novel.

The political plot, for example, revolves round the decoding of a secret document which has reached Lord Oldborough's attention. Even after Cunningham Falconer, brother of the adulterer and secretary to his lordship, has deciphered most of the papers there remain some puzzling sentences which Edgeworth passes on to her readers. For example:

If the Gassoc be finally determined against the *Eagle*, means must be taken to accomplish the purposes alluded to in paragraph 4, in green (of the 7th ult.), also those in No. B in lemon juice (of September last).[18]

At this point the identity of the Gassoc is unknown, though the Eagle has been recognized as Oldborough himself. These are matters of the highest diplomatic importance, and the outcome of wars – by implication the Napoleonic wars – are in the balance. Yet, virtually in the same breath, we are given a résumé of the views held by Falconer and Oldborough, views which in turn indicate the decisively political implications of Mr Percy's openness with his children – 'they agreed in the principle that free discussion should be discouraged, and that the country should be governed with a high and strong hand'.[19] Thus the theme of private education is contrasted with that of political corruption, not just through the fact of Oldborough's acting as patron to the Falconers, but through a web of interconnecting scenes, incidents, conversations, and observations. A benign part of this is characterized in the formidable rectitude of the Percys. But, as if to mimic the effects of repression in the state, there is also scatter-gun fusillade of incomplete names, of initials, partly quoted documents, massively obscure allusions, hints and feints.

This cryptic quality, and its implication for the novel's ultimate view of the world, is instanced in a neat metatextual detail. Cunningham Falconer has ingratiated himself further with his master by publishing a book – on a topic which Edgeworth declines to disclose. Unfortunately, Falconer has not actually written the book himself, but hired a learned and patron-less lawyer to ghost it for him. The real author's name is Temple, and Falconer's deception is unmasked when he fails to identify a classical tag used in his own publication. Oldborough tries to lure Alfred Percy into replacing Falconer by obliging him to identify the source:

'*Thus the fane of heroes is at last neglected by their worshippers, and left to the care of the birds of heaven, or abandoned to the serpents of the earth.*'

Alfred fortunately recollected that this alluded to a description in Arrian of the island of Achilles, the present Isle of Serpents, where there is that temple of the hero, of which, as the historian says, 'the care is left to the birds alone, who every morning repair to the sea, wet their wings, and sprinkle the temple, afterwards sweeping with their plumage its sacred pavement.'[20]

Cunningham is unhorsed by this recognition, though Alfred declines to take up the vacancy. Yet the passage is of more interest in the text than in the plot. The real author's name is Temple, a 'poor starving genius in the garret' yet one whose rightful place is in the legal profession – that is, The Temple. Moreover, the temple occurs twice in the gloss added to the passage from Arrian indicated by Lord Oldborough. The genius, Temple, shines through *nominally*, and this might be read as the undoing of the pseudo-author.

Anyone familiar with Edgeworth's Irish fiction will recognize this characteristic. Just a moment before Caroline Percy is reunited with her true love, she and her sister discuss the merits of Thomas Percy's *Reliques of Ancient Poetry*. Even more startling is the virtual duplication of Oldborough's name in the German Altenberg, a process drawn closer to the history of Enlightenment in England by means of the name of the German-born first secretary of the Royal Society – Henry Oldenberg. Such nominalism at once confirms and jeopardizes the possibility of fictional characters having historical originals, and drives a wedge between 'character' and inimitable, unique personality.

Oldborough is said to be based in part at least on William Stuart (1755-1822), archbishop of Armagh, though aspects of his presentation in the novel also derive from Edgeworth's reading of William Coxe's biography (1798) of Robert Walpole (1676-1745), prime minister and *bête noire* of Jonathan Swift. These concealed sources for Oldborough are oddly replaced in the novel's text with the seemingly aimless precaution of indicating very minor figures as dear Lady B —, Lord N — and Mr G —. In a wholly cynical world, something demands to be concealed – a token secret, a name stripped of all but its initial, a savaged text. At the same time, however, the transparency of what is here termed the novel's cynicism reproduces at the level of style that disjunction between the historical and contemporary to which the term 'vector' was applied. Oldborough is not Walpole, nor is he the archbishop of Armagh; he does, however, oscillate between existence as a historical and public character and as a contemporary, private portrait, and such oscillation sounds a disturbing note of tension. The monochrome virtue of the Percys, like the folly of the Falconers, is offset by the distances which constantly open up between apparently congruent details.

A little less than mid-way into the novel, Edgeworth allows herself the observation that 'in the education of a beauty, as of a prince, it is essential early to inspire an utter contempt of flattery'.[21] The allusion to princes has been preceded by only the most tangential of sub-themes: in the opening pages, a shipwrecked French diplomat recounted a story to the Percys concerning a foolish German prince and his chief minister, Count Altenberg. This stratum of the novel's complex geology will return to the surface, but for the moment the comparison of Caroline Percy and a prince stands oddly aside, as one further instance of disjunction in the prose. To grasp its significance one can reach into Edgeworth's correspondence and working papers, particularly those dating to her residence in Paris in 1802-3.

In the Bodley Library, Oxford, are preserved a number of notebooks in which is found 'revolutionary education' as a heading. If we regard this as a shorthand for the topic of education in a period of revolutionary turmoil, then an associated heading 'the education of Princes' may seem out of place. The apparent dichotomy leads into brief allusions to various written sources – the memoirs of Madame de Bariere and of Mrs Robinson, for example. But even more cryptically and insistently appears the name simply of Mazarin.[22] These sparse details require elucidation through evidence of Edgeworth's movements earlier in her continental tour. In mid-October 1802 the family stopped at Cambrai where she inspected the preserved head of the Abbé Fénelon (1651-1715), the town's celebrated bishop in Louis XIV's days. The veneration of relics was not characteristic of the Edgeworths, and her interest in Fénelon offers unique access to a stratum of historical and philosophical inquiry which runs below the surface of her fiction. Mazarin, for example, features not so much in his own historical right, but as the most recent figure admitted to the dramatis personae of Fénelon's *Dialogues des morts* (1700-18). Under the heading 'Extract for Patronage', Edgeworth transcribed five consecutive speeches from the dialogue between Richelieu and Mazarin, underlining one sentence of the former, which reads in translation, 'I see that true glory shuns those honours which crude vanity seeks and that one is dishonoured by too much seeking honour.'[23]

Modesty is all. To the education of Alfred Percy, an unnamed character contributes much through a few conversations on the subject of rhetoric and style. These are topics to which the Edgeworths devoted many pages in their *Essays on Practical Education*, first published in 1798, the year of revolutionary turmoil in

Longford. In *Patronage*, the Chief Justice (as he is called) appears to draw on this authority as well as an unpublished 'Essay on the Genius & Style of Burke', which Maria Edgeworth never developed beyond staccato notes.[24] The Chief Justice, as befits one who remains unnamed, is accommodated exclusively within an *oratio obliqua* narrative:

> A man accustomed to speak to numbers perceives immediately when his auditors seize his ideas, and knows instantly, by the assent and expression of the eye, to whom they are new or to whom they are familiar. The chief justice discovered that Alfred Percy had superior knowledge, literature, and talents, even before he spoke, by his manner of listening. The conversation presently passed from *l'air noble* to *le style noble,* and to the French laws of criticism, which prohibit the descending to allusions to arts and manufactures. This subject he discussed deeply, yet rapidly observed how taste is influenced by different governments and manners – remarked how the strong line of demarcation formerly kept in France between the nobility and the citizens had influenced taste in writing and in eloquence, and how our more *popular* government not only admitted allusions to the occupations of the lower classes, but required them.[25]

The Chief Justice is engaged in more than commonplace discriminations between English and French ways of doing things. In speaking of different forms of government, and of the relationship between political form and oratorical style, he is invoking an eighteenth-century theme which runs back ultimately to debates about the relative merits of the ancients and moderns.

In Edgeworth two features of this venerable *querelle* are wholly absent. First, there is little reference to the heroic individual or sovereign. It is true that Percy might tap Oldborough's patronage, but the thrust of the novel is that he should not do such a thing. Instead, he is to rely on innate abilities and personal resources which the transparency of the prose does little to substantiate. Even Oldborough is a servant, not so much to his king as to an administrative system of which he only appears to be master. The independent gentleman of independent means, as presented in *Patronage*, is in crisis; and an unstated but pervasive theme declares the Percys' need to acquire a useful profession and some clients, Oldborough's need to develop a private life.

Second, there is no evidence of satire in the Swiftian manner. In place of lofty emulation and scatological humour there is middle-class rectitude. There is excellent comedy of manners, of course, but without any sense of ambiguity or oxymoron, the novel recounts the making of 'le bourgeois gentilhomme'. The historical moment of publication is crucial; in 1814 a fictional chief justice might easily refer to the English form of government as 'more *popular*' than the French, whereas twenty years earlier the comparison would have operated in the other direction and would scarcely have approved the popular element in French institutions.

With this we return to the notion of a structural vector in Edgeworth's fiction, the intervention of an exclusion, identified under complementary names as history or ennui. *Patronage* does not strike one as possessing any features of the historical novel as it was simultaneously launched by Walter Scott. (*Waverley* appeared later in 1814, and few recognized its debt to *The Absentee*.) Yet this contemporaneity of action in *Patronage* is only the measure of its profound concern with a newly forceful and ideologically charged sense of history. The novel's setting at a time of the breaking of nations is signalled not only in political urgency in the matter of decoding documents, but also in the sudden return and equally sudden marriage of Colonel Hungerford, who, like his brother in the navy, has been distinguished in battle.

Insurrection is 'the return of the repressed', and *Patronage* registers this feature of the Enlightenment paradox. The marriage of Caroline Percy and Count Altenberg is twice delayed, first by his sudden need to renegotiate a marriage settlement prepared by his father in the German court where they exercise some kind of political function, but second by the threat of 'revolutionary symptoms'. As in *Castle Rackrent*, the closing pages of the novel are punctuated with allusions to the mob and to insurrectionary feeling. Just as the Irish location of insurrection in *Ennui* is textually usurped and glossed by the discussion of Frederick the Great, Robespierre and other alien matters, so here in this novel of English middle-class education there emerges evidence of a more complex and extensive *place of interpretation*.

THE PLACE OF INTERPRETATION

The critical discussion of realist fiction has naturally devoted much attention to the question of setting, while at the same time it has tended to regard setting as an uncomplicated *donné*. The recognition of symbolic landscape in – say – the Brontës or Dickens has undoubtedly led to greater sophistication. But in relation to what we may crudely call Irish fiction, complications arise. For example, the progressive transfer of setting from Ireland to England in certain fictions by Sheridan Le Fanu (and others) requires the concept of an Anglo-Irish *provenance* in which not only a palpable setting is acknowledged but in which is also accommodated a recognition of ideological origins. At this latter level, one deals with text rather than topography. The business of the transfer from setting to provenance is thus a form of translation, instinct with politics and generally with historiographical issues also.

Edgeworth's *Castle Rackrent* is rightly celebrated for its introduction of a regional Irish setting. Le Fanu's *Uncle Silas* (1864) epitomizes the Anglo-Irish textual provenance. But such a novel as *Patronage* requires a third degree of conceptualization. The question of text becomes critical, and implicates the dynamics of readership or – to be precise – of rival, even irreconcilable readerships. Let us consider this first in connection with Count Altenberg, whose first departure left Caroline with nothing but a slip of paper, tucked into a life of Sir Philip Sidney, to mull over. The slip bore 'a passage copied in his hand', reading:

> Algernon Sidney, in a letter to his son, says, that in the whole of his life he never knew one man, of what condition soever, arrive at any degree of reputation in the world, who made choice of, or delighted in the company or conversation of those, who in their qualities were inferior, or in their parts not much superior to himself.[26]

This stands in odd relation to the positive emphasis on 'mixed government' made by several exemplary figures in the book and on the value and necessity of allusions to the occupations of the lower classes in the idiom of the British constitution. Even more startling, however, is the referential swerve away from Sir Philip Sidney, the embodiment of late chivalry and self-sacrifice, to his kinsman, the ardent republican, and victim of judicial execution as a traitor.[27] At one level, the text links Altenberg with Philip Sidney (he has been reading a biography) but at another with a contrasting figure (whose name he inscribes). This may be taken in various ways, but the least helpful is a mere identification of a source for the passage transcribed. It is in Altenberg's hand, but it is not declared unambiguously either to be transcribed from some external source *or* to be Altenberg's personal response. To put it graphically, Algernon Sidney colours seemingly trivial details in *Patronage*. Considered in this way, he exemplifies the intervention of an absence.

Sidney's most significant writing was the *Discourses Concerning Government* (published by John Toland in 1698), which was written in answer to Sir Robert Filmer (d. 1653). Now 'Filmer' is not a name one encounters frequently but . . . there it is on a memo provided by Commissioner Falconer when Alfred Percy takes over management of his ruined affairs – 'No. 1. Deed of assignment to Filmer Griffin, esq.'[28] This occasion is crucial for the Percy family because, with massive implausibility, the missing lease which will restore them to their own property is found among Falconer's papers, alongside Filmer's name, and Algernon Sidney's shadow. Considering the posthumous status of the works by Filmer and Sidney for which they are known, and considering the vestigial, even spectral, manner in which their names enter a list of alluded characters in *Patronage*, one can see in such minute textual details traces of the classic, Enlightenment dialogue of the dead, offered as a form of education for an era of revolutionary symptoms. Further examples of this fragmented stratum in the fiction could be examined through Mr Temple's reading of a life of Chancellor North, his anonymous writing of a pamphlet for Cunningham Falconer, and Alfred Percy's recognition of Arrian as a source of allusion.[29]

The very fragmentariness of the method deserves attention in itself. In the second chapter, Cunningham Falconer and his father set about deciphering Tourville's papers, which they have handed over to Lord Oldborough. By the eighth chapter, only the 'Gassoc' passage resists their hermeneutical efforts. With the *Eagle* of these papers decoded as Oldborough himself, a *Gosshawk* is suspected, and numerous coats of arms are searched for the emblematic bird. Linguistic corruption is acknowledged as a factor to be taken into account in dealing with French diplomacy.[30] But we must wait until the twenty-fourth chapter for Mr Percy to provide a solution. It seems that the initial G of 'Gassoc' might have been a mistake for C: thus we have 'cassoc' (a notion which earlier led to suspicions of a clerical conspiracy against Oldborough):

> Assuming, therefore, that it was *Cassock*, Mr Percy found the initials of six persons, who stood high in Lord Oldborough's scale of probabilities: Chelsea – Arnold – Skreene – Skipworth – Oldfield – Coleman – and the last k, for which he hunted in vain a considerable time, was supplied by Kensington, (one of the Duke of Greenwich's title), whose name had been scratched out of the list . . .[31]

The plotters against Oldborough do not impinge on the action of the novel, but the manner of their encoding characterizes much of its texture. Figures in social life are 'nameless bodies', as if to complement the countless names – Bacon, Sidney, Leibnitz, Mazarin – who enliven the allusive fabric. At the level of action, writing is forged by Mrs Falconer, even seals of office are imitated in bread-moulds. But consideration at a deeper layer, where more significant interpretation can occur, also implicates questions of morality which the Percy family could answer only with embarrassment.

As befits a novel reworking Enlightenment themes, the focus of moral concern is textual. At the outset, the diplomatic papers are irregularly transferred to Oldborough: the morality of this, and of the Falconers' behaviour generally, does not pass without comment. The Percys, by contrast, provide no covert assistance to government and seek no favours in return. They are paragons of independence, advocates of 'disinterestedness'. Yet when Alfred Percy seeks the hand of Sophia Leicester, he also acts on behalf on her widowed mother in pursuit of debts owed by Buckhurst Falconer. Privately he visits Buckhurst, and extracts the money by arguing that going to law will cost everyone a greater sum. Even less edifying is his conduct at the moment when Commissioner Falconer hands over his papers: when the missing Percy lease emerges, Alfred slips it aside without announcing what he is removing from his client's file. This *legerdemain* may be an exigency of the fictional plot, but it must have its effect on the presentation of the hero's ethical standards. More seriously, it indicates the essentially ambiguous operations of Enlightenment values at a time of violent transition. Perhaps Edgeworth acknowledges something of the kind when she writes in the *Memoirs* of 'the misery necessary in the passage from one state of civilization to another'.[32]

The place of interpretation, therefore, is fundamentally textual; in this case, the swerve from Philip to Algernon Sidney indicates a politico-ethical transition which cannot be fully admitted. But in *Patronage*, the place is also metatextual; that is, it concerns the fate of certain texts within the fiction – diplomatic papers, code-words, philosophical dictionaries, leases. These may display a high degree of arbitrariness in the face of interpretation, or they may become subject to transfers and negotiations of an ambiguous kind. Nothing quite so emphatically dramatizes this process in the novel than the treatment of adultery and illegitimacy.

Very early in the novel, Godfrey Percy is smitten by Miss Hauton. Lord Oldborough's highly intelligent and graceful niece, however, is evidently the daughter of a divorcee. This involuntary fault on her part is followed up in the narrative by a conversation about 'natural daughters' and their often excessive dowries. Miss Hauton, it is true, plays some unladylike songs on the piano, but her conversation with Godfrey indicates a superiority to her surroundings. In time, she is married off to an old marquis, and is reported to have had an affair afterwards. Godfrey, one should note, remains absent from the novel for most of the action, having been despatched to the West Indies. Now, at the dénouement, Oldborough himself is discovered to have an illegitimate child, who turns out to be the admirable Mr Henry, once Godfrey's comrade-in-arms. What distinguishes the illegitimate Henry from the legitimate Miss Hauton to such a degree that she should be progressively disparaged throughout the novel?

Here the 'place of interpretation' readopts a literal meaning, and we resume contact with the question of setting. The final pages of the novel are undoubtedly rushed, and Austenite purists will find the creation of new and very minor figures not to their taste:

> Dr Percy had been lately attending Mr Gresham's porter, O'Brien, the Irishman; who had been so ill, that, imagining himself dying, he had sent for a priest. Henry was standing by the poor fellow's bedside when the priest arrived, who was so much struck by the sight of him, that for some time his attention could scarcely be fixed on the sick man. The priest, after he had performed his official duties, returned to Mr Henry, begged pardon for having looked at him with so much earnestness, but said that Mr Henry strongly reminded him of the features of an Italian lady who had committed a child to his care many years ago. This led to farther explanation, and upon comparing dates and circumstances, Mr Henry was convinced, that this was the very priest who had carried him over to Ireland; – the priest . . . knew only, that he had been handsomely rewarded by the Dublin merchant, to whom he had delivered the boy – and he had heard that this merchant had since become bankrupt and had fled to America.[33]

Yet, if we leave aside the sudden bustle of recognitions and recollections, other, more significant features of the prose emerge. Among these one should certainly note the absence of directly reported exchanges between any of the participants. Here is exemplified again that remoteness between details of apparent intensity and intimacy which recurs in the fiction, a dissociation of event from affective discourse. Second, one notes the brief inscription of Catholicism into the serenely Anglican world of the novel, this effected through the humble priest who has been preceded by a more exotic 'Neapolitan Abbé'. The latter is officially visiting Lord Oldborough in a diplomatic capacity but also bearing from his uncle, a cardinal, a private letter which initiates the business of identifying his lordship's unsuspected son as the offspring of an (unmarried) Italian lady long ago abandoned to conventual seclusion. These profuse, if highly localized, evidences of Catholicism are, however, counterbalanced by yet another exclusion. Henry's guardian is here described as an Irish merchant whom bankruptcy drove into exile. In an earlier account of the child's upbringing, it has been suggested that 'he was the son of a Mr Henry, who had taken an unfortunate part in the troubles of Ireland, and who had suffered'.[34] This explanation is never substantiated, and the story of the Italian lady and her adulterous liason with the young Lord Oldborough finally replaces it. The exclusion of the Irish troubles must be regarded as a major emotive force in the novel if it compensates for sexual irregularity in a great minister. Oldborough's happy discovery of his son, together with the approval implicit in every detail of the novel's conclusion, constitutes an intervention to which insurrection plays the part of potent material excluded.

Having discovered that the place of interpretation in which *Patronage* can be fully appreciated is not congruent with its English setting, we could proceed to examine one final aspect of the novel – its resemblance at crucial moments to 'secret memoirs, and private anecdotes'.[35] Two minor characters provide an opportunity to consider some of the theoretical problems arising out of the distinction between history and fiction which Edgeworth outlined in the preface to *Castle Rackrent.* One of these is distinctively named Mrs Hungerford. Some readers who opened the *Memoirs of Richard Lovell Edgeworth* six years after their first engagement with *Patronage* may have recalled the character's name when they read, in the first volume of memoirs, how the youthful Edgeworth accidentally learned that a very elderly and still beautiful Englishwoman was a Catholic. The penitent whom he discovered upon her knees in front of a crucifix was named Mrs Hungerford.[36] By contrast, the second minor character in *Patronage* who excites attention in a related manner is nameless.

O'Brien, whose illness reunited Mr Henry and his priestly conductor, was once employed by an irascible painter much given to the denunciation of a patron acting the 'Mecaenas'. No clue is given of the artist's name, though his fondness for huge canvases and allegorical themes is emphasized, together with a hint of work left unfinished. Were one to merge the nationality of O'Brien with the intemperateness of the painter, the compound figure would resemble James Barry (1741-1806), whose *Inquiry into the Real and Imaginary Obstructions to the Acquisition of the Arts in England* (1775) denounced patronage, though with a welter of personal abuse which the novelist could only have deplored. Like her imaginary painter, Barry held portraiture in contempt, and left the chief portraitist of the age (Joshua Reynolds) nameless in the *Inquiry*.[37] But the point at issue is not whether one can spot the historical James Barry: as with the two Mrs Hungerfords of memoir and fiction, the question is essentially one of readership.

As with the minutiae of Irish social history in *Castle Rackrent* and *The Absentee*, these characteristics of *Patronage* suggest that Edgeworth's fiction addresses a fractured, or multi-layered, readership. At one level, fiction is virtually hermetic, having only its author as reader. Elsewhere, certain specialized or arcane references come into play through the activity of a few, informed readers. The plot concerning a plot against Oldborough thus has a larger, metatextual significance as it lays out the difficulties of interpretation in what one might now take as a model or ideal text, the papers lost by M. de Tourville during the shipwreck. The subsequent loss of the Percy family's deed leads to their eviction from Percy-Hall; they must take to The Hills, but Mr Percy's correct decoding of the diplomatic papers (where Mr Falconer has failed) is accompanied by the (otherwise inexplicable) discovery of the deed among Falconer's papers. The correct reading of a text is equivalent to the restored existence of a text.

But no single reading of *Patronage* is possible, and so the novel's resolution of issues concerning property, sexuality, ethics and class continues to elude any neat resolution. Whereas Jane Austen's narratives work to confirm the propriety of existing social relations, by eliminating intrusive fashion or 'improvement', and so present English society as a seamless and proportioned garment, Edgeworth's fiction more often resembles a quilting technique in which textures of different ages and tonalities are organized to serve a particular, never absolute, end. Herein lies the political thrust of her work, and this can be acknowledged even by readers who point to discrepancies between the disinterestedness preached by the Percys and the many strategems by which they severally advance in their professions. Patchwork is an art of contraries and 'Without contraries is no progression.'[38]

Given this sense of the novel's concern with interpretation, and with the politics of readership, we can look finally at the scene with which it opens. '"How the wind is rising!" said Rosamond. "God help the poor people at sea tonight!"'[39] The ensuing shipwreck initiates the metatextual action with the loss of Tourville's papers and their subsequent falling into the hands of the Falconers. Even the later loss of the Percys' deed is explicitly traced back to the night of the shipwreck, through the carelessness of a rescued Dutch marine carpenter. More immediately, Tourville discredits himself in the eyes of his rescuers, the Percys, by mocking the altruism of Count Altenberg, adviser to a German prince besotted with a scheming actress. When Altenberg pops up twenty-three chapters later, he is discovered in the London docks strenuously seeking the release of his servant, who has been press-ganged into the British navy. Such irregular negotiations with the sea – shipwreck and press-ganging – complement one another precisely through their political associations. Tourville is a foe of Britain, a scheming courtier, and Altenberg eloquently pleads for his servant in the name of British justice. The ironies of these configurations can hardly be missed – the schemer is entertained in an English country house and the spokesman for justice is a foreigner.

Patronage includes other, seemingly unnecessary incidents of a similar kind. In a letter from Godfrey Percy to his brother, dropped by Edgeworth after the first edition, there is reference to his sailing for the West Indies after six weeks' delay 'waiting for some order, which some secretary had forgotten to expedite'.[40] When Altenberg arrives in England he insists on being brought to the place where Tourville's ship ran aground, and even on being taken out to sea in a small boat as if to reoccupy the scene of the shipwreck. These particulars are excessive. But they underline the metonymic association between the line which links/divides land and sea, and the line (so to speak) which links/divides action and text. If it seems excessive also to regard *Patronage* as in this manner attending to the relationship of Ireland and England, history and fiction, insurrection and ennui, we might recall a striking passage from Maria Edgeworth's correspondence. She refers to her family and their response to *The Absentee*:

> I long to hear whether their favor continues to the end and extends to the catastrophe [,] that dangerous rock upon which poor authors even after a prosperous voyage are often wrecked sometimes while their friends were actually hailing them from the shore.[41]

Shipwreck . . . landing . . . embarkation . . . these actions of the surface plot in *Patronage* shadow a deeper, excluded meaning. Superficially one of the 'English novels' of contemporary life, it embodies a hermetic theory of reading to which Ireland, Catholicism and history make vectoric contributions. Only by such complex means could the contrary values of Enlightenment be revalued at a time when the Anglo-Irish society of 'sceptical gentry who . . .

consider truth as an unstable, relative, individual term little connected with the active circumstance of this world' had been caught up in a universal struggle of the most intense military and commercial aggression.

SIX

'A SHADOWY NARRATOR': HISTORY, ART AND ROMANTIC NATIONALISM IN IRELAND 1750-1850

Luke Gibbons

I

Asked on one occasion to describe the tone of the *Nation* newspaper, Chancellor Plunkett is supposed to have replied: 'Wolfe Tone.' An association established through wit is hardly convincing, but if we bear in mind Freud's claim that humour discharges some of the latent tensions in the psychic system, then it may be that political jokes afford a glimpse into what Fredric Jameson has termed 'the political unconscious'.[1] The yoking together of romanticism and republicanism in Plunkett's witticism signals, in effect, the return of the repressed in Irish history. Indeed, insofar as it acknowledges a fusion between romantic nationalism and the separatist idea promulgated by republicanism, it represents the irruption of history itself as a volatile force in Irish cultural politics.

Republicanism in Ireland – in its formative stage at any rate – is often presented as effecting a radical break with the past and with romantic nostalgia. R.B. McDowell quotes a pronouncement of the United Irishmen that 'mankind have been too retrospective, canonized antiquity and undervalued themselves', sentiments shared by the Dublin society of the United Irishmen, which declared: 'We have thought little about our ancestors and much of our posterity.'[2] The notion that republicanism turned its back on the past is consistent with the forward-looking thrust of the Enlightenment at the end of the eighteenth century, but in one area even the most revolutionary currents in republicanism abroad drew freely on the rhetorical legacy of antiquity. This was in the visual arts, and took the form of a resolute commitment to history painting in mobilizing the self-images of both the American and the French Revolutions. It is hardly surprising then that in the early days of *The Nation*, when republicanism was still treated with caution in its pages, this was the one aspect of its ideological repertoire that appealed to Thomas Davis.[3]

In a series of essays calling for the establishment of a vigorous national art movement in Ireland, Davis invoked Sir Joshua Reynolds's influential argument that the ennobling power of art derives from its concern with the ideal rather than the actual conditions of life. 'Painting is but a shadowy narrator,' Davis wrote, and is little suited to providing a mere 'coloured chronicle' of events. Its treatment of subjects is closer to that of the historian than the journalist:

> As the historian, who composes a history out of various materials, differs from a newspaper reporter, who sets down what he sees . . . so do the Historical Painter, the Landscape Composer (such as Claude or Poussin) differ from the most faithful Portrait, Landscape, or Scene drawer.[4]

Davis's concern that evocations of the past transcend the prosaic details of journalism led him to conceive of history itself in terms of the grand sweep of history painting, as is clear from the metaphors which recur in his elaboration of the task which faces the Irish historian. 'Let us by all means have then a "graphic" narrative of what was,' he writes in his essay on 'The History of Ireland', 'Yet the man who would keep chronicling the dry events would miss writing a history':

> He must let us see the decay and rise of great principles and conditions . . . He must paint – the council robed in its hall – the priest in his temple – the conspirator – the outlaw – the judge – the general – the martyr . . . He who thinks it possible to dash off a profoundly coloured and shaded narrative like this . . . will find himself bitterly wrong. Even a great philosophical view may much more easily be extemporized than this lasting and finished image of past times.[5]

In emphasizing the ideal rather than the actual as the prerequisite of history painting, Davis was, in fact, making a virtue of necessity for, as he candidly admits, the mundane realities of Irish life – 'an indifferently made, ordinary, not very clean, nor picturesquely-clad people' – did not lend themselves to the requirements of the grand style. For this reason, he insisted that painting in Ireland take its bearings not directly from nature but from the great art of other periods, in particular, from the masterpieces of the classical age. It was the availability of a gallery in Cork, possessing one hundred and seventeen of the finest casts in the world, which was responsible for producing artists such as Maclise and Forde, rather than any peculiar traits in the character or climate of southern Ireland. Were this precedent to be developed under public patronage on a national scale, Davis averred, it would be a major step in shifting the balance of cultural power from the imperial centre towards some form of local or national autonomy. 'We do not hope to see art advance much till national character is restored by the break up of two or three of the huge and hateful empires.'[6]

II

Davis's enlisting of the aura of classical antiquity in the cause of a national art movement is ironical, given that the whole basis of the neo-classic revival in the eighteenth century was that it addressed universal themes, allowing artists to escape the limiting horizons of a particular culture or society. Davis's reading of Sir Joshua Reynolds's *Discourses on Art* (1769-90) would have reminded him that in specifying native topics such as 'The Landing of the Milesians' or 'St Patrick brought before the Druids at Tara' (not to mention 'Molyneux's Book Burned' or 'Tone, Emmet and Keogh') as fit subjects for the gravitas of history painting, he was contravening the precepts of the grand style as outlined in Reynolds's canonical treatise. In his Fourth Discourse, Reynolds takes issue with Dutch painting for lowering its sights from the general to the particular, and for dwelling on the surface details of local experience rather than the underlying constants of the human condition:

> The painters of the Dutch school have still more locality. With them, a history-piece is properly a portrait of themselves; whether they describe the inside or outside of their houses, we have their own people engaged in their own peculiar occupations; working, or drinking, playing, or fighting. The circumstances that enter into a picture of this kind, are so far from giving a general view of human life, that they exhibit all the minute

particularities of a nation differing in several respects from the rest of mankind . . . The painters of this school are excellent in their own way; they are only ridiculous when they attempt general history on their own narrow principles, and debase great events by the meanness of their characters.[7]

In these disparaging remarks on Dutch art, it will be seen that the grounds for discouraging the servile imitation of everyday life also rule out the very possibility of a national art. For Reynolds realism means an attachment to the local, to particular details, and national differences are the political equivalent of the trifles and ephemera of daily existence. The equation of the attention to detail in realist art with the constraints imposed by custom and locality on human nature was part of the common fund of neo-classical wisdom, due mainly to the magisterial influence of Dr Johnson's critical writings on literature.[8] Painting, however, was better placed than literature to address universal themes, and hence was under greater pressure to distance itself from the confines of local experience. In this lay one of the main obstacles to the appropriation of the visual arts for nationalist ends – the obstacle which Davis attempted to surmount in his forays into art criticism.

Painting was considered to be well disposed towards the universal for a number of reasons. Primary among these was its deployment of what might be referred to as 'the esperanto of the eye'. It was a truism in eighteenth-century aesthetics that pictorial expression was not bound by the sort of cultural constraints which limited the intelligibility of language. 'A Picture bears a real Resemblance to its Original, which Letters and Syllables are wholly void of,' wrote Joseph Addison. 'Colours speak all Languages, but Words are understood only by such a People or Nation.'[9] As critical debates progressed throughout the century, the analysis of the contrasting merits of words and images took the form of aligning language with time, and vision with space: verbal expression facilitated the passage of time through narrative, whereas visual form, by contrast, allowed an exploration of space within the three-dimensional limits of the pictorial frame. In Lessing's *Laokoon* (1766), one of the great landmarks in the history of aesthetics, this distinction amounted to the virtual exclusion of any sense of temporal succession from pictorial representation, the emphasis instead being placed on heightened action, the kind of elevated moments which compress an event or even a whole epoch into a concentrated point in time.[10] It was in this manner that history painting came to articulate the heroic mode, capturing those turning-points in the affairs of men which constituted the loftiest expressions of human character. Universalism in form and style thus gave rise to the universal in subject-matter.

The dignified concept of human nature eulogized in history painting owed its origins to a tradition of civic humanism which entered English political discourse from Renaissance political theory. Central to this tradition, as J.G.A. Pocock points out, was a concept of *virtue* based on the classical republican ideal of a dedication to the common good through full participation in political life.[11] The common good in this sense was not to be identified with any particular interest, whether it be that of a private individual or even a particular nation. This was another way of saying it did not exist in the real world but was an ideal, an abstraction from the interests of the various individuals and social groupings which comprised the body politic in the most general understanding of the term. It was at this point that the aspirations of history painting coincided with the republican ideal, for both eschewed the particular in pursuit of a general norm, what John Barrell refers to as 'the republic of taste'.[12] This convergence between the aesthetic and the political, both grounded in a universal humanism, received its classic formulation in Reynolds's *Discourses*:

> We pursue the same method in our search after the idea of beauty and perfection in each; of virtue, by looking forwards beyond ourselves to society, and to the whole; of arts, by extending our view in the same manner to all ages and all times.[13]

Reynolds took his own idealism to heart by admitting candidly that in his practice as a painter, he could not live up to the exalted standards of history painting and hence was forced to make do with portraiture – a self-imposed limitation which was not without its financial rewards. The republic of taste had to await the dawning of revolutionary consciousness in France of the 1780s to find its most forceful political expression. The emblematic images of this intensification of republican ideology are David's monumental paintings, *The Oath of the Horatii* (1784-5) and the *Brutus* of 1789. *The Oath of the Horatii* represents the ultimate affirmation of patriotic virtue: in it the three sons of Horatius pledge loyalty to Rome, even though it entails a fight to the death with their opponents, the Curatii, to whom they are related twice over by marriage. The fatherland takes precedence over the family, in keeping with the anti-domestic bias of history painting. If this exhausted the meaning of the painting, it would be simply a mani-

Jacques Louis David, *The Oath of the Horatii*, The Louvre, Paris

festation of patriotism, and hence might even be consistent with a pledge of loyalty to the king (the incident was set, after all, in the pre-republican period when Rome was still a monarchy). The very fact of invoking a distinguished Roman precedent, however devoid of any historical connection with the present, converted it from being an act of local, political expedience into the kind of universal vindication of the civic ideal that made sense only within republican ideology. This covert republicanism, and subordination of the family (and hence the aristocratic means of transmitting power) to an abstract conception of the state, is made more explicit in David's *Brutus*, a historical tableaux which pays homage to Lucius Junius Brutus, who sacrificed his own sons in the course of overthrowing the tyrant Tarquinius Superbus, and establishing the Roman republic. It was exhibited in the momentous year of 1789, the strangely absent centre of the painting itself testifying to a world in which the centre could no longer hold.

It is hardly coincidental that in asserting the constancy of a virtuous human nature, and in devaluing localized expressions of historical change, David's great set-pieces should transform the (narrative) flow of historical time into abstract configurations of spatial form.[14] The geometrical precision exercised in the arrangement of figures, the angular display of the bodies and the rigorous demarcation of emotional space, all point to the moral equivalent of the metric system, precisely the type of Euclidean politics which Edmund Burke was to equate with the abstract theorizing of republicanism.[15] But the rarefaction of classical republicanism into the austerity of form at both the aesthetic and political levels served another purpose. It denied, as we have seen, a historical link or continuum between ancient Rome and France, suggesting at the most that antiquity furnished moral exemplars rather than the historical foundations of virtuous actions.[16] The neo-classical concept of the past was not bound up with the search for origins or remote ancestry which fired romantic antiquarianism and, by extension, cultural nationalism. Such was the blithe disregard for unearthing the original sources that one imaginative critic, George Turnbull, could devote an entire treatise to a meticulous comparison of the paintings of the great Greek painter Apelles with those of Raphael – despite the fact that not a single trace of Apelles's work had survived the classical age.[17] From this perspective, the use of the past in republican imagery, or its French variant, at any rate, was not incompatible with a political philosophy which set its eyes firmly on the present, if not the future. As Thomas Crow has argued, the eventual outbreak of the revolution obviated the need to camouflage republican sentiments in antique costume: in David's *Oath of the Tennis Court* (1791), the Oath of the Horatii is re-enacted on a mass scale as a declaration of the popular will, complete with contemporary dress.[18] As with all forms of idealism, the very success of history painting led to its own dissolution. Its exposure to lived history proved its undoing.

The cult of antiquity, then, was governed by moral rather than strictly historical imperatives, and it was precisely for this reason that the earliest advocates of the visual arts in Ireland ruled out native mythology and subject-matter from the hallowed precincts of history painting. In his 1767 pamphlet, *An Essay on Perfecting the Fine Arts in Great Britain and Ireland*, Thomas Campbell argued that native or traditional culture does not afford a sufficient basis for cultivating 'the learned eye', or acquiring 'that second sight we call taste'. The case of music was instructive in this regard. Someone might grow up 'in the country' appreciating 'the street madrigal or itinerant violin', but when he was equipped with a genuine musical sensibility, 'what before was melody will now prove discord to him'.[19] Campbell returned to this theme in his acerbic *Philosophical Survey of the South of Ireland*, published ten

Jacques Louis David, *Oath of the Tennis Court*, The Louvre, Paris

years later. In the intervening period, his hostility to native culture had somewhat abated – a temporary aberration, as we shall see, and a consequence, perhaps, of the renewed interest in Irish history prompted by the publication of works by Thomas Leland and Sylvester O'Halloran.[20] Campbell defended the claim, against the aspersions of historians such as David Hume, that Ireland was one of the oldest civilizations in Europe and was particularly keen to vouch for the Irish credentials of Ossian against the posturings of Macpherson: not alone is there no mention of Ossian in Scottish history, Campbell argued, but his songs are still 'familiar to the aboriginal natives of Ireland' and are not simply embalmed in historical texts. Yet his enthusiasm for ancient Ireland was qualified, since it lacked those elements of moral purpose and narrative coherence which attracted others to the study of classical antiquity. In pre-Christian Ireland, as depicted in the surviving records:

> There is no variety of events, no consecutive series of action, no motives to war, or inducements to peace, but the adultery of some queen, the rape of some virgin, or the murder of some chief. In fine, there is no exemplary morality, no colour of just history.[21]

This was said more in the way of an aside, but Campbell's commonsense aversion to historical speculation – a trait which grew more emboldened following his acceptance in Dr Johnson's distinguished literary coterie[22] – led him gradually to consider the avid researches of contemporary Irish antiquarians as having more in common with the fictions of Macpherson than with the dispassionate pursuit of historical truth. In a learned, but far from dispassionate, polemic published in the changed circumstances of 1789, when the Catholic issue had polarized Protestant public opinion, he ridicules the special pleading of native historians such as Charles O'Conor and Sylvester O'Halloran who sought to confer respectability on the pre-historic past by arguing, not alone that the ancient Irish were conversant with classical civilization, but that they actually introduced, by virtue of their Phoenician origins, the use of letters to Greece. Such was the credulity of O'Halloran, Campbell writes, that he was prepared to believe that Ireland was entitled 'the island of saints' even before the coming of Christianity – a perverse misreading on his part of the tag 'insula sacra' which classical commentators applied to Ireland.[23] As his strictures proceed apace, the partisan quality of Campbell's own argument emerges, based as it is on a Protestant deference to the written word and a profound suspicion of tradition. In an ideological turn derived ultimately from Locke, he draws on Whitaker's *History of the Britons* to support his contention that tradition is closely allied to superstition in its unreliability and proneness to fantasy: 'Ireland remains to this day superstitiously devoted to her ancient history, sullenly turns away from the light of reformation that is spread over the neighbouring island, and wraps herself in the gloom of her own legendary annals.' The indeterminate and fragmented nature of tradition is sufficient, according to Campbell, to vitiate its claims to truth: 'The savage knows nothing but from living memory, or from fading tradition. The wild song of the barbarous bard may be repeated for some ages, but not with exactness.' Had Ireland really a distinguished past, there would be ample evidence in surviving written records and imposing monuments. Instead there is only the utter desolation of Tara and Armagh, a silent reproach to those who would build historical castles in the air without any solid foundation in fact. This lack of substance is evident at both a material and moral level: in relation to Armagh, he enjoins us to

> Witness the prime favourite of the bards, Concovar MacNessa, emphatically so called from his criminal commerce with his own mother Nessa! A perfidious savage, stained with almost every vice that could degrade and disgrace human nature. Yet Mr O'Conor would persuade us that he was 'a prince, whose heroic actions and patronage of the sciences made amends to the public for great personal failings'.[24]

The contrast between text and tradition in Campbell's writing is easily converted into the standard Enlightenment opposition between universal reason and local custom. The relevance of this to the impoverished state of painting in Ireland hardly needed underlining, but unsympathetic observers nonetheless lost no opportunity in drawing attention to the obstacles presented by the native culture to those who sought to promote the visual arts. According to Anthony Pasquin, writing in 1794, the fickle nature of the Irish national character did not lend itself to the solemnity and moral elevation of history painting:

> Considering Ireland as a nation, she possesses a more than ordinary portion of genius; but that genius is exemplified in an aptitude of merriment according with momentary social desires. Irishmen are, generally speaking, too mercurial in their propensities for the habitudes of profound thinking . . . the seeds of their actions are fraught with the noblest qualities; but the issue from that seed is too repeatedly blighted by the elements of custom – they have some enlightened and philosophic men among them, who have done much towards suppressing the remnants of barbarism, which are even now too prevailing; but their efforts are not effectual; hence the good taste of the country is limited, and not equal to the maintenance of the highest orders of imitative merit.[25]

III

As Tom Dunne has observed, it has become a commonplace to link the social conservatism of cultural nationalism in Ireland to Edmund Burke's formulation of a theory of community and tradition based on custom and the inherited wisdom of the ages.[26] What is interesting from the point of view of visual arts, however, is that the full weight of Burke's formidable critique of the Enlightenment made its presence felt in England rather than in Ireland, and, in fact, met its most sustained opposition at a cultural level from an Irish painter and one-time protégé of Burke, James Barry. The vehicle for shifting the theoretical basis of English painting from universal reason to local and national custom was the later lectures of Joshua Reynolds's *Discourses on Art;* but if, to adapt an aphorism from a later era, the voice was that of Joshua Reynolds, the mind was certainly that of Edmund Burke. Burke was Reynolds's intellectual mentor and closest friend – so close, in fact, that he was at Reynolds's bedside on the artist's death in 1792, and was entrusted with making his funeral arrangements and acting as executor of his will. Reynolds regularly sent his lectures to Burke for examination and revision before delivery, and indeed to Irish readers, the affinities between Burke's and Reynolds's critical opinions seemed so strong that as late as 1810, the *Hibernian Magazine* was still claiming that Burke actually wrote the *Discourses*.[27]

Be that as it may, the discernible shift in Reynolds's *Discourses* after 1776 from the universalism of civic humanism to a language of custom and natural sentiments was prompted, as John Barrell has suggested, by the appearance on both sides of the Atlantic of a spectre that was to haunt the Whig imagination: the outbreak of revolution in America and, more particularly, in France.[28] By 1790, when history painting had met its nemesis in the Oath of the Tennis Court, Reynolds was in a position to exonerate himself from the charge that his own creative investment in portraiture did not live up to the high ideals enunciated in the early *Discourses*. In his final lecture (1790), he pointed out that the universal rhetoric of the grand style, and by extension republicanism, was simply not suited 'to my abilities, and to the taste of the times in which I live' – the best of times for republican Paris being the worst of times for London, at least where history painting was concerned.[29] Reynolds was, in fact, able to disengage himself from the more radical implications of civic humanism without any great loss of face, for even in his most explicit pronouncements on the ideal of universalism, there was always a latent commitment to custom and tradition. This was because of his resolutely empiricist approach to 'abstraction' and 'general ideas'. In keeping with Hume's celebrated attack on causality, Reynolds held that the 'essence' or 'general form' of any object was not immanent in nature, but was simply what most people from habit and experience had agreed to be the case. What we perceive as general or universal is the residue of custom and accepted practice. The tenuous connection between this idea of universality and local custom was sufficient to permit Reynolds to argue that in certain cases local interests merge with the common good of humanity. What he had in mind, of course, was England's national interest. As John Barrell summarizes it:

> To indulge . . . a nation within a universal republic, 'with the privilege of abiding by their own customs', is inevitably to allow them not to subscribe, in certain particulars, to the universal law; but if that nation is England, the case is entirely altered, and the indulgence will be difficult to withhold, for it involves the very survival of English liberty.[30]

What was good for general humanity apparently was also good for the empire. The hidden premise here was the assumption that custom in its political guise – the unwritten constitution and the tradition of common law – bequeathed the proud legacy of the free-born Englishman. The recourse to tradition which was dismissed as an outcrop of Catholic superstition in Ireland was thus reclaimed in England under the pretext of liberty. It was this traducing of both republican ideals and Irish history which galvanized the Irish émigré James Barry into an unremitting – and, in terms of his own self-advancement, very costly – attack on the British art establishment that led ultimately to his expulsion from the Royal Academy in 1799: the only painter to enjoy that dubious honour.

Barry's strategy was simple if audacious: it was to deny that England had any right to be regarded as the custodian of liberty, and to propose instead that the very features of Irish society which English rule had systematically repressed were the true inheritors of the spirit of freedom. The idea that the torch of liberty had passed from England to Ireland was familiar enough in Volunteer rhetoric of the 1780s,[31] but Barry took this a stage further by arguing provocatively that *Catholic* Ireland was the true repository of the kind of freedom and virtue enshrined in republican discourse. Presented with an Irish society based on tradition and community, it would have been easy for Barry to relapse into Burkean homilies on 'the little platoon', and to counterpose the merits of local custom to English pretensions to universal liberty. But this was not his approach: he distanced himself explicitly from the kind of parochialism which, as he put it, on 'being made acquainted with the domestic detail of one neighbourhood', states 'we shall profit very little by extending our enquiries to another'.[32] With this in mind, Barry sought to rehabilitate the native Irish for the cause of progress and to bring about a fusion – a highly combustible one, as it turned out – between the forces of Catholicism and republicanism in Irish culture.

In 1776 Barry published a striking print entitled *The Phoenix or Resurrection of Freedom* which was intended to mark the flight of liberty from England to a new home in an America still basking in the light of independence.[33] The dramatis personae gathered in the foreground around the bier of Britannia were stock figures in the annals of republicanism – Algernon Sidney, John Milton, Andrew Marvell, John Locke and, not a little presumptously, Barry himself. At the left-hand side, Father Time pays homage to the cradles of classical republicanism – Athens and Rome – but more important

James Barry, *The Phoenix or Resurrection of Freedom*, British Museum, London

for Barry's ideological project is the barely perceptible trace in the mid-ground of Florence, the birthplace of modern republicanism. It was in Florence, and more generally in renaissance Italy, that the discourse of civic humanism and 'virtue' was revived,[34] and not least of the factors promoting its rebirth in Barry's eyes, and facilitating the extraordinary flowering of the visual arts in this period, was the presiding influence of the Catholic Church. Barry had no hesitation in delineating the unacceptable face of Catholicism, and in his great painting *Elysium and Tartarus or the State of Final Retribution* he took some pleasure in placing the visage of what he called 'a political pope', along with a monarch and a wretch holding the sectarian 'Solemn League and Covenant', in the depths of Tartarus, his vision of eternal damnation. But he took particular exception to the imputation in the writings of thinkers such as Montesquieu that Catholicism was incompatible with the sense of public spirit fostered by republicanism.[35] For Barry, the break-up in the whole idea of public life, what a modern critic has referred to as the fall of public man,[36] began with the rise of individualism and unbridled self-interest during the Reformation.

The extent to which the Protestant ethic brought about the collapse of the public sphere was a complex and controversial question, but in one area there was a measure of agreement among

James Barry, *Elysium and Tartarus or the State of Final Retribution*, etching and engraving (1792), National Library of Ireland, Dublin

Barry and his contemporaries that the Reformation had led to a deterioration in the quality of civic life. This was in the decline of a public role for the visual arts, particularly the disappearance of the kind of church art practised by Michelangelo and others during the Renaissance which raised painting to new levels of moral grandeur. It was fashionable to lament the baneful influence of puritanism on the visual arts – even Reynolds saw fit to condemn this modern form of iconoclasm[37] – but Barry considered this as having disastrous consequences not just for art's relationship with the public but also for its relationship to time and history. In place of the sweep of narrative painting, pictorial styles had degenerated, he maintained, into 'portraits of ourselves, of our horses, our dogs, and country seats'.[38] It was fitting that this type of painting should lend itself to the depiction of inanimate objects, for it involved an attempt to step outside the remorseless flow of time into the private repose of the still-life. Soon after his death, a critic sought to disparage Barry's greatest works by comparing them to the narratives of stained glass,[39] but this would have been welcomed as fulsome praise by Barry himself. He lauded the arrangement of pictures in Italian churches as 'serving at once for books, intelligible to the unlettered',[40] in a word, for having a democratic mode of address. It was for this reason that the abject failure of an ambitious scheme in 1773 to decorate St Paul's Cathedral with an extensive series of history paintings proved a turning-point in Barry's life. Barry, Reynolds and Benjamin West were among the six distinguished painters chosen to carry out the project, but its ignominious collapse due to lack of interest and patronage convinced Barry that the republic of taste was a lost cause where Britain was concerned.

Partly out of desperation to execute a series of history paintings on a grand scale, Barry offered in 1777 to decorate the Great Room at the Adelphi, the new headquarters for the Society for the Encouragement of Arts, at no cost to the Society, save his own expenses. This monumental project, which in one way or another consumed Barry for the rest of his life, required the completion of six epic paintings charting the progress of the arts in western civilization, culminating in a vast sprawling canvas, over 42 feet long, entitled *Elysium and Tartarus or the State of Final Retribution*. This provided him with an opportunity to fasten the links between republicanism, liberty and Catholicism that underlie so much of his work. As he expressed it himself: 'It was my wish to bring together in Elysium, those great and good men of all ages and nations, who were cultivators and benefactors of mankind; it forms a kind of apotheosis, or more properly a beatification of those useful qualities which were pursued through the whole work.'[41]

It might be expected that such a cosmic vision would be prepared to fix its gaze only on the everlasting things, or the most dignified expressions of human nature, and indeed as the eye

Illustration by A.C. Pugin, T. Rowlandson and J. Bluck of The Great Room of the Royal Society of Arts (showing a section of Barry's monumental *The Progress of Human Culture* on the walls)

traverses the canvas it encounters many of the notable historical figures who devoted their lives to liberty: for example, Junius Brutus, Cato the Younger, Shaftesbury and his adviser, Locke. The centrepiece is provided by William Penn, the founder of American liberty, who is imparting his code of laws to other great legislators, such as Numa, Solon and Lycurgus,[42] and towards the right of the painting overlooking the precipice of Tartarus, the assembly of the faithful is comprised of the greatest writers and artists who have graced human history: Apelles, Homer, Shakespeare, Milton, Michelangelo, Raphael, and so on. As we look beyond the familiar figures, however, it transpires that not only has Barry given a Catholic tincture to the entire panorama – in the form of various popes, monks, Jesuits, and Catholic monarchs such as Francis I – but there is also a distinctive Irish sub-text running through it. Situated at the very apex of the painting is Ossian, or rather Barry's intervention in the Macpherson controversy, for having gone to some lengths to consult those authorities who argued in favour of Ossian's Irishness, he equips him with a historically accurate Irish harp.[43] Further down the painting, behind Junius Brutus and facing the group of legislators, is William Molyneux, complete with his *Case of Ireland Stated,* the first systematic presentation of the case for Irish legislative independence. The emblematic harp on the cover of Molyneux's book calls attention to Ossian's harp at the top of the picture, as if the claim to legislative independence is bound up with a vindication of ancient Irish civilization.

Molyneux, or for that matter William Penn, did not quite fit in with the Catholic contribution to liberty and progress, but in 1792-3, in the first flush of the concessions made by the government to the Catholic Committee in Ireland, Barry amended the original centrepiece in an engraving. Penn was forced to give pride of place to a nobleman with an Irish title, the Catholic Lord Baltimore, who as early as 1649 had anticipated the eminent Quaker by passing the Maryland Act of Toleration, which established a pioneering legal framework for human rights and civic harmony between Catholics and Protestants.[44] In the top left-hand corner, as if benefiting from the passing of the Act, one of the most unlikely groups ever assembled in a history painting is taking part in a convivial discussion: Benjamin Franklin, Pope Adrian, Bishop Berkeley, the Jesuit Mariana[45] and Cardinal Reginald Pole, the arch-opponent of Henry VIII's break with Rome.

The choice of figures in this engraving may seem idiosyncratic but in fact it was keenly attuned to the thinking of some of the

Detail of James Barry, *Elysium*, showing William Molyneux (bottom left, behind hooded figure, holding book) and Ossian (above centre, leaning on harp), etching and engraving, National Library of Ireland, Dublin

James Barry, *Lord Baltimore and the Group of Legislators* (1793), etching and engraving, National Library of Ireland, Dublin

most prominent supporters of the Catholic Committee in Ireland. Berkeley, for example, had provided a model for Charles O'Conor's observations on the Popery laws,[46] and in a letter to Joseph Cooper Walker in 1787, O'Conor mentions how, on seeing a portrait of Reginald Pole, he found his praises of the Catholic prelate reciprocated by Lady Moira.[47] Even more to the point, William and Edmund Burke had given the spirit of toleration in Maryland their imprimatur by citing it as an early example of the American pursuit of liberty, and this was seized on by Charles O'Conor in 1777 as an alternative to some of the republican excesses in the American Revolution.[48] As George Sigerson was later to point out, the importance of the example of Maryland for Catholic apologists was that it had offered a haven to both Catholics and Protestant dissenters escaping persecution in Ireland – thus forging a common interest between them in the face of English oppression.[49] The idea that Catholics had prepared the ground for Protestant conceptions of liberty and national independence proved immensely attractive to Barry, and it was with this in mind that he included Molyneux in the corner of the Baltimore engraving. As he himself commented on Molyneux's contribution to the cause of Irish liberty:

> It must, however, be acknowledged, that the Roman Catholics, in Ireland, had led the way, in the vindication of those rights of their common country; as they had, some years before, prevailed with king James to give his assent to an act entitled, *An Act for declaring that the Parliament of England cannot bind Ireland, and against Writs of Errors and Repeals out of Ireland into England*. But the happy adjustment of these matters was reserved for a more liberal, philosophic age, when all occasions of disunion, strife, dependence, and desolation should be for ever banished, together with those mischievous horrors of Popery which gave rise to them . . . We may now fairly hope that Ireland will, at last, permit itself to be free; and that the great majority of the natives of that country (and the majority and the country are synonymous terms) will no longer have the bitter mortification of being prescribed [*sic*] the enjoyments of those constitutional rights (derived from the virtue of their ancestors, under the Henry's, John's, & c).[50]

It is possible, then, to see in this vast work a series of oblique but politically charged comments on the state of Ireland, as if only the breadth of vision furnished by history painting could show the way out of the impasse presented by British rule in Ireland. Barry himself admitted that this was the motivating principle in the work: 'I have no small satisfaction in reflecting', he wrote, 'that the business transacted in the group of legislators in the Elysium, goes all the length of the remedy for the disorders of Ireland, the application of which remedy has been so long desired, prayed for, and hoped for.' When the public acclaim which Barry had expected for the monumental work did not materialize, but turned instead into a series of bitter recriminations that led to his expulsion from the Academy, he had no hesitation in linking the fate of his painting to that of his oppressed country.

It does not surprise me [he wrote] and I feel no sorrow or repentance to find my work and myself involved in the same fate with my country, in the struggle for that political happiness which results from genuine freedom of equal laws, uncontaminated with either personal, party, or local feelings . . . I felt myself the very focus of that influence which is so unwisely, and so much against its true interest, operating ruin and destruction in Ireland.[51]

Though contemporary critics did not object to, or even notice, the subversive networks which Barry had threaded through his narrative, it can be shown that what they did object to at a stylistic and thematic level had a direct bearing on his attempt to smuggle his Irish preoccupations through the stately portals of history painting. In his response to the *Elysium*, Richard Ryan (who had ridiculed the stained-glass quality of the Adelphi series) also took exception to the fact that the controlling gaze of the eye is overwhelmed by the proliferation of details and discordant rhythms of the work:

Surely, nothing in painting was ever so utterly *unpicturesque* as this work in its general effect. The picture is rather an index to the book of explanation, than the book to the picture; and the eye wanders in vain amidst a promiscuous throng of kings, quakers, legislators, and naked Indians, for a centre of interest and a point of unity.[52]

Barry's tendency to let the surge of the narrative overpower the visual cohesion of his paintings was an affront to the neo-classical sense of order and decorum, and featured regularly in negative appraisals of his work. But it did not simply challenge the rule of order: it also prevented a painting from achieving the kind of spatial unity which allowed it to arrest the flow of time, and hence to disengage itself from history. It was a central tenet of neo-classical aesthetics that a painting be taken in by a single act of perception: if the apprehension of work required the passage of time this meant that time itself, in the form of contingency, had entered the frame.[53] Part of David's appeal to republican ideology was that by foreshortening time into space, he released classical republican themes from the flux of history, and converted them into abstract moral exemplars. But this option was not available to an Irish painter. Classical antiquity may have been dead and gone, but the appeal of ancient Ireland to nationalist historiography lay in the belief that it was part of a lived historical experience, a product of an embattled collective memory. The rediscovery of Pompeii and Herculanium yielded still-life remains under the calcified lava of Vesuvius, but when the antiquarian Joseph Cooper Walker stirred the embers of the past in Ireland, he wrote that

> it was hinted to me by a friend, who perused my manuscript, that I dwell with too much energy on the oppressions of the English; treading, sometimes, with a heavy step, on ashes not yet cold.[54]

It was not, moreover, as if the relationship to the past in Ireland was one of unbroken succession, forming a stable, integral heritage. This was the organic view of tradition upon which Burke modelled his view of the English constitution, and it was what Joshua Reynolds had in mind when he remarked of custom that it 'does not grow upon a new made, slender soil, but is fastened by strong roots to ancient rocks, and is the slow growth of ages'.[55] Yet try as they would to emulate this image of continuity by insisting that ancient Irish civilization had come down to the present in an uncorrupted state, native historians had to face Edmund Spenser's taunt, quoted with evident satisfaction by Thomas Campbell: 'If such "old scholars", why so unlearned still.'[56] Why, in other words, was there so little to show of the glories of remote antiquity? The obvious answer was the destruction wrought by conquest – but to acknowledge the disruptive effect of successive invasions was to concede the discontinuous, fragmented nature of Irish history. For this reason, native historians such as Keating, O'Conor and O'Halloran were at pains to point out, as Joseph Cooper Walker put it, that 'many volumes of well-authenticated records have escaped the ravages of time and foreign spoilers'. Yet Cooper Walker himself admitted, with regard to the numerous copies of the legendary *Seanachas Mór*, or Great Book of Antiquity, that, 'most of these copies were destroyed, during the ravages of the Danes and English', and only 'several inestimable fragments' survived into the present. Even more ruefully he laments in a footnote:

> St Patrick, in the excess of his zeal, committed to the flames several hundred volumes, relating to the affairs of the Druids in particular, and the kingdom in general. This literary conflagration occasioned a wide chasm in our annals.[57]

The ideological shorthand which equated tradition with continuity, a sense of history with an enduring set of values, overlooked the fact that lived historical experience is amorphous and open-ended, and hence is at the farthest possible remove from the stability of the conservative canon. The past provides a sense of security only when it does not spill over into the present. As Samuel Weber expresses it:

> To determine History as totalisation, as a single self-same narrative, as a process of unification and of integration – ultimately, in short, as a movement of *identity* and *presentation* – is to assume a point of view from which the whole can be comprehended, a position, therefore, that must be essentially detached from and outside of what it seeks to contemplate.[58]

Tradition as conceived in England, then, was a closed system, a form of equilibrium, and one could step back from it as one stood back to contemplate an ordered work of art. But it was not possible to stand back from an Irish history painting: the spectator was confronted with the visual equivalent of Cooper Walker's 'inestimable fragments', and plunged into a mass of inchoate details and unresolved action.

Characteristically, it was Edmund Burke who sensed that there was more to Barry's work than met the eye: 'a space which extends beyond the field of vision', he wrote anonymously in a perceptive critique of the *Elysium*, 'only serves to distract and mislead the eye, and to divide the attention'.[59] It was as if the action was not capable of being contained within the frame, but was instead bound up with an historical reality which was resistant to the very idea of closure. This was the force which comes into play in Barry's only explicit incursion into Irish history, an oil sketch entitled *The Baptism of the King of Cashel by St Patrick* (1799-1801). An earlier treatment of this theme, exhibited at the Dublin Society in 1763, first brought the young painter to public notice, and can lay claim to be the earliest recorded painting on an Irish historical subject. By its very conception, it represented a triumph of history over art, for in looking to the native past rather than classical exemplars for inspiration, it broke with the axiom that art was born of art rather than the vicissitudes of history.[60] Barry's painting can be seen as part of a general tendency in Irish republicanism to revitalize the abstract universe of classicism by an active engagement with the past. Since his early acquaintance with Ulysses, the United Irishman William Drennan wrote, 'the love of my country has been in my breast, not merely a classical image, or a cold principle, but an animating spring of action'.[61]

James Barry, *The Baptism of the King of Cashel* (1799-1801), Dublin Castle

This tension between classicism and nationalism is worked into the second version of Barry's *St Patrick* painting (1799-1801), in which he attempts to coalesce classical republicanism with Ireland's heroic past. Since Barry linked Catholicism with classical virtue, the spatial logic of the painting would dictate that the Greek temple be placed on Patrick's side. The fact that it is part of the local landscape, and visually simulates the dolmens in the background, suggests that Ireland was already imbued with the glory of ancient Greece – a conviction Barry derived from his reading of Geoffrey Keating, Charles O'Conor and Sylvester O'Halloran.[62] (The specific inclusion of doric columns would indicate that heroic Ireland was ripe for, but had not yet attained, the republican ideal.) The unity of the scene is further destabilized by the multiple points of view, or lines of vision, which intersect the picture plane: Patrick's followers are looking up at the baptism, but those in the company of Aongus, the King of Munster, are pointing down in horror at the immolation of his foot by Patrick's crozier (his stoical countenance, as William Pressly remarks, itself attesting to the noble fortitude of Ireland's ancient rulers).[63] If at one level there is continuity between pagan and Christian Ireland, at another level, as Cooper Walker recognized, there is profound discontinuity. It is as if the left-hand side of the picture does not know what the right-hand side is doing, and our attention is accordingly dispersed towards the amputated figures at the margins, indicating a temporal reality that escapes pictorial entrapment.[64]

That reality has to do with another experience of discontinuity which made a deep impression on Barry. The second *St Patrick* picture was painted during the passing of the Act of Union, which Barry initially welcomed on the ground that it would bring Catholic emancipation. It is no coincidence that in his version of emancipation, the lethal alliance between the Catholic cause and republicanism is reactivated and the crown has been removed from the king. The turbulent forces at work in Irish history towards the end of Barry's life are riven with apocalyptic energy in one of his last drawings, *Passive Obedience* (1802-5). A dark cloud of destruction shatters the centre of the image, hurtling the details of the action like shrapnel towards the edges of the frame. Besieged and mocked by ghoulish monarchs invoking the divine right of kings, and even by the ghostly spectre of Edmund Spenser, who devastated Barry's native county during the Elizabethan conquest, a tormented figure is forced to look outside the boundaries of the picture for a narrative to make sense of it all.[65] That narrative lay in history itself, a history which, unlike the classical past, could not be sealed off from the present and was far from a state of completion.

IV

The problem posed by history painting to the idea of a national art was similar to that presented by republicanism to romantic nationalism: how to convert the universal into the local, and historical abstractions into a living relationship with a fractured past. In terms of the artistic principles outlined in Joshua Reynolds's *Discourses on Art*, this became a problem of how to integrate particular details and different points of interest into a scene without undermining the unified structure of the work. Barry too was concerned to avoid the utter contingency of the detail, and to

James Barry, *Passive Obedience* (1802-5), drawing, The Art Museum, Princeton University

redeem the particular in terms of the general, but this was achieved not through spatial logic but by means of an indeterminate pictorial narrative which went beyond the limits of the frame. In one of his final lectures to the Royal Academy, Barry questioned the organic completeness of the neo-classical ideal, emphasizing instead the importance of what, following Burke, he terms:

> the artificial infinite, where ingenuity may have so many recourses of *suggested* beauty or sublimity; where the imagination, when satisfied with the scene before it, might, by the concatentated secondary lights, be led on to the conception of something still further out of the picture.[66]

– an effect which can be achieved by flooding the entire frame with light, rather than using the kind of lighting which, as in Caravaggio, pinpoints one centre of action. Thus, as his friend and editor, Edward Fryer, wrote, even though particular objects and details were raised in Barry's mind 'into one vast and sublime, yet connected and systematic whole', his 'range was so ample that it appears without limits'.[67] To the extent that he believed in system-building, Barry was a republican; but insofar as his system was governed by historical time rather than universal space, he paved the way for romantic nationalism.

In his essay on 'National Art', Thomas Davis reserved the highest accolades for Barry, and the spirit of Barry would seem to preside over his manifesto on 'Hints for Irish Historical Paintings'.[68] But Davis was not the first Irish romantic who sought an accommodation with the prestigious genre of history painting. Over fifty years earlier, and largely in response to the same expressions of patriotic fervour which drew Barry back to native Irish themes, the antiquarian Joseph Cooper Walker published a pioneering pamphlet: *Outlines of a Plan for Promoting the Art of Painting in Ireland: with a List of Subjects for Painters drawn from the Romantic and Genuine Histories of Ireland* (1790). Cooper Walker's proposals for the arts in Ireland are animated throughout by a desire to reconcile national sentiments with the virtuous, classical temper. Recommending the provision of an academy in the manner of Davis, suitably stocked with paintings and casts, he remarks:

> Soon as the young artist has by this means acquired the idea of that central form from which every deviation is deformity, he may then venture to range abroad amidst the works of nature in quest of subjects for his pencil, or seek them amidst the annals of Irish valour or Irish patriotism.[69]

Citing the authority of the Greek painter Pamphilius, and no doubt with the example of the Great Room at the Adelphi in mind (Pamphilius is, in fact, among the elect in the *Elysium*), Cooper Walker emphasizes the importance of a well-stocked library and adds:

> This room should owe its decoration to the pencils of the students or of the masters, whose choice of history ought to be confined to Irish history or Irish romance – *nobly partial to our native earth,/Bid* Irish *pencils honour* Irish *worth*. Thus would the Academy not only be the nursery of infant genius, but be regarded as a school of public virtue. [70]

'Public virtue' is thus recast in terms of 'Irish worth' and this is brought to bear on the programme of instruction which Cooper Walker envisages for the students. Whereas Reynolds, for example, had stipulated that in history painting drapery 'is neither woollen, nor silk, sattin, or velvet: it is drapery',[71] Cooper Walker was adamant that the painter pay careful attention to costume as the means of expressing 'with true precision the time and place in which his scenes are laid' – an extension of Barry's view that genuine history painting admits 'all those transitory though happy accidental effects and graces, which may be extended to the most unimportant things, even to the folds of a drapery'.[72] A further incentive to the 'exertion of genius' in the academy would be the revival of the type of annual exhibition which first brought Barry to light, and it is in this context that he explicitly enlists Barry in the cause of cultural nationalism:

> In those exhibitions I would recommend the giving particular encouragement to history painting, not only for the reasons already assigned [i.e. it would encourage genius] but because it is, as Mr Barry sensibly observes, 'one of the tests by which the national character will be tried in after ages'.

This provides the cue for an inventory of memorable tableaux 'drawn from the romantic and genuine Histories of Ireland', which are deemed suitable for history painting. It begins by emphasizing the gap between Christianity and Druid culture – 'St Patrick encompassed with Druids, Bards and Chieftains, explaining the nature of the Trinity by means of the shamrock. A Druidical temple *overthrown*, at some distance. The sun rising.'[73] – and ranges across subjects such as the death of Conloch, the battle of Clontarf, 'The Parley between Essex and Tyrone in the county of Louth', and so on. It is not until the end of his idiosyncratic list that the full extent of Cooper Walker's desire to bring the grand style down to earth becomes apparent. History painting was subject to an interdiction against representing contemporary scenes – unless they were transferred, like West's famous *Death of General Wolfe* (1770), to a distant, exotic location.[74] When this rule was breached, as in David's *Oath of the Tennis Court* or, at a less incendiary level, in Francis Wheatley's pioneering renditions of the patriot movement in Ireland in the early 1780s, it signalled a crisis not only in the system of pictorial representation but in the political system itself.[75] It is in this light that we should view Cooper Walker's penultimate theme, a studied violation of the prohibition on representing living individuals:

> The venerable O'Conor meditating over the grave of Carolan in the church-yard of Kilronan. Part of the church appearing, with the skull of Carolan in a niche . . . Mr O'Conor might be a portrait.[76]

The inspiration for this scene came from a letter written shortly beforehand by Charles O'Conor of Belanagare to Cooper Walker, when he was staying with his son, also Charles O'Conor, at Lough Allen, Co. Roscommon, a short distance from O'Carolan's grave. James Barry's attempt to fuse Catholicism and republicanism led him, as we have seen, to posit an extra-pictorial reality, a more turbulent historical narrative beyond the boundaries of the frame.

Engraving of O'Carolan's grave at Kilronan (*c.* 1840)

There is a certain irony in the fact that the historical events of 1792-3 which convinced him of the possibility of such a fusion owed not a little of their momentum to the contributions of the O'Conor family. It was, in fact, Charles O'Conor snr (1710-91), the eminent historian, who first attempted to reconcile civic humanist discourse, at least in its liberal Whig variant, with the achievements of native Irish culture, in the several editions of his *Dissertations on the Ancient History of Ireland* (1753), a foundation-text of Irish cultural nationalism which Barry had actually read. O'Conor was also a founding member of, and a leading propagandist for, the Catholic Committee, whose eventual success in dismantling the Penal Laws in 1792-3 reactivated Barry's interest in Irish politics.

Charles O'Conor snr kept his distance from radical republicanism, but the same cannot be said of his son, Charles of Mount Allen (1738-1809), an active supporter of the United Irishmen. It was his communications with Thomas Russell and Wolfe Tone in 1791, pledging the support of the Catholics of north Connacht to the principles of the United Irishmen, which led both Tone and Russell to redouble their efforts in favour of Catholic emancipation.[77] Writing in the immediate aftermath of the 1798 rebellion, Thomas Addis Emmet recalled the initiatives of the Catholics of north Connacht, organized mainly by the O'Conors, in terms that could just as easily be used to describe the kind of insignificant detail which detonates the equilibrium of a history painting. When the Belfast Volunteers adopted a resolution in favour of Catholic emancipation that was to be announced publicly during the Bastille Day celebrations in July 1791, Emmet writes:

> The resolution that drew from the Catholics of Elphin and Jamestown, others, expressive of their thanks which were forwarded to Belfast; and this at the time almost-unheeded event, was the first foundation of a union which in its progress seemed destined to strike a tremendous blow against [the] British connection.[78]

This was the unfolding panorama which led Barry in 1793 to add one significant detail to his imaginary Elysium: by placing Lord Baltimore instead of William Penn at the centre of the picture, the Catholic cause was moved to the forefront of the struggle for universal liberty. The inclusion of the detail, the 'unheeded event' in Irish history, was sufficient, at least where Barry was concerned, to produce an insurrection on canvas.

SEVEN

GENEALOGIES OF ENGLISHNESS: LITERARY HISTORY AND CULTURAL CRITICISM IN MODERN BRITAIN

Stefan Collini

Let me not confound the discriminating character and genius of a nation with the conflux of its individuals in cities and reviews. Let England be Sir Philip Sidney, Shakespeare, Milton, Bacon, Harrington, Swift, Wordsworth; and never let the names of Darwin, Johnson, Hume fur it over. If these, too, must be England let them be another England; or, rather, let the first be old England, the spiritual, Platonic old England, and the second, with Locke at the head of the philosophers and Pope [at the head of] the poets, together with the long list of Priestleys, Paleys, Haleys, Darwins, Mr Pitts, Dundasses etc etc, be the representatives of commercial Great Britain. These have their merits, but are as alien to me as the Mandarin philosophers and poets of China. (S.T. Coleridge, *Notebooks*, 1805)[1]

The life of nations no less than that of men is lived largely in the imagination. (Enoch Powell, speech at Trinity College, Dublin, 1946)[2]

I

Living largely in the imagination, we may begin by letting our minds play over two entirely imaginary scenarios from an English history that never was.

The first is set in 1866, which, in this imaginary world, is the fiftieth anniversary of the Napoleonic conquest of Britain. The official language of government and education has now for two generations been French; the counties have been replaced by *départements*, and the real administrators are the *préfets*, appointed direct from Paris, though a regional assembly of co-operative notables has been allowed to stage a pastiche of parliamentary debate in annual gatherings at Canterbury. But by the 1860s we have, as in so much of Europe, stirrings of nationalist discontent: and, as in so much of Europe, questions of language and literature and even philology are very much to the fore. Militant young members of the Guild of Wessex address each other in a laboriously learned version of Anglo-Saxon; meetings of the Early English Text Society are officially illegal, yet the recovering and re-editing of ancient English texts is pursued with patriotic ardour. Clandestine reprintings of a popular edition of Asser's *Life of King Alfred* can barely keep pace with demand. A dictionary of the English language on historical lines is planned, attempting to do for an imagined 'English nation' what had been done for Germany by her philologists and lexicographers in the previous generation and was being done by Hungarians and Bohemians in this.

Of particular significance for my concerns, one fruit of what was later to be known as 'the English Revival', is a proposal to publish a series to be called something like 'English Writers' or 'English Men of Letters', designed to subvert and eventually replace the official curriculum of Racine, Corneille and Voltaire. Naturally, the discussions of this proposal become very heated: one group within the Early English Text Society insists that only authors who wrote in Old or Middle English are to be considered. Representatives of the League of St George, on the other hand, insist on the need to include authors who can stir the consciousness of the less scholarly classes: they regard the novels of Dickens as the equivalent of several regiments, and they engage one Frederick Elgar, whose son was to become an even more famous nationalist composer, to set some of Wordsworth's simpler lyrics to music. But eventually a compromise list is agreed, the basis for a literary education for properly patriotic Englishmen (and, suitably modified, for English women). The modern section begins, naturally, with Shakespeare; there was then much debate about Milton, finally rejected for republicanism, latinity and excessive use of *enjambement*. Dryden and Pope are excluded as literary quislings, practitioners of a French aesthetic, just as, among contemporary poets and critics, greatest hatred is reserved for Matthew Arnold, whose literary toadying has recently been rewarded with election to the Académie Française. Others who have written in the English language but who have expressed the consciousness of other peoples are of course excluded: no Hume, no Burns, no Scott, no Carlyle, and no Swift, no Sheridan, no Goldsmith, no Burke. The premises where the Gibbon volume was being printed were attacked one night and burned when it was discovered that he had written his first book in French. But finally the flames of nationalist sedition were spread through Wessex and Mercia and the other ancient kingdoms by a series of inflammatory little books on Bede, Langland, Shakespeare, Camden, Dr Johnson, Wordsworth and Dickens.

Now imagine a second, no less fictive but perhaps no less plausible, scenario. Here, the year is 1898, the centenary, in this imaginary world, of the (second) English Revolution, which had, like so many revolutions, begun with mutinies in the navy in 1798, and been aided by the circumstances of war with a foreign power and intense economic hardship. Several republican régimes had succeeded each other in the first seventy years of the century, but then the army, the Church and the landed classes had staged a successful counter-revolution and installed one of the least unacceptable descendants of George III on the throne. The arrival of the centenary of the Revolution, therefore, was bound to be a highly charged affair, marked by intense political and sectarian rivalry. Once again, questions of literature and the curriculum assume great political and nationalist significance. For the Right (a term, incidentally, used with as much familiarity by nineteenth-century Englishmen, in this account, as by any other European citizens), the pantheon of national heroes leans heavily towards soldiers, expansionist statesmen, Erastian churchmen, and court poets; the Left naturally favours republicans, anti-clericals, popular novelists, and professors of philosophy. Once again, there is a proposal to launch a series of volumes to be called 'the English Men of Letters', something that could provide the backbone of what the Right called (as it always does) the 'national curriculum', a proper source of patriotic pride. But here the two sides are unable to agree a common list, and the Left, traditionally stronger (according to this fantasy) in London and the provincial universities, finally issues its own series to counter the official selection commissioned by the Right, largely from Oxford and Cambridge (especially, perhaps, from All Souls).

The divisions are revealing. The Right proposes, above all, court poets, dramatists, and wits such as Chaucer, Spenser, Dryden, Walpole, and Southey; among prose writers, those they would see read in every school in the land include Cranmer, Hooker, Lancelot

Andrewes, Clarendon. Its list is a little weak on novelists, though it is prepared to include the series of novels that had been secretly commissioned by the aristocratic opposition in mid-century to idealize the traditional hierarchical relations of the English cathedral town, commissioned from a then little-known novelist called Trollope. The Left, whose series is called, inevitably, 'Writers of the English People', also has a strong list of poets, running, contentiously, from Marvell's Cromwellian odes to the work of Crabbe, Clare and Shelley (proposals for a volume confined to the young Wordsworth were eventually dropped). But the great strength of its series is in prose writers, including Bunyan, Defoe, Paine, Dickens and Hardy. Only one author is common to both series, namely Shakespeare, but whereas the volume commissioned by the Right, and written by a young writer called Kipling, concentrates on the patriotism of the history plays and the reconciling message of the great tragedies, the volume commissioned by the Left – started shortly before his death by the aged William Morris, and finally finished several years later by a very young unknown writer called Herbert Lawrence – stressed instead the popular energies of the comedies and the subversive nature of Shakespeare's questioning of the limits of language.

One could, of course, extend this story into the twentieth century, showing how the Right is finally brought down by its catastrophically incompetent conduct of the First World War, and how in 1919 the English Third Republic is established, which, as well as dispossessing the Church of England and breaking up large landed estates, bans the use of the 'reactionary' 'English Men of Letters' series in schools and universities. The whirligig of time, of course, brings in its revenges, and many decades later the greatest popularity among the young is enjoyed, despite or perhaps because of official disapproval, by a new series called 'Old Accents'.

I trust that by now the point of both these imaginary accounts will be evident. To put it negatively, one could simply say that during the period I am concerned with in this essay, the late nineteenth and early twentieth centuries, 'the English' (I shall come back to that familiar metonymy later) experienced neither the most common promptings to a self-conscious nationalism nor the kind of systematic and repetitive political and ideological division which makes all aspects of a society's life matter for partisan dispute. As a result, the dominant relation to the English past during this period, its intellectual and literary no less than its political and constitutional past, was conceived along the lines of what might be called the

'National Trust' model, a repository of treasures which all members of a united nation can enjoy as part of their uniquely glorious heritage. The muffling inclusiveness of this view is beautifully caught in the almost liturgical cadence of a passage in Eliot's *Four Quartets*:

> These men, and those who opposed them
> And those whom they opposed
> Accept the constitution of silence
> And are folded in a single party.

And here the eirenic gentleness of 'folded', culpably disguising the violence of the actual processes by which conflict is rendered liveable, begins to suggest some of the tendentious purposes which can be served by this invocation of the encompassing membership of the national community, 'folded in a single party'.

My own starting-point is that English cultural nationalism has in fact been a vast presence in British history of the last two centuries (I think that is the right relation between the two adjectival forms), even though it has largely not been recognized as such or systematically articulated. Indeed, to some ears there may still be a discordant oddity in speaking of 'English nationalism' at all. Certainly, the conventional view was for long that 'in England patriotism takes the place of nationalism'.[3] In part, this view rested on taking a rather restrictive view of nationalism itself: all the while it is defined as 'the reaction of peoples who feel culturally at a disadvantage',[4] the identification of its presence in modern English history will scarcely seem like an urgent task. But understood more largely as the dynamic or activating power of the assertion and confirmation of national identity, a power operating, often unobserved, across a wider range of activities than the narrowly political, English nationalism is, I would argue, a pervasive feature of the history of this period.

Beyond this, I want to suggest that, for reasons that would need further exploration, a crucial vehicle for establishing and negotiating the relevant sense of national identity has been provided by that symbolic and emotionally charged selection of writing known as 'English literature'. (This is perhaps the unstated premise underlying the common observation, usually given in the form of a complaint, that much of the elaboration of moral and political values which has been carried on in some other European countries in a more explicitly theoretical vein has been conducted in Britain in the twentieth century through the medium of discussion of the national literature.) As part of this wider cultural activity, what developed as the academic study of English literature was thus freighted from the start with an exceptional intellectual and even moral significance, a condition attested to in part by the violence of so many of its ostensibly critical debates. In particular, the question of sustaining, reworking or challenging the central 'canon' of English literature has become a crucial mode of legitimization in the cultural politics of the later twentieth century, as well, of course, as an inexhaustible source of rancour among those charged with the design and reform of syllabuses. To understand how this has come about we need to look beyond the confines of the academic discipline and to adopt a longer perspective than that provided by the familiar debates of recent decades. I wish to propose that a very important strand of this perspective would be provided by a sketch of the so far unwritten history of English cultural nationalism.[5] This essay is, therefore, a very preliminary and tentative exploration of one aspect of that history, and I hope it will serve as a kind of historical introduction to the later question of how literary criticism came to function as cultural criticism in twentieth-century Britain.

The rest of the essay, therefore, falls into two parts. The first offers a few highly general and largely unargued assertions about the relations in the late nineteenth century between dominant senses of English national identity and constructions of its intellectual and literary past. The second part then tries to isolate a few of the changes which led, by the 1920s and 1930s, to the literary-critical engagement with that past becoming one of the chief resources for conducting larger disputes in British culture, in the course of which the whole business of constructing genealogies of Englishness acquired an altogether more self-conscious and more contentious dimension.

II

Although it is obvious that Victorian England will hardly fit the classic pattern of nineteenth-century European nationalism, it is worth beginning by observing that it was not immune to all the forces and impulses that fuelled more explicitly nationalist movements elsewhere. Consider, by way of example, a feature insisted upon in Benedict Anderson's synoptic account of the rise of nationalism, when he observes that the activities of 'vernacularizing lexicographers, grammarians, philologists, and littérateurs . . . were central to the shaping of nineteenth-century European nationalisms'.[6] Many such activities were, of course, pursued in mid-nineteenth-century Britain also, but with not quite the same political resonances or sectarian functions as in my imaginary accounts. I mentioned, for instance, the nationalist significance of undertaking to compile a great vernacular dictionary on historical lines. Such a project was one of the major scholarly enterprises of the Victorian period, and it is clear from Elisabeth Murray's detailed account that the *New English Dictionary*, with its declared ambition to capture 'the genius of the English language', was not without its patriotic overtones.

Indeed, in some ways, its moving spirit, James Murray, had the identikit profile of a nineteenth-century liberal nationalist in its British mutation: he was a Nonconformist; he was an ardent Liberal; he was an admirer of Garibaldi; he enthusiastically greeted Kossuth with a banner written in Hungarian; and he called his sons names like Ethelbert and Aelfric.[7] In addition he was, one might say, the Stubbs of English philology, charting with appreciative patience the slow, impersonal growth of the rich intricacy of the national vernacular. But the comparison with Stubbs – the Whig historian of ancient English liberties who voted Tory and gave up his Oxford chair to become a bishop[8] – also signals some of the complexity of the English case. It is not merely flippant to begin to indicate that complexity by pointing out that this great monument to Englishness was compiled by a Scotsman (who was knighted for it) and dedicated to a monarch of recent German descent. For the example not only indicates how far this was from being an oppositional project, but also suggests one recurring difficulty for any putative English nationalism in modern times, namely the absence of an easily identifiable or separable ethnic basis for the actual British polity – it has hardly been a pure example of the nation-state, after all.[9]

But just because it has been difficult to hold on to any steady definition of the nature and limits of the political entity that is in question – while at the same time the core of that polity has experienced a relatively settled and continuous history in modern times, devoid of both revolutions and foreign invasions – less narrowly political images of national identity have assumed correspondingly greater importance. There is no need to labour the tensions and contradictions that have been involved in using the term 'the English' to refer to the citizens, or more properly the subjects, of a supposedly 'united kingdom' which was also for most of this period the nucleus of an empire. But it is also clear that there have in fact been certain core notions of 'Englishness' which have provided the dominant images and assumptions not only in relation to other parts of the British Isles but also within England itself, idealizing a rather vaguely located rural south – what Patrick Wright has aptly termed 'Deep England'.[10] There has clearly been work for notions of cultural nationalism to do here.

Perhaps I can most economically indicate the chief lines of the development of ideas about English identity up to the end of the nineteenth century by giving ruthless two-sentence summaries of a couple of the most significant recent studies of this theme. Gerald Newman, in *The Rise of English Nationalism*, argues that self-conscious English nationalism is first fully elaborated in the late eighteenth century as part of a largely middle-class, to some extent radical, and eventually Evangelical protest against the Francophile culture of a cosmopolitan aristocracy; and that the celebration, by Johnson, Warton and others, of a distinctive English literary tradition, to set against the previously dominant models of French classicism, was an important part of this process. Newman's highly contentious conclusion is that what we know as 'Victorianism' is really the successful take-over of the wider culture by this initially oppositional 'nationalist' movement, as a result of which the English come to congratulate themselves on their unique blend of liberty, sincerity and moral earnestness.[11] Those who know John Burrow's highly nuanced account of the elaboration of the Whig interpretation of English history in the Victorian period will acknowledge that it is not easily susceptible to such schematic summary, but a recurring motif is the Victorian celebration of the way in which England's native genius for liberty and representative government had brought it a far more fortunate history than had been the lot of less happy peoples (again, the contrast with France is revealed as a crucial part of national self-definition). Burrow's story, too, is one of a growing consensus, showing how by the end of the century what had begun life as a partisan account of, in particular, the constitutional and religious struggles of the seventeenth century, finally becomes accepted as the basis for what Butterfield later called the 'national' interpretation of English history.[12]

One could supplement both these accounts with further evidence of what may be called the 'nationalization' of English culture in the second half of the nineteenth century, that is, the softening of many of the political and religious divisions that had marked the first half of the century, and the elaboration of a self-congratulatory portrait of the 'national character', a category of analysis with acknowledged claims to scientific status during this period.[13] This development was, presumably, further encouraged by the sense of foreign competition and imperial rivalry which is such a marked feature of the pronouncements of the educated classes in the three decades before 1914.

I want to suggest that the noticeably greater attention devoted to arranging and celebrating English literary history in the last few decades of the century, including moves to establish it as an academic subject, may be seen as part of this wider process of national self-definition. Indeed, the consolidation of a 'national' interpretation of England's political history in this period can, it seems to me, be roughly paralleled in the celebratory accounts of English literary distinctiveness, to the point where we might usefully refer to 'the Whig interpretation of English literature'. A certain native genius for individuality and sincerity would make its appearance here, too, and the contrast with France would yet again be a constitutive part of the self-definition, the role of the French penchant for the political dialectic of despotism and revolution being matched by the linked characteristics of formal artificiality and moral doubtfulness in French literature – indeed, all the qualities that can be ambiguously referred to as 'French polish'.

Attempts to define the national literary character notoriously run the risk of circularity: only those authors who display the putative characteristics are recognized as authentically English, a category whose definition relies upon the examples provided in the literature written by just those authors.[14] What is perhaps less obvious is the way in which the promotion of a certain conception of the distinctiveness of English literature reinforced the cherished notion of the supposed English incapacity for systematic abstract thought. Pride in the national literature's special talent for expressing a rich diversity of life and feeling, symbolized not only by the essentially Romantic elevation of Shakespeare over Racine but also by the more recent acclaim for English achievements in the novel, easily shaded into self-congratulation that such fidelity to the complexity and concreteness of life should resist reduction to the abstract categories of a system. This in turn provided an important buttress for those soaring claims about how English individualism and its admirable respect for eccentricity provided particularly favourable soil for the propagation of political liberty.[15]

This elaboration of the national literary character obviously involved some selectivity. Johnson and Wordsworth proved to be better exemplars than Dryden and Pope. Moreover, the characterization of the informing spirit of the national literature was subject to constant adjustment depending upon the particular scale of moral values to which it had to be accommodated. The following passage from Henry Morley's very popular *A First Sketch of English Literature*, published in 1873, provides a representative example:

> The literature of this country has for its most distinctive mark the religious sense of duty. It represents a people striving through successive generations to find out the right and do it, to root out the wrong and labour ever onward for the love of God. If this be really the strong spirit of her people, to show that it is so is to tell how England won, and how alone she can expect to keep, her foremost place among the nations.[16]

Morley's primer was also representative in being aimed at the rapidly expanding educational market, which needed accredited guides for its first ventures into literary history. Similarly, this market was hungry for approved selections of vernacular texts, and the growing trade in anthologies of English poetry in the second half of the nineteenth century gave influential expression to 'the Whig interpretation of English literature'.

Perhaps the most notable example, certainly the most influential, was Palgrave's *Golden Treasury*, the first edition of which appeared in 1861. Palgrave's explicit purpose was to produce 'a true national anthology', though by the standards of the modern, post-Eliot, canon the selection is highly idiosyncratic: Donne is absent and Herbert gets only twenty lines, whereas Walter Scott gets three hundred and forty-five and the comparatively minor Romantic Thomas Campbell gets no fewer than four hundred.[17] There were, inevitably, disputes on aesthetic and moral grounds between various schools of contemporary writers, but the dominant relation to England's much-celebrated succession of poets and novelists, at least as evinced by the most widely used accounts, seems to have been to accept that they could be 'folded into a single party'.

This was perhaps most evident in the actual 'English Men of Letters' series, launched by Macmillan's under the general editorship of John Morley in 1877. Needless to say – at least, to anyone who has ever been involved in such publishers' series – contingency played some part in determining the eventual range of both subjects and contributors: we know that the publishers tried hard but unsuccessfully to get George Eliot to do Shakespeare, for instance, and there were no doubt other big fish that got away.[18] Nonetheless, the series bore all the marks of a consciously designed national monument: the list is inclusive, unsectarian and predictable. No restrictive view of the achievement of English letters is being pushed, though of course some covert criteria were operative, such as an understandable mid-Victorian prejudice in favour of the Romantic poets and their chief eighteenth-century predecessors. In the thirty-nine volumes published in the first series, eighteen were devoted to poets, seven to novelists and fourteen to other prose writers. If one classifies by century, a certain bias towards the more modern figures emerges, in part, no doubt, for simple commercial reasons: there is one fourteenth-century author, two from the sixteenth century, five from the seventeenth, sixteen from the eighteenth, and fifteen from the only three-quarters-completed nineteenth century. In the twenty-six volumes of the second series, published in the first few years of the twentieth century, there were ten poets (or poet-playwrights, like Shakespeare), six novelists, and ten other prose writers, and now fifteen of them came from the nineteenth century, many of the great Victorians having died in time to be placed in this national mausoleum. Unselfconscious inclusiveness of another kind is suggested by the fact that of the original thirty-nine 'English Men of Letters' five were Scottish, four were Irish, and one American, while of the second series of twenty-six 'men of letters' four were women.

While I cannot claim intimate acquaintance with all sixty-five volumes in these two series, it is safe to say that the common format was very largely biographical: there was relatively little of what a more recent generation might expect by way of literary criticism, though a certain amount of what might more properly be called 'appreciation' makes a frequent appearance.[19] The tone in which these lives were for the most part recorded also suggests that the series embodied an assumption that was common to much mid- and late-nineteenth-century biography, namely a conviction that familiarity with the lives of outstanding individuals tended to have an inspirational effect, above all a morally elevating effect, as an incitement to the development of 'character'.[20] The individual volumes were not, in fact, all written by Leslie Stephen, but he was naturally one of the most frequent, and characteristic, contributors, and the series spawned many imitators in the next couple of decades, similarly constructing genealogies of English achievement, including Longman's *English Worthies*, Scott's *Great Writers*, and on into the 1900s with Hodder's *Literary Lives* and others.[21] At the same time, a very important part of giving such a canon an effective existence lay in the greater number of cheaply republished editions of English classic authors for which the expansion in education in the last decades of the century created strong demand. The place of such enterprises in the larger national self-consciousness I am describing may be gauged from the way the most popular of these series of cheap editions, Cassell's *National Library*, under the editorship of Henry Morley, was prompted, as his biographer recorded, by 'an article in the Daily News in the summer of 1885 calling attention to the fact that we have nothing in England corresponding to the famous threepenny series in Germany'.[22]

III

I have been suggesting that in the late nineteenth century, the dominant manner of arranging or invoking the canon of English literature served purposes which were primarily celebratory and patriotic. Insofar as this body of literature was called upon to support criticism of features of contemporary Britain, it was chiefly on the familiar Romantic grounds of providing a repository of aesthetic and moral values felt to be neglected or threatened by the operative forces of a commercial or industrial society. Although in practice the values appealed to may have been rather parochial, they were ostensibly invoked in the form of universals, such as altruism as a corrective to egoism, and so on. For these purposes, it should be noted, the appeal does not necessarily have to be to the national literature, nor was any such restriction implied in most of those classic nineteenth-century invocations of the value of 'letters', 'culture', or 'art'.[23] Similarly, many of the early proposals for teaching literature as an academic subject appealed to these larger moral justifications, and accordingly not all of them envisaged confining the syllabus to English literature. In this respect, it can be particularly misleading to lump Matthew Arnold with later proponents of the discipline of 'English', as historians of the subject commonly tend to do.

Not only did he frequently place English literature on a lower pedestal than French and regard both as inferior to the Classics, but he actually objected, when consulted near the end of his life, to the establishment of English literature as an entirely independent subject within the university.[24] Moreover, he had also shown himself to be a little sceptical about attempts to infuse the treatment of literature with explicit patriotism: his one reproach to Stopford Brooke's otherwise excellent primer of English literature had been that it was all a bit 'too much to the tune of Rule Britannia'.[25]

However, despite the reservations of Arnold and others, the realities of vernacular education and the pressures of late-nineteenth-century chauvinism did increasingly encourage concentration on what was familiarly referred to as 'our national literature'. Even so, there was one further element which limited the contemporary purchase of such literary history as a source of social criticism in the late nineteenth century, an element which also to some extent qualified its nationalist character, namely, the dominance of the study of literature not just by the historical method in general, but above all by Germanic philology. One effect of the scholarly Teutonism of the mid-Victorian decades was to link the narrative of English literary history, at least in its earlier stages, more closely to the actual Whig interpretation of English political history as that was in turn modified and extended by researches into Anglo-Saxon and ultimately Teutonic origins.[26] But although Old English literature, as it was usually called (not without polemical intent), could and did provide material for speculations about an enduring national character, it could only with some awkwardness be deployed in support of direct criticism of contemporary political and cultural preoccupations. William Morris might be cited as one who did attempt to harness philological enthusiasm directly to radical social criticism, though the awkwardness was evident and Morris anyway remained far outside the circles of respectable academic philology.

Moreover, the prestige of philology tended to limit the potentially parochial tendencies of the study of the national literature in another way. Philology, especially when pursued in the comparative manner fashionable in the mid-nineteenth century, was inherently international: its practitioners were members of trans-national scholarly associations, devotees of a cosmopolitan science, and there was nothing improbable in becoming an expert on the philology of a language other than one's native tongue. (Many of the teachers of philology in late-nineteenth-century British universities, for example, were German.) It is surely far easier, even perhaps normal, for literary criticism to confine itself to the responses and cultural preoccupations of native speakers of the relevant language. Criticism in this sense does not travel well, certainly does not translate well, generating the problem of what might be called 'criticism in one country'.

The institutional establishment of that mixture of historical, biographical and philological inquiries that made up the study of literature in the late nineteenth century did not, therefore, necessarily provide fertile ground for the nurturing of contemporary cultural criticism or the elaboration of rival accounts of the national identity. Nor, more obviously, did the fingertips-together style of aesthetic appreciation of the non-academic Edwardian bookmen. But the part played by the First World War in my argument has necessarily to be more ambiguous. The war encouraged, even demanded, the expression of an aggressive nationalism (again overwhelmingly English rather than British or imperial), and the men of letters and literary professoriat were not slow to make their contribution here.[27] The mobilizing of the canon of English literature to serve the nation's cause in the First World War is a subject for study in its own right. Two remarks about it are particularly relevant to my argument. First, far from revealing previously neglected divisions in the legacy of the nation's literary past, the war encouraged the propagation of the idea of a deeply unified literary tradition, predominantly pastoral in its register.[28] Indeed, Paul Fussell's book suggests not only that the experience of the war was, to a very striking extent and for a surprisingly wide social range, mediated through a shared range of literary allusion, but that as a result the war served to strengthen the position of literature as a privileged location or bearer of national consciousness.[29]

Secondly, one casualty of the vehement anti-Germanism stirred up by the war was the tradition of Germanic philology and the emphasis on the common Teutonic roots of English and German literature (an emphasis which had already become rather dated by 1914). Part of the consequence of this was to shift attention away from philology and the earlier period of literature generally, a process reinforced by other pressures towards a more 'relevant' or 'accessible' education after the war. Again there is a much longer story to be told here, which would encompass the foundation of a distinctively modern English course at Cambridge in 1917, and would concentrate particularly on the cultural nationalism of the so-called 'Newbolt Report' on the teaching of English, which appeared in 1921. The spirit of the report is most economically represented by the proposal of one of its members, John Bailey (a past Chairman of the English Association and future leading light of the National Trust), for a kind of 'English Greats' course which would provide, he hoped, 'a School of national culture'.[30]

The Newbolt Report was symptomatic of, and itself greatly contributed to, a sense that English literature was a national resource that could and should be deliberately employed for present cultural purposes (the chief of which, for the Newbolt Committee, was the encouragement of national unity and social harmony between classes). At the same time, 'English', which had barely been recognized as a proper subject for instruction in 1850, now occupied a central place at all levels of education. But to understand how polemical interpretations of this literary legacy came to be an important form of cultural criticism in modern Britain, there are two further developments that need to be mentioned, though again each is a large and complex issue.

The first is that constellation of changes which prompted in many members of the educated class a profound cultural pessimism. Alarm at the power of the so-called 'yellow press' at the beginning of the century was extended by anxiety about the techniques employed in advertising, the potential power of new media like film and radio, and a wider unease at the cultural consequences of greater social equality. The importing into the language at this time of the terms 'highbrow' and 'lowbrow' indicate this perception not just of a gulf between the classes – that there had in some form always been – but of a sense (however well- or ill-grounded we might now take it to have been) that culturally the educated class was on the defensive. One common response to this sense was a conviction that a cultural heritage which was under threat or disappearing had to be rescued and made vital and effective in the present.[31]

The other crucial, and in fact related, development was the advent of literary Modernism. Insofar as the canon of texts and the underlying conception of the English literary character which was elaborated and refined in the nineteenth century had had its roots in Romanticism, it is hardly surprising that the great anti-Romantic shift of sensibility labelled 'Modernism' should involve some challenge to the received arrangement of the 'national literature', a challenge most notably exemplified as well as theorized by T.S. Eliot. In principle, the aggressive internationalism, or even anti-nationalism, of Modernism expressed a repudiation of the parochialism of pre-war English literary chauvinism, but the eventual form taken by the associated 'critical revolution' could be said both to have enhanced the role of literary critics as professional explicators of increasingly opaque texts, and at the same time to have contributed a more contentious note to English cultural politics than had been found in the earlier historical forms of literary study. An interesting aphorism by Gustave Lanson, the doyen of academic literary study in Third Republic France, may be pertinent here, especially since Lanson's own scholarly efforts before 1914 had been so explicitly devoted to deploying the French literary past for nationalist and republican purposes: 'Literary criticism divides; literary history unites.'[32]

An essay of this sort obviously cannot have a 'conclusion' in any conventional sense, but I want to end with an expansive gesture towards some of the many possible ways of continuing. The issues I have touched on here seem to me to provide one relevant framework in which to consider the cultural criticism of many of the figures who have been important in twentieth-century British intellectual history. The most predictable name to suggest at this point would, I suppose, be that of F. R. Leavis, though I think our sense of even his place in that history would benefit from a fuller understanding of just what views of English history and literature he took himself to be challenging, since his early work is these days rather too simply regarded as a familiar form of cultural conservatism, without its original oppositional and dissident, almost Dissenting, character being properly recognized. But a little less obviously, one might consider Eliot's revision of the canon, undertaken in the light not only of his own poetic practice but also of a conception of England's place in Christian Europe, and thus a means of criticizing a society he described as 'worm-eaten with liberalism'.[33] Or, less obviously still, we would find another literary definition of lineage at work in Orwell's attacks on what he derisively called 'the Europeanized Left intelligentsia' of Britain in the 1930s and 1940s, attacks conducted partly through essays on some of those earlier English writers with whom Orwell identified and who made up what Bernard Crick has nicely described as 'God's great awkward squad of unorthodox, dissident Englishmen'.[34] Or, bordering on the implausible, one might place Raymond Williams, too, in this framework as a reminder of the continuing centrality of attempts to appropriate and reappropriate an enabling tradition of English literature even for someone hardly committed to promoting 'essential Englishness'. In each of these cases, it will be evident, the reordering of English literary history had an insurgent and oppositional character precisely because these critics believed that the dominant tendencies of contemporary culture represented a betrayal of an earlier England.[35]

Ranging more widely still, one might also consider the ways in which the fond dwelling on England's 'incomparable' (and unrepeatable) literary heritage can be seen as a modulation of that pervasive nostalgia many observers have detected in English culture since 1918.[36] The tendency to cope with loss by resorting to elegy is surely deeply intertwined with the immense cultural presence of that particular body of writing, and writing about writing, that is known as 'English literature', with its varied and recurrent forms of pastoral, a genre predicated upon nostalgia. 'Nostalgia', the *OED* tells us, is 'a form of melancholia caused by prolonged absence from one's home or country.' That 'England of the mind' which, in several of its twentieth-century forms, draws so heavily on images from 'the national literature' is so constructed, it seems to me, that one can only be 'absent' from it. What nostalgia longs for, in English nationalist pastoral, is a time when one's relation to 'England' was not a matter of nostalgia. While reminding ourselves of that *OED* definition we ought perhaps also to remember that the same entry tells us the word originated as a term of what was called 'mental pathology'.

Finally, it is a truism to observe that the more troubled sense of English national identity evident in the late twentieth century encourages the search for other 'usable pasts' as alternatives to what is often hypostatized as the 'official' account. But in part this involves only a fresh adaptation of what is now an established tradition of cultural criticism, one that seeks its own legitimating ancestors and tries to constitute its own canon. Our heightened sense of inheriting a divided and contentious history may prompt us to look with new respect upon Eliot's teasing remark, made in 1947: 'The Civil War is not ended: I question whether a civil war ever does end.'[37] But if the spirit of that remark contrasts with some of the more blithely consensual assumptions I was ascribing to the late nineteenth century, the fact that it was made in the course of a reassessment of Milton suggests one important kind of continuity, and reassessments of major authors have continued to provide some of the most highly publicized occasions for addressing questions of national cultural identity.

In more mournful (perhaps even elegiac) vein, it may seem that the chief manifestation of the increased sensitivity to questions of English cultural nationalism in Britain today is, alas, a rash of papers by academic historians and literary critics uncovering some of the ways in which our less self-conscious ancestors derived their identities from their less complicated relation to their chosen past. Still, there may be some unacknowledged continuities here, too, since the seductions of nostalgia are not altogether absent even in such reflections on a lineage twice removed. In other words, the scholarly study of 'Englishness' can, in some cases, be yet another way of perpetuating that fond absorption in the alleged distinctiveness of the English past which it ostensibly desires to criticize. But this sceptical observation does not entail the conclusion that we should regard the forms of self-definition discussed in this essay simply as part of a world we have lost. If it does nothing else, the fact that 'our' recent Secretary of State for Education chooses to promote his triumphalist version of 'England's' (predominantly military) history by publishing an anthology of English poetry, should at least suggest that the impulse, and perhaps the need, to conduct some of our cultural criticism through the medium of literary criticism is likely to be with us for a while yet.

EIGHT

'REPULSIVES VS WROMANTICS': RIVAL VIEWS OF THE ENGLISH CIVIL WAR

Ian Green

When Sellar and Yeatman first published their spoof history of England in 1930, it was still possible to bridge the gap between rival views of the English Civil War by claiming that the Royalists were 'wrong but wromantic', whereas the Roundheads, though 'right', were clearly 'repulsive'.[1] A mixture of support for limited monarchy and dislike of Puritan spoil-sports was enough to satisfy the nostalgic love-affair with the past which historians like J. R. Green and G. M. Trevelyan had nurtured among their readers. Half a century later, such a balanced view is hard to find. Since the 1930s, the debate on the origins of the English Civil War has become not only much more wide-ranging but also increasingly bitter. In the last twenty years alone at least two major reinterpretations have been offered, both of which have been met by heated criticism and a vigorous, not to say violent, restatement of older views. Indeed, in recent years the quakes have become so frequent and severe that undergraduates studying the subject might justifiably feel that they are being asked to camp on top of the San Andreas fault with no guarantee that they will survive to see the end of their course.

Nowadays one might well find a 'revisionist', like Jonathan Clark, denouncing as 'romantic' – in the pejorative sense of the word – the neo-Whig belief that the early seventeenth century was a crucial period in the assertion of liberty, while some senior historians, like Jack Hexter and Lawrence Stone, would probably condemn as 'repulsive' and even dangerous the 'revisionist' view that constitutional principles were less important than political ineptitude and mutual misunderstanding in bringing about civil war.[2] What has led some British and American historians to hone their quills to razor-sharpness in this way? Is it more than accidental that the first phase of hostilities, from the 1930s to the early 1950s, coincided with differing reactions to the rise of fascism and communism and the start of the cold war, whereas the second coincided with the disenchantments of the late 1960s and early '70s and the divisive policies of Ronald Reagan and Margaret Thatcher? I suspect that the answer in the case of the first phase is that there was a clear political dimension to the historiography, though not necessarily quite what one might have expected; but that in the case of the second, when the temperature of the debate reached new peaks, this dimension is not so easily demonstrated, and we may have to settle for alternative or supplementary explanations.[3] To set both phases in context, however, it may help to offer a few comments on the interpretation that prevailed until the 1930s.

The first point to note is that the Civil War does not seem to have left an indelible impression on the minds of the majority of English men and women, compared to, say, the impression of the civil wars in America and Ireland, or the revolutions in France and Russia, on the inhabitants of those countries. How divided English society was during the 1640s and '50s is still an open question,[4] but when it comes to the period after 1660, even allowing for the dearth of sources and to some extent of research, there does seem to be relatively little sign of popular interest for the next two or three centuries. To some extent a memory was preserved through the annual festivals of the Church of England commemorating the execution of Charles I and the return of Charles II in 1660, which were held well into the nineteenth century; but this was perhaps a matter of an officially inspired ceremony being welcomed by the populace as a holiday.[5] There is also some evidence of folk memories of striking incidents, such as Charles II's dramatic escape after the battle of Worcester, or of a key figure like Oliver Cromwell, whose name was perhaps used more often as that of an ogre to frighten naughty children than as a popular hero to rally the downtrodden.[6] But these motifs were only part of a larger score – popular memory also contained echoes of the Norman Conquest and Magna Carta – and in our own century memories of the Civil War seem to have largely disappeared, unless one counts the names of pubs ('The Royal Oak') or of rock groups ('The New Model Army'), or the antics of groups like the 'Sealed Knot', which each summer refights the battles of the Civil War.[7] In the opening years of this century, R.H. Tawney may have found his students in the Workers' Educational Association curious about the development of capitalism in the early modern period, and in the years after 1945 members of the Communist Party Historians' Group may have been anxious to give the workers an account of 'the Good Old Cause' of popular radicalism; but it seems that they could not count on much specific knowledge or insight being there already.[8]

By contrast, the interest of at least part of the educated sections of society was evident as early as 1647 with the controversy caused by the publication of Tom May's vindication of the parliamentary cause. It can be further traced through the sales of the rival accounts of Tories like Echard and Whigs like Oldmixon in the early eighteenth century, down to the allegedly Tory history of David Hume and the triumphantly liberal accounts of Macaulay and Trevelyan.[9] There were some very talented or technically proficient historians among those who wrote in detail about the early Stuart period, notably Clarendon, Hume and Hallam, but much of this literature was, of course, produced for different reasons or in different ways from the work of the last half-century.

In the first place, it was in many cases designed to teach moral lessons or political wisdom or to score party points; and since the object of the exercise was to confirm the truth of existing opinion, there was relatively little attempt to find new sources or develop new lines of approach.[10] Secondly, differences of opinion were confined within relatively narrow limits, since Whigs and Tories, for all their sparring, had a good deal in common, and were not averse to stealing each other's clothes from time to time.[11] Thirdly, in so far as there was an interest in the seventeenth century as opposed to other periods, it was probably in the events of 1688-9 rather than those of 1640-60. Churchmen and Tory politicians might use the events of the 1640s to press home the sinfulness of pride and the dangers of rebellion against ordained authority, but the Whigs, who were dominant for much of the period, were more concerned to remind voters of the part the Whigs had played in securing and defending the allegedly Glorious Revolution of 1688. No fewer than four leading Whig politicians of the early nineteenth century wrote books on the late seventeenth century,[12] and the best of them, Thomas Babington Macaulay, epitomized the attitude current in early Victorian times when he wrote that it was because England had had her revolution in 1688 that she did not have to suffer the revolutions that had afflicted France in 1789 or much of Europe in 1848.

Macaulay, the politician, when speaking in public could come out with such comments as: 'To the Whigs of the seventeenth century we owe it that we have a House of Commons. To the Whigs of the nineteenth century we owe it that the House of Commons has been purified.'[13] But Macaulay, the writer, had the ability to metamorphose a party view of the past – a pragmatic, Burkean, gradualist view of politics – into the English view of that period.[14] In many ways, his great-nephew, G. M. Trevelyan, that last flowering of Victorian country-house liberalism, merely consolidated this development by stressing the need for interplay between Whigs and Tories in achieving constitutional progress, and thus integrated the Tories into an essentially Whig view of the rise of parliament and the growth of liberty.[15]

Finally, accounts of the mid-seventeenth century also tended to be very selective: very few historians were prepared to defend the Levellers or the Quakers, or to vindicate the execution of the king, the abolition of the House of Lords, and the declaration of a republic. Even accounts favoured by Whig readers tended to squint at the events of the 1640s: hence the shock in the late 1760s when Catherine Macaulay in the course of her Whiggish, eight-volume history of Stuart England openly defended the execution of the power-crazy Charles I as 'an eminent act of justice'; to argue otherwise, she said, would 'betray the cause to Liberty, and confound both truth and reason'.[16] What most readers, either Whig or Tory, appear to have wanted was a carefully tailored view of the past which they and their political leaders could use to vindicate the maintenance of their perception of the constitutional and religious *status quo* and to justify their policies or – more commonly – lack of policies. What we have here in a sense is not just 'history as political ideology' but 'politics as history', that is, the practice of politics being in part based on a specific historical view of the past, though it was also, of course, based on other, more pragmatic considerations such as survival in office.

By the mid-1930s such views were still held, but by a dwindling number of people. They were trotted out on public occasions, as in 1935 when Trevelyan was asked to write the speech delivered by George V at the opening of Parliament. It read in part:

> It is to me a source of pride and thankfulness that the perfect harmony of our parliamentary system with our constitutional monarchy has survived

the shocks that have in recent years destroyed other empires and other liberties . . . The complex forms and balanced spirit of our Constitution were not the discovery of a single era, still less of a single party or of a single person. They are the slow accretion of centuries, the outcome of patience, tradition and experience constantly finding channels . . . for the impulse toward liberty, justice and social improvement inherent in our people down the ages.[17]

Such sentiments continued to enjoy a middle-brow market in England well into the 1960s and later, as can be seen by the large sales of Trevelyan's *Social History* and *Short History of England* and of works by authors such as Winston Churchill, Sir Arthur Bryant and C. V. Wedgwood. But in many circles, even as George V spoke, they were being denounced as inaccurate and anachronistic.

For those acquainted with the developments in the writing of history that emanated from nineteenth-century Germany, there is no need to dwell on the changes in attitude and technique and in personnel that had taken place in the historical profession in Europe and America between the mid-nineteenth century and the 1930s. In the case of early Stuart England its fruits can be seen in the multi-volume history of England from 1603 to 1656 which, following Rankean principles, it took Samuel Rawson Gardiner over forty years to produce, the last volumes appearing after his death in 1902.[18] Gardiner set out to write this history partly as a reaction against what he saw as the exaggerations of the old Whig version, though he himself displayed some weaknesses, especially on matters of definition or when he raised his eyes to the far horizon, and gave way to the temptation to write about the spirit of the English constitution 'marching steadily forwards' over the centuries 'under the influence of a great principle', namely 'the rule of law'.[19] But in many ways his work remains a bastion of the more sophisticated neo-Whig historiography of the twentieth century, from Notestein to Hexter. Working in the shadow of Gardiner, Trevelyan had his reasons for persisting with an older approach which stressed style and empathy and the uplifting lessons to be learnt from history.[20] But it cannot have been altogether a surprise when in 1931 Herbert Butterfield launched his famous attack on the Whig interpretation of history for its selectivity, its moralizing, its preoccupation with progress and its tendency to be on the side of Protestants and parliaments. Though Butterfield later said that his barbs were aimed at Lord Acton, not Trevelyan, many were sure that it was his own Regius Professor that he was attacking.[21]

In political circles, too, the idea of working in 'the present under the spell of the past' was probably much less widespread in practice in 1935 than it had been a hundred or even fifty years before. By the turn of the nineteenth century both liberals and conservatives had come to terms with the need for the state to intervene more often than before, while the new Labour Party was from the outset committed to state action on behalf of the workers, albeit in practice rather less drastic action than their opponents had feared.[22] Moreover, given the threats posed in the 1930s by economic slump and the rise of fascism and communism at home and abroad, it would have been surprising if politicians as hard-headed and hard-pressed as Baldwin and MacDonald were convinced by Trevelyan's reassuring references to the many examples of the 'good sense of the English people' in the past or by his talk of 'kindly old England' having never tolerated '"fascist" experiments' at suppressing the opposition.[23] And many of those to the left of MacDonald had certainly no faith in the self-satisfied jingoism or belief in divine providence that had coloured the political outlook of much of the historical writing of previous generations. It was in this context of rapid change both in historical technique and in political and religious perceptions that the first major assault on the established interpretation of the English Civil War was produced; and, given the strength of radicalism among young intellectuals in the 1930s, this assault predictably came from the left.

It was embodied in a theory that had obvious links with the views of Marx and Engels, which had hitherto received little attention from academic historians in Britain, and it also, at the outset, had many parallels with the social interpretation of the French Revolution already advanced by scholars like Jaurès, Lefebvre and Soboul.[24] Indeed, events in England in the 1640s and '50s were soon being referred to again as the 'English Revolution' in a conscious bid to downgrade the events of 1688-9 to the status of a mere *coup d'état*.[25] The evolution of a social interpretation of the English Civil War represented a major break with previous historiography, and proved to be the pace-setter for the next thirty years. Thus it is worth taking a look at the political opinions and historical conclusions of three of its most influential expositors: R.H. Tawney, Christopher Hill and Lawrence Stone.

Tawney was unusual in that he combined a fervent belief in socialism with an equally strong adherence to High Church Anglicanism: it was a combination of concern at the dreadful poverty he witnessed in the slums and a strong sense of the need for remedial action that made him a Christian Socialist. He was also one of that second generation of scholars who did so much to set up the study of economic history as an independent discipline in England in the first half of this century.[26] His earlier work was on agrarian problems in the sixteenth century, in which he identified the aggressive tactics of exploitative landlords, and on the relationship between religious ethics and the attitudes of capitalism, which reflected his hope that Christian influence on economic and social behaviour might again be felt in a broader arena.[27] By the 1930s, however, perhaps pushed by the challenges of the post-war decades, he had moved to an examination of how far changes in the economy and social formation could affect political stability. Through his reading of the political theorist Harrington and his own work on manorial holdings, he came to advance the thesis that the revolution of the mid-seventeenth century was due not to clashes over political and religious principle between Charles I and Parliament, but to 'impersonal forces too strong for both', in particular the rise of a class of bourgeois landlords – the rising gentry – and the corresponding decline of the old aristocracy. Tawney thus inserted a Marxist component into the debate, though he himself was concerned about the possible elements of determinism in Marx (and of irreversibility in Weber).[28]

It would be a mistake to think that Tawney was trying to force the past into a shape to suit his present political purpose. He sometimes drew analogies between the Tudor-Stuart period and his own century – smallholders, he said, were 'trade unionists' to a man – and he clearly thought that political man should be informed about the past, about the origins and ideological props of capitalism or the relationship between property and power. But he was too much a Christian to ignore the ethical side of politics, and too good a scholar to ignore the unpredictable cause or the unwitting effect in history. He also seems to have been a modest man, who did not expect his work to stand for ever: 'All flesh is grass,' he once sighed, 'and historians, poor things, wither more quickly than most.' Yet he probably did not expect to be berated quite as forcefully as he would be later by Trevor-Roper.[29]

Politically, Tawney was a marginal figure. He wrote some classic tracts for the Labour Party, but neither these nor his historical writing had much influence on the heart of a labour movement which, despite the efforts of a number of left-wing intellectuals, including G. D. H. Cole and Harold Laski as well as Tawney, remained cautious about advancing truly socialist solutions, and, given his own hopes, it is ironic that Tawney's greatest impact was not on the working man or on labour politicians but on an academic world which he viewed with very mixed feelings.[30]

Tawney had opened the door wide enough to permit a sharp wind of change to blow across the English Civil War and full advantage of this was taken by two very different scholars, Christopher Hill and Lawrence Stone, who both acknowledged Tawney as their inspiration. Hill's story is that of a lifelong dialogue with Marxism during which, it may be suggested, his political views have been affected almost as much by his historical studies as the other way round. Born in 1912, Hill was one of that group of young men who were appalled by what they saw happening at home and abroad, and joined the Communist Party. He wrote his first account of the 1640s in 1940 in a mood of great anger and despair at the onset of another world war. Dissatisfied with what he saw as the compromises made by Attlee's government, he later became a leading light in the Communist Party Historians' Group until it split up in the wake of the Soviet suppression of the Hungarian rising.[31]

From the 1940s to the mid-1960s, much of Hill's work was designed to demonstrate that there had been, as Marx and Engels had said, a bourgeois revolution in mid-seventeenth-century England. The rapid growth of trade and industry and the commercialization of agriculture in the century after the Reformation had led, he argued, to a confrontation between on the one hand a rising middle class, which for Hill embraced not only Tawney's progressive gentry but also clergy and lawyers, yeomen and merchants and some skilled artisans and husbandmen, and on the other hand a feudal court and aristocracy pursuing reactionary economic and social policies. Even the geography of the Civil War reflected this tension, as the economically advanced south-east triumphed over the backward north and west. Though some of the trappings of the old order were restored in 1660, the English economy and society would never be the same again.[32]

Hill faced a good deal of criticism from both right wing and centre in the 1950s and '60s, and by the 1970s and '80s more detailed work on a number of aspects had exposed the weakness of many of the bolder assertions that he had made as a result of flying high above the landscape to gain a bird's-eye view. He has made concessions: claiming that he never meant to suggest that the revolution was bourgeois in intention, only in effect; and he would now perhaps put less stress on the role of the gentry among his revolutionary 'middling sort'. But if pressed, he still says that he finds the adoption of a Marxist model the most helpful way of making sense of the events of the mid-seventeenth century, and this, together with the sense of social injustice he infuses into his writing, has left him open to the simplistic charge of teleology by the hard-headed pragmatists of the right.[33]

In focusing on the 'bourgeois revolution' thesis, however, Hill's critics do him an injustice in that the focus of his work has become increasingly wide over the years; such critics also run the risk of missing the subtlety of his thought and how far he has moved – under his own steam mainly – from his original position. Like other members of the Communist Party Historians' Group, he has always argued that a crude economic determinism was a mindless vulgarization of Marxism, and that the writing of history should be not simply scientific, but also poetic and aware of moral dimensions.[34] As a result he has written extensively on the changes in theology and scientific ideas in the seventeenth century, and on many of the great literary figures of the age, such as Milton and Bunyan. Moreover, he has moved from an early position where such ideas tended to be treated as superstructure to a position in which the complex symbiosis between economic realities, social aspirations, religious belief, intellectual trends and political action is treated much more sensitively. His Marxism has been described recently as 'of the "radical Arminian" rather than the "high Calvinist" kind'.[35] I must confess to having reservations about the way in which he has constructed a number of his case-studies: my reading of Bunyan, for example, suggests a zealous evangelical rather than a social radical. But many literary critics have found his readings pertinent and helpful, and of the stimulus provided by much of Hill's work in these areas there can be no doubt: he has opened the camera shutter even wider than Tawney did.[36]

There is one further change in Hill's work that is relevant. Like other members of the C.P. Group, Hill had also been keen to show that there was a tradition of popular radicalism in England, but after he left the Party, possibly under the influence of Gramscian ideas, he increasingly turned his attention to the history of the lower orders.[37] Hill had always thought that there had been a potential revolt within the English Revolution, as England's persistent underground radicalism surfaced again in the Levellers and Diggers, the Seekers, the Ranters, Fifth Monarchy Men and Baptists. These groups proposed a wide variety of social and other changes but were thwarted by Cromwell and Ireton, who deserted the Good Old Cause in its hour of need. In the 1970s, Hill suggested that there had been not two but three cultures in mid seventeenth-century England: the old reactionary one, a new bourgeois one, and a truly plebeian radical one, the importance of a figure like Milton being that, like Blake and William Morris later, he acted as a bridge between the last two.[38] I think it can be fairly said that it is due to Hill more than any other scholar that what used to be dismissed as the 'lunatic fringe' of the 1640s and '50s is now taken much more seriously; but it must also be conceded that if he was looking for genuinely plebeian social radicals, he has run into difficulties. The attitudes of many of the people in the 1640s were clearly royalist and anglican rather than radical; the Levellers are now seen as being less democratic and egalitarian than was once thought; and many religious radicals, like the Ranters, appear to have been too concerned with defeating sin to pursue social equality.[39] Indeed, it seems to me that any attempt to detect the thinking of the illiterate 80 per cent of the population through the medium of the printed pamphlets which are Hill's forte is bound to run into serious problems.

The impact of his political ideals on his writing are evident in Hill's choice of topics, his technique of research, and the tone as well as the specific content of his conclusions. But he is not a dogmatic Marxist, and he has not used his work to preach an overt political message. In fact, like Tawney, he has found it difficult to produce books which would be taken seriously both by fellow academics and by the Party leadership or rank and file of the left. Even before 1956 he was in danger of being marginalized, and if since then he has switched his attention to disproving the anti-Marxist case of rival academics he has not been totally successful in that direction either. Indeed, so sustained had the assault on his views become by the 1970s that a recent volume published by a new generation of his admirers talks of having to 'revive' the notion of an English Revolution that in the 1960s seemed to have become a permanent feature of the historical landscape.[40]

Only slightly less prolific and influential than Hill has been Lawrence Stone. Born seven years after Hill, Stone had also grown up under the shadow of the Depression and fascism, and been strongly influenced by Tawney's hostility to the ruthless landlords, entrepreneurs and money-lenders of early modern times. Conversations with Tawney in the early 1940s, he says, convinced him of three things: that 'the documents for early modern history were preserved in sufficient quantity to make it possible to enter into the very minds of the actors', that 'nearly all the greatest transformations in the history of the West' had taken place in Tudor-Stuart England (the shift from feudalism to capitalism, from a single Church to religious pluralism and secularism, the first radical revolution, the creation of the first liberal polity), and, finally, that 'history can be a moral as well as a scholarly enterprise, that . . . cannot be disassociated from a vision of the contemporary world and how it should be ordered'.[41] But in other respects the path he followed was far different from Hill's. The son of an artist, Stone's first work was on medieval architecture, and despite showing a liberal's concern for the hardships of the people he has always retained an interest in élites rather than those at the bottom of society. Again, where Hill's dialogue was with Marx alone, Stone admits to having being influenced also by Weber, the *Annales* school and a number of the social sciences, the latter giving him an enthusiasm for model-building he later came to feel was exaggerated.[42]

Stone clearly sees himself as something of a maverick, and in many ways he is. He tends to be scornful of the Ph.D. system, which he himself avoided. He has not wanted to be tied down but has zoomed around, physically and mentally, trying new ideas and angles, though he says he has consciously sought a mean between the 'unverifiable global speculations' of those adopting a bird's-eye view – what Emmanuel Leroy Ladurie has termed the parachutist's approach – and the narrowness of vision of the traditional scholar, snuffling through the archives for undiscovered treasures – Ladurie's truffle-hunter. Unwilling to be trapped in an academic ivory tower, he has reached out to a larger audience by reviewing in journals with a national readership and by reproducing his scholarly conclusions in cheap paperback abridged versions. But despite his enthusiasm for new ideas, he has remained at heart 'something of a dinosaur', a child of the Enlightenment, and the last of the Whigs, a mixture of the individualistic and the anachronistic; and for the purposes of this survey we should be cautious about claiming that he represents anything but himself.[43]

The paths of Tawney, Hill and Stone crossed periodically in the 1950s and '60s. For a premature article on the decline of the Elizabethan aristocracy, Stone, like Tawney, was attacked by Trevor-Roper; in 1958 Stone and Hill teamed up with other Marxists and liberals on the board of the journal *Past and Present*; and in their different ways the two have continued to defend the significance of social change in the early modern period. Stone remains convinced that the idea of a rise of the gentry in the century before 1640 is largely true, though like Hexter and Zagorin he rejects the equation of those gentlemen with a rising bourgeoisie. He also feels that one cannot move directly from the demonstration of a rising gentry and a crisis in the aristocracy to the conclusion that constitutional change reflects these shifts, since 'ideological enthusiasm, military force and traditional habits of obedience . . . may often outweigh crude economic pressures'.[44]

Stone's contribution has been to open up the discussion on the origins of the English Revolution in directions that neither Tawney nor Hill had tried. He started, he says, from the premise that great events must have not just important causes (a statement with which Gardiner and other Whigs would have agreed) but multiple causes.[45] He has also promoted the idea of overlapping time-scales for long, medium and short-term causes, and has argued against linear sequence and hierarchical causation for a dynamic interaction between material factors (such as the economic and demographic base and the social structure) and cultural factors (such as ideology, religion and mentalities).[46] This programme is extremely ambitious, straddling as it does the social change and neo-Whig schools. Not only has he faced severe criticism on technical grounds, but he himself admits that he may sometimes have been guilty of neglecting to show exactly how these mutually reinforcing trends interacted. Indeed, further work by Stone has forced him to rethink his position to some extent.[47]

Stone's political opinions are less well-defined than Hill's or Tawney's, but they may account not only for the way he developed but also for his influence, especially in America. He is by his own admission a nineteenth-century Whig, with 'an abiding faith in reason, in the possibility of limited material and moral progress, in paternalist responsible leadership, and in the rule of law not men'.[48] A persistent critic of Marxism and a committed popularizer, he has determined to prove to a wide readership the importance of events between 1500 and 1700, and in this sense his interpretation is open to the charge of being an updated version of the 'romantic' account of Trevelyan.

In the case of our first three historians, then, it can be seen that all of them responded to the political ideas of their own day, but in an idiosyncratic way, so that none can be said to have influenced its politics to any great degree. Moreover, each continued to employ concepts which have left him open to attacks – albeit sometimes of a simplistic or even carping kind – from those of different political persuasions, both then and since.

By the time that Stone's main historiographical contribution to

The Causes of the English Revolution was published, in 1972, doubts about the social-process interpretation were mounting. Challenges had been made in the 1950s and '60s, but until the 1970s these seem to have had limited effect. Trevor-Roper had followed up his attack on Tawney with one on Stone which, its victim says, 'connoisseurs of intellectual terrorism cherish to this day', while J. H. Hexter's periodic attempts to demolish Tawney and Hill left some filled with admiration and others feeling sympathy for his targets.[49] Peter Laslett offered a rival model to Hill's class tension,[50] and Geoffrey Elton blew a couple of raspberries at a view which he felt was turning Elizabethan and early Stuart history into a 'high road to civil war'.[51] Namierite studies of the membership of the Long Parliament cast further doubt on the theory of a social divide between royalists and parliamentarians,[52] and John Kenyon stressed the importance of issues of principle and of high politics as well as political and legal structures in his study of *The Stuart Constitution*.[53] But these blows did little more than dent the armour of the social-process historians, partly because the attacks, though based on scholarly research, were spasmodic and uncoordinated, and because the attacks came from historians whose political views varied almost as widely as those of the historians they were attacking. In part also it may have been because the violence of some of the attacks did not appeal in an age of rather anodyne politics in which, in Britain at least, a new consensus had emerged within which collectivist conservatives and pragmatic labourites might throw punches at each other without meaning to draw blood. But perhaps it was also because the man most suited to be the Elton or the Namier of early-seventeenth-century studies – Hugh Trevor-Roper – did not really want the part.

Trevor-Roper had waged trench warfare against Tawney, Stone and Hill, but in terms of a willingness to try a new approach or take a broader look, his trench was remarkably close to that of the other side. His attempt to replace the 'rising gentry' by a 'mere' or declining gentry put him closer to Tawney and Hill, and his insistence on the importance of ideas and individuals has put him closer to Stone than he might have found congenial.[54] One suspects that it was the thrill of the chase alone that appealed to Trevor-Roper. Much preferring fruitful error to unimportant truth or arid scholastic consensus, he was temperamentally unsuited to set up a new school of orthodoxy.[55]

From the late 1960s to the late 1970s two new interpretations were developed, both of them by scholars who for the most part had grown up after the traumas of the 1930s and '40s. One was the localist perspective developed by scholars like Alan Everitt and John Morrill. This took a much closer look at the counties in early Stuart times, and found not an incipient divide along political or socio-economic lines but a series of closely knit and largely self-sufficient communities exhibiting a conservative provincialism that resented intervention from the centre, either by the crown in the 1630s or parliament in the 1640s: hence the title of Morrill's survey, *The Revolt of the Provinces*.[56] There developed a split inside this school between those like Everitt, who felt that the local communities were so introverted that they were virtually apolitical, and those like Morrill, who felt that the gentry were concerned by national issues but were pulled in different directions by local and national interests. Indeed, the idea that a community or an individual might feel a tension between national and local loyalties formed a bridge between the local school and the exponents of the other new interpretation of the 1970s, that of the so-called 'revisionists'.

These are a motley group of historians led by Conrad Russell and Kevin Sharpe in the 1970s, but now including Morrill and Jonathan Clark, who have relatively little in common apart from a conviction of the need to challenge both the old Whig orthodoxy and the newer social interpretation. They have argued that early Stuart parliaments were surprisingly feeble bodies, riddled by faction and dominated by the Lords rather than the Commons; and that what was of crucial importance in precipitating the crisis of 1640-2 was not deep-seated social or economic changes, or disputes over clearly articulated constitutional principles, but unforeseen, short-term political and administrative problems, brought to a head by the rebellions in Scotland and Ireland, and rendered insoluble by personal antagonisms and mutual misunderstandings.[57] One wing of the 'revisionists', led by Tyacke, Russell and Morrill, also believes that from the late 1620s there was a new source of religious tension – a doctrinal rift between Calvinists and Arminians; but the other wing, led by Sharpe, sees the abrasiveness of this debate as having been exaggerated by contemporary propaganda rather than reflecting a major rift in early Stuart society.[58]

The rise of the local school and the 'revisionists', however, soon prompted a restatement of older views and the development of new, post-revisionist opinions. In the first place, over the last dozen years there has been a forcible if somewhat modified restatement of the old Whig view that the early seventeenth century was a crucial period in the history of the English parliament and of English liberty, though it is notable that the chief exponents of this neo-Whig position are either Americans or British scholars working in America, like Jack Hexter, Theodore Rabb and Derek Hirst.[59] Secondly, there has been an attempt to revive the social-process interpretation by scholars like Liam Hunt and Geoff Eley, and sympathy for it from a historical sociologist, Mary Fulbrook.[60] Lines were once again being drawn, and perhaps the peak of hostility was reached in 1986 when Jonathan Clark delivered a stinging attack on what he has described as the 'rogues' gallery' of Marxists, radicals and liberals who for decades had been purveying their disastrously mistaken view of the early modern period.[61]

Some taste of the current state of affairs can be had if we look at the views of two of the more outspoken participants in the current debate – the neo-Whig Hexter, and the revisionist Clark. Jack Hexter is something of a throwback to an earlier age, in that he was born earlier than both Hill and Stone, and published his first book, a study of John Pym, in 1941.[62] Since then he has published only essays and reviews on the seventeenth century, but many of them have been hailed as important reappraisals. Indeed, according to a *Festschrift* published in 1980 he 'has served as the conscience of his fellow scholars' over the last few decades.[63] If so, to some of his victims he must have appeared less of an indulgent father-confessor than an agent of the Spanish Inquisition. Thus when Hill protested that in one attack Hexter was accusing him of 'distortion and cheating', Hexter replied that only those who were aware that they were selecting the passages of a source that suited their case could be accused of cheating, and since Hill seemed to do this unconsciously this accusation did not apply.[64]

During the cold war it was the Marxists and the social-science-orientated historians that were Hexter's particular *bête noire*, though he never tackled them on their own special patch – the later 1640s and the 1650s. But since the rise of *détente* his particular brand of wrath has been directed increasingly at those to his right, the repulsive 'revisionists'. Hexter feels that by playing up the role of faction and accident and by playing down political ideology they have been guilty of throwing the baby out with the bathwater. He would agree with Theodore Rabb that by contextualizing so narrowly, the 'revisionists' have distorted the 'shape' of history – those 'larger movements' which, Rabb feels, give sense to our understanding of the past.[65] Hexter may not be guilty of the crude Whiggish teleology of which he has been accused by Clark, and, unlike classic Whigs, what he finds under the early Stuarts is less a winning of the initiative than the defence of certain liberties which the political nation felt it had enjoyed for some time.[66] But he has written that the early Stuart period witnessed the 'birth of modern freedom', and that what was at stake in the early Stuart period was 'not only the liberty of seventeenth-century Englishmen but our own liberty'. Indeed, he has virtually accused the 'revisionists' of being not only intellectually obtuse but morally deficient as well.[67]

Why has Hexter become so agitated? Does he feel that an interpretation which suggests that Charles I and Archbishop Laud have been misunderstood, and that Puritans like the Pilgrim Fathers were a bunch of eccentrics whom England could do very well without, falls into the category of un-American activities? Is it a gut reaction to Watergate that prompts Hexter to see a very real threat to the rule of law in Charles I's England? Is it part of a growing sense of insecurity among the liberal left in America who now see their past achievements questioned and their future in doubt as support moves to groups to the right and left of them? Or is it simply a means of protecting the considerable investment, both of money and effort, which American scholarship has placed in the subject of English parliamentary history since the days of Notestein, McIlwain, Judson and others?[68] Whatever the reason, neo-Whiggery today is an essentially American phenomenon, and the venom of Jonathan Clark's attacks on it may represent another nail in the coffin of the special relationship.

Clark himself is much younger than the others discussed here, having grown up in the relatively tranquil era of Macmillan and Wilson before attending that nursery of 'intellectual Toryism' – Peterhouse, Cambridge – moving onto a post in the City and then to All Souls.[69] In his reviews and interviews, he often sounds like a crusader for the New Right.[70] The tone of the book in which he has tried to emancipate the Civil War debate from the 'old orthodoxy' is less strident, yet it is striking how Clark tries to seize the moral high ground in regard to the unprejudiced analysis of the sources, how regularly his opponents are denounced for sins of 'teleology' and 'reductionism', and how silent he is about the events of the later 1640s and the '50s. What he actually says about the English Civil War – that it was due to problems in high politics, the Scottish and Irish rebellions and complications caused by religious disquiet – contains little that has not already been said by Russell, Sharpe and Morrill.[71]

Those familiar with the historiography of other periods may see parallels between the growing speed of change and the greater bitterness illustrated here and in their own area of special interest.[72] Closest parallels seem to be with the historical treatment of the French Revolution, where the earlier doubts of Cobban in the 1950s about an over-simple social explanation were reinforced by Furet and Richet and a number of French and American 'revisionists' who from the late 1960s stressed the importance of ideology and politics, which in turn provoked replies and new arguments, especially from those still persuaded by a social interpretation.[73] There are possible political parallels as well. In the case of Britain and America, one might link these historiographical changes with the transition from the relative prosperity and internal calm of the 1950s and early '60s to the growing social and political crises of the late '60s and early '70s, and to the polarization of politics which led to the triumph of the right and the rise of the moral majority in the late '70s. In Britain, for example, the localist perspective on the English Civil War came to the fore about the time that many voters were showing distaste for 'Big Brother'-type government and industrial management by supporting some devolution of power to the regions and some partnership in industry. Similarly, the increased interest in early Stuart theological debate in the work of Tyacke and Morrill has coincided with a minor revival of religious commitment, and the ultra-right views of Jonathan Clark reflected the changing world of which Thatcherism was both a symptom and a cause.[74] In America, the reassertion of the neo-Whig cause may have owed something to a feeling that the broad national consensus and the rule of law were at risk from the hard right as well as the new left.[75]

In a broad sense such links probably have some validity. But it is not clear in the case of the English Civil War whether they can be made as firmly in the case of the post-war generations as in regard to those who grew up in the first half of the twentieth century. It is hard to imagine Tawney or Hill reaching the conclusions they did without their strong political convictions, but it is possible to read the work of Gerald Aylmer or Anthony Fletcher without getting strong impressions of their current political opinions.[76] The chronology of change is also not quite right. In Britain the rise of revisionism was well under way before the hegemony of the broadly based centrist parties was challenged by the New Right or by coalitions of the left and non-parliamentary bodies in the late '70s and early '80s. Moreover, a number of its exponents, like Russell and Morrill, would probably see their affiliation as being to the centre or even above party politics.

Another possible political dimension that does not work so well on closer examination is the contrasting attitudes to the social sciences of those on the left and on the right: many of those who were most attracted to social science ideas in the past were often left-wing in sympathy, while a number of those who reacted against them tended to be from the right.[77] To a degree the historians discussed here seem to confirm the tendency of left or liberal-left historians to be parachutists, prepared to adopt new techniques and new angles of approach in order to view society as a whole and to identify neglected areas which might yield new results. The topics they chose were often concerned more with the collective than the individual. To a lesser extent the Civil War debate also confirms the tendency of those on the right, or antipathetic to the left, to be truffle-hunters, taking on finite, manageable topics and focusing on the individual or the operation of political machinery. But this dichotomy between the techniques of left and right should not be taken too far.

There have always been exceptions: on the one hand, Trevor-Roper, though a conservative in many ways, has not been afraid to explore social change theories; on the other, neo-Whigs like Hexter have been suspicious of the social sciences; while, in between, individuals like Lawrence Stone have moved from warm support to a more cautious position. Also, when the challenge to the social-process theory came to its peak in the 1970s, it came from historians nearer the centre than the right.[78] There may be a social or academic reason for the divide, namely the tendency of students already attracted to a particular subject or a particular line of argument to seek out the existing exponents of that line as their supervisors and to pursue the lines of research they suggest. But the tendency to adopt or reject a sociological approach is not an infallible test of political belief.

The main reasons for the heating-up of the debate in the last two decades lie rather in the changing character of the profession and in the temperament of a few of its leading members. By the 1930s the divide between academic history and amateur or popular history was already well under way due to changes in attitude and personnel among the professional historians discussed earlier. But by the 1970s that process had moved several stages further: the universities had experienced another burst of expansion, during which history retained its popularity, indeed reached new peaks; techniques of research had become more varied and more demanding; and the Ph.D. system had achieved a virtual stranglehold on postgraduate study.[79] Many new avenues of enquiry were thus opened and both the quality and the quantity of research rose. Moreover, in England many old landowning families deposited their papers in newly constituted County Record Offices, encouraged by historians and for private reasons.[80] In one sense there has been more disagreement because there has been more to disagree about as the range of materials explored has become broader and has raised more searching questions.

Yet much of the new work was written by and for academics in a style that only other scholars could comprehend or enjoy and a great deal of research was narrowly conceived and executed. The Ph. D. system has many merits but it creates pressure for quick results and original conclusions, which, combined with the need to publish regularly and an increasingly tough search for jobs, is not conducive to embarking on large or co-operative projects or to being generous in reviewing other historians' work. Rather than integrate their conclusions into an existing framework or delay judgment until a wider angle or larger sample can be explored, as in the French doctoral system, English-speaking postgraduates of recent years have too often been tempted to bring down the walls of Jericho through a single blast on a rather small trumpet. In short, the bifurcations and eructations of the last two decades owe a certain amount to the increasingly introverted and competitive nature of the academic profession.[81]

The question remains as to how far this increased competitiveness is a reflection of the society in which these academics live. It is a truism that all historical writing is beset by a series of epistemological dilemmas. How far in looking at the past can we cut ourselves off from our own personal present? How far can the relative truths that we may establish about the past be used as a basis for comments about the present? If an historian with pronounced political opinions (of whatever hue) also displays a tendency towards dogmatism, may this not be due as much to temperament as to training or to any innate connection between historical study and political conviction?

To use a theological parallel, the politico-historian is one who is inclined to be apodictic rather than apophatic. The apophatic churchmen (as in the Byzantine Church) says all we know about God is how much we are in the dark about what He is really like; but his apodictic counterpart in the Western Church says this is what we know for certain about God and there is no reason why one should not believe it. A theological analogy is not out of place here since the leading historians I have discussed all seem to have made what Kierkegaard called the leap into faith and to be anxious for others to imitate that leap. In a reply to J. C. Davis's criticism of his work on the Ranters, Christopher Hill asked, 'What is he afraid of?'[82] The implication was that Davis might be politically or temperamentally unsuited to get to the heart of the Ranters' world; but what the question also revealed was that Hill knew (as an act of faith, as it were) that radicals were really people and that once one got to know them their ideas were not really so frightening. The same faith is implicit in Stone's belief in the moral value of history and in his seeking great causes for what he believes are great events; it is there in Hexter's statement that it is our own liberty that is at stake and in Clark's determination to be emancipated from what he sees as the heresies advanced by social-engineering leftists or social-science inspired liberals.[83] Historians who have not taken the leap into faith or have a more apophatic faith are less likely to be so dogmatic about what happened in the past.

The historical debates of recent decades may owe more to a combination of academic rivalry and contrasts in personal temperament than to political circumstances or ideas, and it may be said that even in so far as there is some intrusion of political belief into historical writing the consequences are not serious. If political commitment has led an historian to make assertions which his peers regard as distortions of what happened in the past, there is at least a dialogue in process rather than a dull consensus. It is probable that the politico-historian does no more than push a debate further in a particular direction than it might have gone without his intervention; certain features of the debate on the English Civil War might well have occurred even if Tawney had not been a socialist or John Morrill a late convert to Catholicism. This centrifugal tendency does not matter much in that there are certain generally agreed standards by which historical scholarship is judged and which tend to have a countervailing centripetal effect. As a result many historians may agree on a range of topics with other scholars whose political beliefs are very different from their own.

It is in fact possible to construct a list of statements about the possible causes and consequences of the English Civil War that, with due care against academic or political rivalry, might receive support from a surprising range of historians. Such a list would recognize that the old Whiggish idea of a parliamentary opposition steadily growing in confidence and power was misleading; but would concede that the revisionist case for the weakness and ideological confusion of early Stuart parliaments has been overdrawn.[84] It would point out that the older view of a coherent and politically active body of Puritans needs to be replaced by one which shows that there was a wide variety of standpoints within English Protestantism and that what we should be examining is shades of anti-Catholicism rather than a simple dichotomy of 'Puritans' and 'Anglicans'.[85] It would not give undue weight to the contingent or the role of individual actions while admitting their significance at certain pivotal moments.[86] It would make efforts to detect the ways in which economic change and social differentiation between 1540 and 1640 affected political events, while recognizing that neither these nor the effects of structural problems in central and local government are easy to pin down or were in themselves likely to provoke a war.[87] It would concede that the task of explaining the constitutional crisis of 1640-1 is not the same as that of accounting for the outbreak of fighting in 1642 and that the lines along which the community divided were probably not the same in 1642 as they were in 1644, 1647 or 1655.[88] It might also suggest that, although there were radical proposals with limited prospects of success, there was a more moderate set of ideas with more realistic chances of being implemented.[89] While acknowledging the considerable degree of variation within English regions, it would stress the need for events in England to be viewed in a British and a European context.[90] It might accept that the most striking legacies of the period were psychological: fear of radicalism, fear of a standing army, dislike of interfering governments.[91]

Yet there is one way in which the intrusion of politics into history does matter and could make a permanent difference in Britain at least. When Jonathan Clark publicly lambasts the historical profession as one dominated by Old Guard Marxists and Old-Hat Liberals he plays into the hands of a government which in the interests of cost-effectiveness has sought radically to overhaul the universities which it seems to want to convert from centres of scholarship and education into training colleges. Its policies have already led to a loss of between 11 and 15 per cent of teachers of history in higher education at a time when student interest has risen by much the same proportion.[92] It may be suggested that nothing would give this government more pleasure than to get rid of even more of the country's historians on the grounds that they are costly and include many undesirable left-wing elements or wishy-washy liberals likely to give students the wrong ideas about the enterprise culture. The future of history in British universities is not bright at the moment. Let us hope that by the time the leaders of the present government [1989] leave the House of Commons to join Lord Dacre and Lord Russell in that other great institution of Stuart England, the House of Lords, there will still be a future for the past in Britain.[93]

NINE

THE FUTILITY OF HISTORY: A FAILED EXPERIMENT IN IRISH EDUCATION

David Fitzpatrick

Ireland's moral and social engineers were at once fascinated and frightened by the rapid diffusion of basic literacy and popular education after 1831. The 'Victorian mind' set great store in the power of teachers and school-books to mould mass mentality, whether for better or worse. This belief was widespread among Catholics as well as Protestants, nationalists as well as loyalists. It did not pass unchallenged, at least in the rhetoric of reforming administrators. Thus in 1900 the new resident commissioner of national education, William Starkie, promised that 'we shall no longer treat the child's mind, according to the old mistaken idea, as a "white tablet" on which may be written whatever the teacher desires'.[1] In practice, however, the manipulative potentiality of teaching remained a basic assumption of educational planning in Ireland until very recent times. Since primary teachers and texts were more closely supervised by central administrators in Ireland than in Britain, the feasibility of controlling mass mentality through the school system seemed commensurately greater. Indeed the prevalent issue was not whether Irish people were susceptible to indoctrination through primary schooling, but whether the *tabula rasa* of the newly literate population would be imprinted with good or evil precepts.

Instruction in religion and the Irish language prompted the noisiest controversy among political educationalists, but the more muted debate concerning the functions of history teaching was equally significant. Moralists and pedagogues in Britain as well as Ireland were widely agreed that patriotism and civilization were sensitive plants, which might be either enriched or poisoned by selective instruction in history. In 1913 a fellow of the Royal Historical Society urged that the life stories of patriots should be instilled 'into every youthful mind until the burning, active love of one's own country should be a powerful factor in the daily life of every true son and daughter of England'.[2] Such was the aim of *The Young Patriot Readers*, advertised in 1916 as 'tending to foster love of country, to suggest the duties that devolve upon true patriots, and to stir the hearts of young readers by holding up before them noble examples'.[3] English interest in history as a source of patriotism was undoubtedly sharpened by the menace and experience of the Great War, which caused propagandists to view with envy the more ruthless exploitation of history by educationalists in France and Germany.[4] In Ireland, however, the political functions of history teaching had long been a matter of public contention. The trouble was that patriotism had distinct and hostile meanings for nationalists and loyalists, meanings closely entangled with religious affiliation. The concepts of 'scientific' and impartial history had few Irish exponents; controversy centred on the choice of ideology worthy of inculcation through the teaching of partisan history. As an English Catholic declared in 1869, 'If it is not taught in a Catholic sense, it must be taught in an anti-Catholic sense.'[5]

The most systematic exploitation of history in the service of Catholic nationalism was undertaken by the Christian Brothers. Their *Irish History Reader* (1905) proclaimed that 'a nation's school books wield a great power'. Teachers should reinforce the text-book's message by dwelling 'with pride, and in glowing words on Ireland's glorious past, her great men and their great deeds', until pupils were persuaded 'that Ireland looks to them, when grown to man's estate, to act the part of true men in furthering the sacred cause of nationhood'.[6] The Christian Brothers had been more circumspect in their previous readers: the Irish section of the *Historical Class-Book* (1859) culminated in celebration of the 'peaceful revolution' of Catholic emancipation, and Cardinal Cullen claimed with justice that its condemnation of past wrongs did not entail hostility to the current administration.[7] Even so, the 'pervading Catholic and Irish tone' of their text-books, replete with 'the glorious names of St Patrick, St Columbanus, St Brigid: of O'Brien and O'Neill; and in later times of Grattan and O'Connell', provided a model for other Catholic educators.[8] A similar tone marked many of the popular histories circulated by the Catholic Young Men's Society, the Gaelic League and Sinn Féin, or recommended by influential publicists such as Michael MacDonagh and the Rev. Thomas O'Donnell. Protestant authorship was not incompatible with a 'Catholic and Irish tone', as shown by the popularity of works by Davis, Mitchel and Alice Stopford Green. But *Our Boys* urged pupils establishing libraries in Christian Brothers' schools to 'be sure, though, that everything you get is recommended by a good Catholic Irishman, and avoid anti-Irish, anti-Catholic books like the over-praised boys' stories of Kingsley': while Fr O'Donnell asked, 'Who can expect a non-Catholic professor of history to treat the revolt of Luther or the deeds of the Spanish Inquisition without bias and prepossessions? . . . In a word, will not a non-Catholic school infallibly ostracise the Catholic faith, undermine its essential principle of authority, uphold the alien principle of private judgment?'[9] In the battle of Catholic truth against Protestant falsehood, history was a small but sharp-edged weapon.

Protestant attempts to popularize an alternative history were more fitful and uncertain. An Irish history reader was adopted by the Church Education Society between 1854 and 1857, while Orangeism generated an outpouring of pamphlets and ballads celebrating the heroic defence of Protestant liberties against reiterated Catholic conspiracies.[10] Yet the manifest difficulty of justifying the past conduct of Irish government encouraged many Protestant educationalists to redirect the focus of history teaching from Ireland to Britain and its empire. Others preferred to have no history rather than two histories taught in Irish schools. Since Catholics were the majority, the costs of allowing inculcation of disloyalty among Catholic children might be deemed to outweigh the benefits of bolstering loyalty among Protestants. An attractive corollary was to condemn all history as being intrinsically subversive in a divided society. In 1808 Richard Lovell Edgeworth approved the prohibition of classical history in the Charter schools, arguing that 'to inculcate democracy and a foolish hankering after undefined liberty is not necessary in Ireland'.[11] Protestant publicists concentrated on denouncing the partisan abuse of history rather than constructing an alternative version. Crofton Croker and the convert William Carleton accused 'hedge' school-masters of employing seditious historical text-books not merely for 'amusement' but for political subversion; as Carleton asked rhetorically in 1830, 'With this specimen of education before our eyes, is it at all extraordinary that Ireland should be as she is?'[12] If history was a weapon for Catholics, it was a menace to Protestants.

Throughout the nineteenth century, the Commissioners of National Education acted on the premise that non-partisan history was unfeasible. Since their rules prohibited lessons that might offend anybody on religious or political grounds, they simply eliminated all systematic teaching of history from the curriculum. It was a cliché of nationalist polemics that this was part of a British plot to anglicize Ireland. John Mitchel wrote in 1858 that 'the intention was not so much to convert Catholic children as to denationalize them'; suggesting elsewhere that the teaching of Irish history 'would have made young faces flush hot with a dangerous passion, mingled of pride and shame, to think of what their country was, what it is, and – God of heaven! what it *might be*.'[13] Likewise, the Christian Brothers argued that the intention of Whately and his fellow Commissioners had been 'to efface from the minds of Irish children all idea of their distinct nationality'.[14] The conspiracy hypothesis might account for suppression of the history of Ireland, but scarcely of Britain and the empire. Until 1898 no historical chronology was taught except for brief compendia in the two highest readers, which were studied by less than one-sixteenth of pupils in 1868.

The *Supplement to the Fourth Book of Lessons* (1862) contained 22 pages on 'modern history', omitting all reference to Ireland and the Reformation but noting that Napoleon was 'totally routed' at Waterloo. The *Fifth Book* (1835) contained a chart listing three 'principal persons or events in each century', including 'the Reformation' but no Irish entry except the 'Union of Great Britain and Ireland'. This reader for advanced pupils drew a clear distinction between 'chronology' and 'history', embracing motives, causes and effects – but prudently confined itself to chronology.[15] In 1858 the Commissioners decided that it was 'expedient to publish a class book' on a hybrid termed 'Chronological history', which must not 'give just cause of offence, either on religious or political grounds, to persons of any denomination in Ireland'. This task being 'of a very delicate and difficult nature', they were still searching four decades later.[16] Apart from a few classical histories, virtually no historical works of unofficial origin were sanctioned for school use between 1839 and 1893, whereas dozens were rejected. The bulk of Catholic as well as Protestant requests were for English rather than Irish text-books, though the inspectors sedulously rooted out works on Ireland by Daunt, Sullivan and Cusack as well as the Christian Brothers when these were discovered in classrooms.[17] The difficulty of finding impartial text-books also inhibited history teaching in England, where, according to the *Educational Times* in 1873, many school boards 'decided to adopt the oral system of teaching, preferring to leave the matter in the hands of the master to adopting any of the existing objectionable Handbooks on the subject'. After the codification of English primary schooling in 1862 history remained a rather unpopular option until the curriculum reform of 1900.[18] Official discouragement of the subject in Ireland echoed English indifference as well as Irish fears.

Opposition to the elimination of history teaching in national schools was significantly muted. Protestant moralists in Whately's tradition placed more faith in literature and political economy as agents of civilization, than in history; whereas Catholic moralists concentrated their campaign against anglicization on the issues of religious instruction and later the Irish language. Thus both parties, while affirming the utility of history as a tool for reshaping Irish mentality, gave it low priority. Since the national system was initially intended to be interdenominational, those participating in it often dismissed history teaching as being impracticable. In 1854 the Catholic bishop of Down and Connor opposed history lessons in mixed schools; while a Protestant witness thought that 'the less they know of the history of Ireland, the better'.[19] As Catholic pressure undermined the interdenominational principle after Whately's resignation in 1853, Church spokesmen became more plaintive about the suppression of history. In 1860 the hierarchy lamented that the Commissioners seemed 'to have determined to leave the rising Catholic generations in Ireland without any knowledge of their forefathers in the faith, and without any traditions whatsoever of country or of family to console, to cheer, and to excite them to virtue' (not, as Mitchel hinted, to revolt).[20] Several witnesses before the Powis Commission in 1868-9 argued that the judicious teaching of Irish history would restrain rather than incite sedition. The bishop of Cloyne felt that if a text-book 'without any objectionable observations' could be devised, Catholics might 'confine themselves to it, and that there would be less appetite for the food supplied by newspapers and other sources'; while Cullen declared that 'Our history presents much that is glorious for our country, and children should not be left in ignorance of it.'[21] Some Protestant spokesmen agreed. A Presbyterian minister, after opposing any incorporation of the Catholic view of history, argued that while 'a true history of Ireland' might cause offence, 'the fact of its not being acceptable to all should not prevent it being tried'. One assistant commissioner regretted the 'jejune manner' in which history was treated, while another ingeniously suggested 'that a history of Ireland written, so to speak, *backwards*' might enable teachers to play down the insidious story of 'ancient misrule'.[22]

By the end of the century, the impact of social and political reform was sufficient to persuade administrators that an inoffensive history programme might after all be constructed. Catholics might be placated by admission of past oppression; Protestants might take heart from Britain's contemporary benevolence. Starkie, the Catholic and unionist resident commissioner, did not spare his predecessors for their 'narrow pedantry in ignoring, as worthless, the whole previous spiritual life of the pupil, and the multitude of associations, imaginations and sentiments that form the content of his consciousness'.[23] The first beneficiary of history's recognition as a fit subject for national schools was P. W. Joyce, a Catholic and former principal of the Marlborough Street training college, whose text-books were the first Irish history readers to be sanctioned for use in national schools. Between 1898 and 1900 teachers were permitted to use approved works on Irish or British history in combination with other readers on the general reading course, and in 1905 a rather more specific historical ingredient was prescribed for the fourth and higher standards. Finally in 1908 history became 'a definite course of instruction' supported by a broadening range of approved text-books on British and Irish history for more advanced pupils.

The new programme envisaged progression from 'conversational lessons' to a 'general outline of the history of Ireland' in fourth standard, rising through study of 'a selected period of history, preferably Irish, with outline of the corresponding period of English history' to more specialized topics in seventh standard.[24] By contemporary standards this was a singular curriculum. No uniform history syllabus had been imposed on the English Board Schools under the new code of 1900. The history option in the Irish intermediate examination (introduced in 1903) had only minor Irish content, predictably begrudged by Commissioner Mahaffy, who argued that 'Irish History is not a fit subject for young people at all.'[25]

Why did the Commissioners of National Education end their decades of indecision by adopting not merely history but Irish history? Their reasoning was set forth in the *Notes for Teachers*, 'recommendations . . . rather than injunctions' which teachers were invited to discard in favour of 'a well defined method of their own'. The author confessed that for 'the general student, whose objective is the history of the growth of civilisation, a detailed knowledge of

English history appears unquestionably to be more valuable than Irish'; yet if history were to be rendered interesting as well as useful, it was 'clearly preferable that Irish history should be the starting point of any formal study of the subject in Irish schools'. The *Notes* echoed Starkie's professed preference for Rousseau rather than Plato by allowing latitude to teachers, advocating non-partisan discussion of 'the struggles and contests of parties and nations from the point of view of each side in turn', and avoiding indelicate references to history as the foundation of patriotism. Nevertheless, historical study was required to make one 'fit to take his share in such civic duties and privileges as fall to his lot', and 'should tend to form the character of the pupil by stimulating the growth of desirable moral qualities, such as love of justice'. Memorizing facts and extracts from text-books was to be 'scrupulously avoided', while student interest was to be aroused by poems and ballads at junior level and local studies bolstered by school excursions beginning at fifth standard.[26] In their assumptions and practical advice, the *Notes* would probably be deemed too radical and ambitious for adoption in Ireland today.[27]

The abrupt introduction of Irish history into the primary curriculum was consistent not only with Starkie's professed determination to inject 'national sympathy' into education, but also with the broader process which has recently been dubbed 'the greening of Dublin Castle'.[28] No doubt it was also encouraged by the continuing if scarcely vigorous campaigning of certain 'Irish-Irelanders'.[29] That campaign did not cease in 1908, partly because the reform of history teaching went largely unnoticed. In 1911 Douglas Hyde remained unaware that Irish history had become a specific subject, so provoking the sneering rejoinder from Bonaparte Wyse that 'Archbishop Whately and his "happy English child", of whom we continue to hear so much, are as dead as Queen Anne.'[30] Clergy and educationalists, though better informed than Hyde, expressed misgivings about the new programme. In 1913 the General Synod of the Church of Ireland proposed that scruples of conscience should enable pupils to avoid historical as well as religious instruction.[31] The editor of the *Irish Educational Review* welcomed the Irish focus of the programme but advocated a less frenetic survey course of two years instead of one, finding fault with the demand for special studies and with the absence of attention to the world beyond the British Isles.[32]

It was the Easter Rising that made the history programme once again a political rather than pedagogical issue. Provost Mahaffy's epithet of the 'Schoolmasters' Rebellion' provoked a frenzy of public and official debate on the political consequences of learning history, anticipating Conor Cruise O'Brien's suggestion in 1972 that 'the seeds of Aldershot' might have been 'sown in some Irish classroom'. Mahaffy blamed Irish school-teachers for transmitting 'the events of long past history calculated to make rebels of those who in the present have no reasonable basis for disloyalty'.[33] The reputation of teachers and history teaching was defended by the *Irish School Weekly* and the Irish National Teachers' Organization, though a proposal was tabled at the 1917 congress that only 'the broad facts of history' should be generally taught. Speakers at meetings of the Presbyterian and Methodist Churches urged abolition of the subject, and in March 1917 the issue was still being debated 'in small Dublin weeklies and in various heretical coteries throughout the country'.[34] The Commissioners managed to avoid major changes to the programme, though the INTO's secretary J.J. O'Connell claimed in 1920 that the board had 'insisted that English history should be taught', so undermining the enthusiasm hitherto associated with the study of Ireland.[35] In the revolutionary years renewed demand was made for the extension of the Irish history programme, with greater concentration on the glorious Gaelic past, less on 'the dreary and saddening political vicissitudes of the last five centuries', and clearer identification of 'the enemies and friends of the democratic nation'.[36] Somehow, the board's attempt to promulgate non-partisan history survived the assaults of scare-mongering loyalists and dogmatic republicans alike.

After partition, both Irish states drew upon precedents established by the Commissioners in devising history programmes for primary schools. Contrary to Roy Foster's suggestion that educational policy in each state reflected 'an equally strong sense of history as a tool, or weapon, to be manipulated through the schools', the missionary zeal of the northern authorities never matched that of their Dublin rivals.[37] It is true that in Northern Ireland, the Lynn committee in 1923 recommended strict control of text-books and inculcation of 'loyalty' through study of the history of one's 'native country'. Yet this entity was wisely left unspecified, pupils being expected to 'acquire an elementary knowledge of the history of Great Britain, and of Ireland, and especially Ulster as part of the United Kingdom'. For 'a variety of reasons', also unspecified, history was to be downgraded from being a day subject to an option available at higher levels in larger schools.[38] Irish history was given little prominence in the 1924 programme, though it was reinforced in

1956 when Catholic schools seldom taught the history programme, while even at secondary level the popularity of the official history option diminished sharply after partition.[39] Thus in practice, the northern Ministry of Education reverted to the nineteenth-century precept that impartial history was unfeasible whereas compulsory partisan history was divisive. Northerners remained as uninstructed in the identity of their 'native country' as ever.[40]

In the Irish Free State, Starkie's emphasis on Irish rather than British history was predictably stiffened. Irish history almost unsullied by foreign associations was taught from fifth standard upwards between 1926 and 1971, after a brief period in which junior pupils also were exposed to Irish stories, legends and inspirational biographies.[41] The effect of restricting formal instruction to upper standards was to reduce the proportions of pupils 'at risk' in a given year from 27.8 per cent in 1908 to 22.6 per cent in 1946.[42] The moral fervour of educational administrators was concentrated upon a fostering of the Irish tongue, but warm language also marked the official guidelines for history teaching. The patriotic functions of the subject were emphasized in the National Programme of Primary Instruction of 1922, which maintained that 'one of the chief aims of the teaching of history should be to develop the best traits of the national character and to inculcate national pride and self-respect'. The 1926 programme, operative until 1971, stressed 'broader issues' such as 'the struggle for national independence and religious equality, and . . . for the land and the language'.[43] But the most eloquent plea for the political manipulation of history appeared in the new *Notes for Teachers* of 1933, which were still being reissued without amendment even of the reading list up to 1971. The *Notes* helpfully provided a skeleton course for 'inexperienced teachers', who were to offer 'vivid descriptions of the evictions', stress 'the continuity of the separatist idea from Tone to Pearse', and castigate the Irish administration for allowing grain exports during the famine. Juvenile interest was to be awakened 'through stories of the heroic or romantic exploits of the national heroes of legend and semi-history', while pupils were to repeat 'telling phrases' such as: 'With the sword I won them; with the sword I will keep them.' In Whiggish fashion, students were to be reassured of the linear development of Irish civilization, 'using the chief events as rungs of an ascending ladder'. The fruits of history teaching should be 'at least, as much moral as mental', with pupils learning 'that they are citizens of no mean country, that they belong to a race that has a noble tradition of heroism, and persistent loyalty to ideals'. Teachers were further advised to tolerate 'no distortion of the facts of history nor any deliberate suppression of facts derogatory to national pride. Irish history has been much distorted by those who wrote from the enemy's standpoint.' Faint echoes of these sentiments still colour the instructions on history in the *Primary Teacher's Handbook*.[44] As Patrick O'Farrell has written, 'It is time the Irish took their history *seriously* . . . the Irish take their history seriously as politics, but not as history.'[45]

Until recent years curiously few protests were raised against the subordination of history to patriotism, though in 1926 W. B. Yeats deplored the 'tendency to subordinate the child to the idea of the nation', while fourteen years later J. J. Auchmuty argued trenchantly that 'history should not be taught primarily for its moral value'. The history curriculum, in common with most educational issues except the Irish language and compulsory schooling, scarcely ever secured the attention of parliamentarians.[46]

The effectiveness of school history as a moral instrument depended not merely on the rhetoric of successive administrations but on the training and eagerness of teachers and the contents of text-books. Before partition virtually no training in Irish history was provided for national teachers, as perusal of the Queen's and King's scholarship papers confirms. The historical content of the nineteenth-century readers was deemed insufficient to require preparation and the only history question in the examination of 1848 simply asked, 'What were the principal events of the eighteenth century?' Virtually no Irish questions seem to have appeared until 1897, a year before the sanctioning of Joyce's text-books. This modicum of Irish content was further reduced in Northern Ireland, and by 1937 trainees at Stranmillis (though not St Mary's) were released from all study of both Irish and Ulster history. [47] In the Irish Free State, students at all levels were required to answer questions in Irish history: but these often constituted a desultory *mélange* of 'well-known saints', 'remarkable ruins', rebellions and examples of misrule. The inadequacy of training was compounded by bias in selection and formulation of topics. Whereas Queen's scholarship candidates in 1897 had been invited to 'give as many examples as you can of unconstitutional government under the protectorate of Cromwell', entrants to the Free State's preparatory colleges in 1927 were asked, 'What were the principal industries injured by English legislation during the eighteenth century?'[48]

Defective training made text-books all the more cardinal. All three administrations applied rigorous supervision of the choice of history manuals, prohibiting the use of unsanctioned histories and mobilizing the inspectorate in pursuit of them. The Commissioners took this task seriously, frequently demanding the excision of tendentious passages before sanctioning publication. The minutes of their meetings indicate that members of the board were accustomed to take text-books home for detailed and penetrating appraisal.[49] The resultant disputes within the board sometimes reached the press: after one bruising conflict in 1908, the defeated Bishop Foley sportingly defended the victorious Starkie against the 'absurd' accusation of 'being opposed to the teaching of Irish History or of anything else Irish. In private as well as at the Board you have been, for the past two years at all events, as strong an advocate of things Irish as any reasonable man could wish.'[50] The eruption of loyalist indignation after the Easter Rising induced the Commissioners to withdraw sanction from at least four history text-books and demand excisions from others.[51] Subsequently, the procedure for sanction was made more rigorous, and from June 1919 the only approved manuals of Irish history were by Joyce and Constantia Maxwell, whose *School History of Ireland* had achieved widespread unpopularity in 1914 by winning a prize from the Presbyterian Church. Publishers of some redundant text-books were, however, allowed to sell their surplus stock for the time being, and a handful of works on British history retained sanction.[52] Starkie had reluctantly accepted the political necessity of sanitizing the curriculum, despite his initial rejection of Mahaffy's 'very serious charge against the teachers', and his belief that 'the great majority of the books are satisfactory'.[53] By April 1918 his diary expressed a less sanguine view:

> Wyse tells me that children in the schools take their histories home and read them to their parents, with the result that their vague beliefs about English misrule are made definite: they generally know little about Cromwell, the Penal Laws, and confound their friends and their enemies in an amusing way: but now they know the facts as told in our miserable textbooks. There may be something in this.[54]

Next month Starkie was reading Mrs Concannon's *Makers of Irish History*, whose tone was 'somewhat hot', style 'interesting', balance 'excessively tilted towards St Columkille [*sic*]', and content likely to 'give colour to Sinn Féin principles . . . I can't understand how these publishers can think we would sanction such books.' [55] In June, Starkie reported a board discussion in which it was remarked that the Chief Secretary's wife 'had been trying to get a history for her children, but could find nothing that was not full of hatred of England. I said he should not take the opinions of a Newcastle Radical on Irish matters.'[56]

The conflict between political and educational priorities was illustrated by Starkie's response to a letter from Barry O'Brien in October 1918, protesting at the board's insistence that he excise references to 'the Destruction of the Irish Constitution' and the conduct of Tudor government. Starkie contested O'Brien's maxim, 'Tell the truth, and shame the devil,' observing primly that 'the unvarnished truth is not necessarily the full truth' and ascribing 'bungling not savagery' to the Elizabethans in Ireland. Moreover, regardless of his personal views:

> I rarely interfere in this very thorny question, and if I did I have only one vote. In defence of this Board, which is very liberal in its opinion, you should remember the circs. of 1916. We were violently attacked by the 'I.T.' Dr Mahaffy, the church of Ireland, and Presb. managers, Ulster papers, and Members of Parliament for 'teaching sedition in the schools'. Many deputations came before us with a rabble of histories in their hands, and proceeded to read all the obnoxious passages they could find: several out of your books figured in the list. The B. acted very well.[57]

Study of public response to the selection of history manuals suggests that these protests were multiplied rather than initiated in the wake of rebellion. The Presbyterian Church had long sought histories 'equally suitable for children of all religious denominations' before realizing its dream in Constantia Maxwell.[58] A Church of Ireland manager from Ballycastle, Co. Antrim, likewise complained that no history manual sanctioned by 1910 was fully acceptable, since even 'the most promising' readers conveyed 'the fallacy that Roman Catholicism was the old religion of this land, or that the Church of Ireland dates from Henry VIII'.[59] Mrs Stephen Gwynn's *Stories from Irish History* attracted particular Protestant vituperation, being denounced as 'very unsuitable' by the general synod's education report in 1914 and 'undisguisedly anti-English as well as anti-Protestant and anti-Unionist' by the *Daily Express*.[60] In humbler surroundings, the battle of the books had also been fought in the Enniskillen board of guardians in 1907. A motion to familiarize the workhouse children with P. W. Joyce, and thus 'Irish history, love of their country, and what their forefathers had suffered', was predictably defeated. One guardian proposed that Joyce be complemented by the anti-clerical tracts of Frank Hugh O'Donnell; while another suggested the still more rabid Michael J. F. McCarthy (whom he confused with Justin McCarthy, 'one of the cleverest of writers') as well as 'the Douay Testament, and so in this way they could have a good blend'. The motion faltered when it was pointed out that nobody in Enniskillen 'knew anything about it', and died when Joyce's protagonists failed to demonstrate that his 'history would be any good at all for training the children for any commercial position'.[61]

After the Easter Rising, as Starkie complained, public debate about the contents of text-books intensified. The Presbyterian education board stepped up its denunciation of sanctioned manuals that 'were fitted both directly and indirectly to foster a spirit of disloyalty'.[62] The Rev. William Corkey, one of its most bigoted spokesmen, published a colourful and detailed dissection of text-book treatment of 1798, which propagated 'the most dangerous political doctrine that every reform or benefit that Ireland has obtained in the past from England came as a reward of conspiracy and rebellion'. He concluded that Irish sedition was 'the result of a well-defined policy of the Church of Rome, carried out in the Christian Brothers' Schools and in many Roman Catholic National Schools as witnessed by the text-books used'.[63] More moderately phrased criticism emanated from the Church of Ireland, which appointed watchdogs to detect and eliminate 'false statements of facts in Irish Histories'.[64] Catholic teachers and managers responded by calumniating Constantia Maxwell, only to be themselves challenged to go further: 'Are they courageous enough to adopt readers which are banned by the present educational boards? . . . A combination of the managers, teachers, and people can do anything they like . . . This question of Irish educational books is probably the most important question of the day [a striking claim on 9 July 1921], for on the education given in Irish schools depends the future mentality of the Irish race. England knows this.'[65] A rare target of united opposition by Catholics and Protestants was the pamphlet *What is Patriotism?*, published by the board in June 1916 and written by Starkie's wife, May. This called for inculcation of the 'passionate love of one's country' and of 'a common morality', as recommended in Plato's *Republic*. Commissioner Starkie, once a passionate opponent of 'Socratic introspection' in education, now remarked that 'it strikes the Platonic note on which I am always insisting, but how can we make the teachers platonists?' Mrs Starkie had been cunning enough to avoid specification of the country to which patriotism was owed, juxtaposing celebration of 'the deeds of the Irish soldier fighting in every corner of the world from the seventeenth century down to the twentieth', with 'Mike

O'Leary's Homeric killing of Germans' and Conn's Hundred Fights.[66] Bishop O'Dwyer, unperplexed by these ambiguities, identified it as a 'recruiting pamphlet'; the Rev. William Corkey sang its praises; but the earl of Dunleath protested to the Chief Secretary that 'According to a pamphlet, recently issued by the Board of Education, "Patriotism" is to be taught as exclusively Irish Patriotism, and the Empire, the King and Great Britain are to be ignored and passed over in silence.'[67]

Thereafter the Commissioners were cautious in their pursuit of patriotism, though the immediate occasion of their abrupt dissolution by the provisional government in January 1922 was their inopportune decision to allow pupils to attend 'a cinema performance entitled "With Lord Allenby in Palestine"'.[68]

After partition, public interest in the selection of history manuals waned. In Northern Ireland the familiar choice of Joyce and Maxwell continued to encompass Irish history in the lists of approved books published in 1926 and 1932, though works by A. S. Green and Standish O'Grady were sanctioned as literary texts.[69] Bonaparte Wyse, a Catholic unionist deemed by Starkie to be 'as anti-clerical as Gibbon' and head of the northern Ministry of Education from 1927, also wanted 'a suitable book on the history of Ulster'. The outcome of his quest was Chart's *History of Northern Ireland* (a less emotive term than 'Ulster'), which was remarkable for its omission of all reference to 'recent controversies' and 'painful memories' and indeed all political events since the Union.[70] In the Irish Free State the new Department of Education was also loyal to Joyce and Maxwell, but a steady trickle of patriotic histories, including those banned after 1916, augmented the list of approved works. Many of these histories were familiar from the reading rooms of the Gaelic League, Sinn Féin and the Christian Brothers; though after 1933 Mitchel's works were reserved for study by teachers while the Brothers' readers were evidently considered too sophisticated for use in primary education.[71] Occasional Protestant grumbles were met by the toleration of Kingsmill Moore's *Irish History for Young Readers* (1914), and by the involvement after 1938 of the Church of Ireland in the selection of textbooks for Protestant schools.[72] The loudest complaints concerned Dora Casserley's *History of Ireland*, which received a prize from the general synod in 1938 but contained placatory judgments such as the comment that disestablishment 'has been in reality, a great blessing for those concerned'. Such concessions to popular sentiment drew from the bishop of Down and Dromore the remark that 'the whole work seems permeated with an objectionable outlook, taking a one-sided view of Irish history'.[73] It was safer for Protestants to war among themselves. Otherwise, dreariness rather than bias was the complaint most often voiced. As one inspector reported in the mid-1920s, most history text-books were 'insipid and colourless' by comparison with, say, Mitchel's *Jail Journal*.[74] This saving insipidity neutralized what might otherwise have seemed blatant and perhaps malign distortion of facts and explanation. This is not, however, an appropriate occasion for defining and classifying bias in primary school text-books.[75] My concern here is with the consequences rather than precise character of the bias.

The impact of history teaching is best chronicled in the reports of the inspectors of primary schools, a group unkindly described by Starkie as 'the lowest specimens of the human race – excepting of course the majority of men teachers'.[76] In fact many inspectors made thoughtful and detailed reports on the conduct of history, reports which were overwhelmingly negative under all three administrations.[77] Some had strong though divergent views on the political functions of history, ranging from enthusiasm for its power to repel the 'insidious attacks' of 'debasing literature', to fury 'at anything savouring of Irish patriotism'.[78] Starkie himself combined summer vacations with tours of inspection, once noting 'a flavour of Sinn Féinism', which he forgave after some good readings from *The Merchant of Venice*. He was sometimes surprised at the interest and vigour of history classes, though despairing when told 'that Sarsfield introduced the potato into Ireland'.[79] Analysis of seventy published reports for the period 1902-14 shows that only seven were wholly favourable, while forty-eight were entirely unfavourable. In descending frequency, the major defects mentioned by the inspectors were as follows: history a mere reading lesson (19), ignorance of teachers (18), inadequacy of text-books (13), lack of context for facts (12) and inadequate linkage with geography (10). Other complaints concerned lack of preparation by teachers, learning by rote, and neglect of important periods and sectors such as local history. A feeble improvement occurred after 1911, when only fifteen of the twenty-seven reports were wholly unfavourable. In a representative report, the inspector of the Enniskillen circuit observed in 1914 that history was 'a subject that teachers have considerable difficulty in making living'.[80] Entirely unfavourable reports were particularly common from Ulster, but there was no overall disparity between the assessments of Catholic and Protestant inspectors.[81]

No perceptible improvement was noted by inspectors in the Irish

Free State, many of whom were survivors of the old régime. Indeed the twenty-five published reports for 1925-30 were marginally less likely to be favourable than those of 1911-14. While teachers' ignorance remained a common lament, greater prominence was given to learning by rote and inadequate attention to local history. The Department's reports had a dispirited tone, as in the complaint that 'until the history of Ireland is properly taught in the schools the work of Gaelicization will be greatly hindered, since there will be no real incentive to urge the pupils to the use of Irish as a living speech'.[82] As an inspector for the south-eastern division reported in 1930, 'many teachers are not greatly interested in History, and, as a consequence, their teaching of it is dry, without life or power . . . It is surprising how little knowledge the senior pupils in many schools have of the history of our own times: one would imagine that they had never heard of Arthur Griffith, for example, or of Easter Week.'[83] Scattered reports for Northern Ireland, before the virtual disappearance of history from the smaller schools, were equally dismal: 'It is probable that there is no subject in the curriculum less well taught than History.'[84]

Historians of history teaching may take heart from the evidence of widespread indifference to the subject at primary level. The fears of Provost Mahaffy and Conor Cruise O'Brien were probably baseless. Shockingly low standards of instruction and class boredom saved most pupils from effective indoctrination within school hours. The would-be manipulators of the Irish school-child's mind left a hasty scrawl rather than indelible imprint on that *tabula rasa*. Teachers in higher-level education retained a fighting hope of correcting the warp.

Part Two

TEN

HISTORY AS A SCHOLARLY DISCIPLINE AND *MAGISTRA VITAE*

Ivan Berend

Is historiography a scientific discipline? For historians themselves this question remains fraught with difficulty. Since the composition of the first historical works in the ancient world, we have had to face doubts and challenges as to whether historiography is scientific at all. In Aristotle's *Poetics* we read that 'Poetry is something more scientific and serious than history because poetry tends to give general truth while history gives particular facts.'[1] According to Schopenhauer, while history is *knowledge*, it is by no means scientific, since the basic feature of science, the subordination of what has been learnt, is missing from it; 'Instead, history offers a mere juxtaposition of what has been learnt.' He confronts history with the 'genuine sciences', which elaborate comprehensive concepts and with their aid 'rule over the singular', while history conceives the singular as such.[2] Similarly, Oswald Spengler states: 'Nature offers itself to scientific analysis, for history a poetical inspiration is necessary.'[3] Many scholars share these views even today.

One could list at great length the related trends of thinkers from the seventeenth to the twentieth centuries, the neo-positivists, agnostics, etc., who have denied the existence of historical rules and asserted that at most only the regularities or constructions of human logic were discernible in and applicable to history. Even some of those who related the explanation of a phenomenon in history to the exploration of fundamental causes, with its deduction from some general law, considered, on the basis of the philosophy of Hume, causality and the 'law' to be a construction of human logic and not the objective reality of history. I refer in particular here to the intellectual current of our own century which flows from Max Weber to Karl Popper. Yet as a matter of fact, the identification of historical relationships with the logical constructions of the individual mind is nothing other than a negation of its scientific character. This remains the case even if some philosophers (like the neo-Kantians) accept the validity of the social sciences (including history), but distinguish them from natural sciences, by contrasting a 'science of laws' with a 'science of events' or a 'generalizing' science with an 'individualizing' science.[4]

Such a denial of the existence of objective historical rules necessarily dictates an approach restricted to the description of events, at most extending to a critical review of facts, or to the presentation of the direct causal relationships and an abstention from value judgments. Moreover, every effort which wishes to channel historiography into the narrow by-path of *factology* leads into the indirect negation of its scientific character even if it emphasizes the importance of scientific methods. To note only one twentieth-century advocate of this old view, let me quote Spengler's famous warning: 'not to praise, not to disapprove, but weigh up morphologically'.

The most distinguished modern representative of this highly restrictive approach to causal explanation and generalization is Karl Popper. In *The Open Society and its Enemies*, Popper formulated his position as follows: 'there can be no historical laws. Generalization belongs simply to a different line of interest sharply to be distinguished from that interest in specific events and their causal explanation which is the business of history.'[5] And almost a quarter of a century later, at the San Francisco international congress of historians in 1975, it was obvious that these views were still prevalent if in different forms and colours. A Dutch rapporteur on that occasion excluded value judgment from the scope of history and instead, in the Weberian manner, considered the comparison of values as well as a general humanistic commitment as the scientific methodological and moral basis of history. Several participants opposed even this moderate standpoint. 'History is not a judge to pass verdicts over the past, its task is to understand the past,' said a German contributor to the discussion. The view that historiography cannot be scientific in the true sense of the word has always existed and is still current.

Of course both historiography and the philosophy of history have often suggested alternative approaches. There have been those which did not seek to analyse the nature of scientific criteria, nor to examine whether it is possible in history to trace back individual phenomena to general rules. They considered that the real value of historiography lay in its capacity to *preserve* everything from the history of mankind which was good or bad, noble or bloody, to resist the human tendency to forget, and to order our past into a well-arranged museum, into which every new generation may enter to wonder and learn. This approach to historiography, too, is at least as old as written history itself. The often quoted words of Cicero offer its most succinct definition: history as witness of time and schoolmaster of life: *testis temporum, magistra vitae*.

Up to the eighteenth century such an attitude toward history remained remarkably influential. History, invariably understood as a collection of 'factual truths', of moral examples, was a treasury of worldly wisdom drawn from such classical authors as Plutarch, Cicero and Tacitus. The emergence of romantic historicism around the end of that century, however, effected an important change within this general approach which developed rapidly in the following decades. History now became a so-called nationalist science: it was not only and not even primarily general wisdom and morality, but rather the nation that gave contents and meaning to the 'secrets of olden times'. In the twentieth century irrational trends and movements used historical analogies, compiled at will. Opposing, progressive trends, however, walked into the same trap and used similar collections of counter-examples. The excellent contemporary observer, Marc Bloch, put it aptly: 'Among the ghosts which hover above our road personifying a mistaken concept of the past . . . I would give pride of place to false analogy.' Such approaches which 'incessantly search in the past for the principles governing the present and justifying the present' are still alive today.[6]

In what sense, then, can historiography be seen as a scientific discipline? In seeking to answer this question, I will start with another observation of Bloch's:

History . . . this newcomer in the field of rational knowledge, is also a science in its infancy. Or to explain more fully, having grown old in embryo as mere narrative, for long encumbered with legend, and for still longer preoccupied with only the most obvious events, it is still very young as a rational attempt at analysis. Now, at last, it struggles to penetrate beneath the mere surface of actions, rejecting not only the temptations of legend and rhetoric, but the still more dangerous modern poisons of routine learning and empiricism parading as common sense.[7]

Though it has existed since ancient times historiography remains very young as a scientific discipline. It reached this stage only in the last century when it was able, in the chaotic whirlpool of infinitely varied individual phenomena, of actions of individuals interwoven with subjective motives, to present the regularities, the determination and causal relationship of events and actions in such a way that the many kinds of single and random events should not get lost in the formation of the freedom, fate and experience of the individual and society.

In this process of history's development as a scientific discipline, principal credit must be attributed to Hegel, who was a pioneer in linking logic with history, and in searching for laws in historical development. From Hegel, historiography started on the road already travelled by the natural sciences, when the application of the logical concept of *regularities* (i.e. the idea that single events can be referred back to a general law) to historical actions provided a possibility for scientific methodology. This approach toward the discovery of social and historical laws, in contrast to the innumerable discrete intellectual experiments allowed by Popper and others, does not apply a logical construction to the explanation of historical processes from the outside, but attempts in contrast to discover the laws as they objectively manifest themselves from within those processes. No doubt, in the understanding of historical processes a huge role is played by the advances made in developing the scientific method and by the various solutions to causal explanations. In fact, even the application of the Popperian 'comprehensive law' as a logical scheme promotes the development of a link between historical description and explanation, for it suggests that seemingly individual explanations also rely on non-explicit generalizations. Thus even if the historian makes no effort to generalize, but tries merely to explain individual phenomena, he still sets out from some unspoken generalizations. Yet, even as they promoted a better interpretation of single phenomena, such methods could not in themselves lift history from its 'pre-scientific' state. They are unsuited for explaining general tendencies. However good an answer we find for single events, or individual acts, even the best explanations do not fit together into an explanation of the historical phenomenon.

Hegel called attention to the fact that behind the single and random event there looms an objective law:

in history an additional result is commonly produced by human actions beyond that which they aim at and obtain – that which they immediately recognise and desire. They gratify their own interest; but something farther is thereby accomplished, latent in the actions in question, though not present to their consciousness, and not included in their design.[8]

The same idea can be found in Engels's famous statement:

history is made in such a way that the final result always arises from conflicts between many individual wills, of which each in turn has been made what it is by a host of particular conditions of life. Thus there are innumerable intersecting forces, an infinite series of parallelograms of forces which give rise to one resultant – the historical event. This may again itself be viewed as the product of a power which works as a whole *unconsciously* and without volition. For what each individual wills is obstructed by everyone else, and what emerges is something that no one willed.[9]

The general law, asserting itself through chance, became recognizable through Marx's discovery of the socio-economic formation as a basic theoretical concept. On this basis he could trace back the phenomena of social structure and its development to the relations of production valid in individual historical epochs, that is, to the mode of acquiring the means of subsistence which serve as a basis of every kind of human coexistence. This analysis uncovered from the set of individual phenomena what was general, the repetitions and regularities. It should be added that, as against the efforts of Hegelian historicism, this was not done on the basis of common and eternal natural laws, which could hardly have amounted to more than trivial generalities.

Marx's theory allowed a transition from the mere description of historical phenomena to their scientific analysis: the relation of events and phenomena to the common features of great historical eras. It thus became possible to trace back the multitude of individual actions to those of groups of individuals determined by their role in the order of social relations, their living conditions and interests, that is, of classes. And it is at this general level that the particular, the individual, obtains a genuine meaning. The work of the historian does not stop, however, at generalizing abstraction. Just as the road to the disclosure of rules, of generalizations, can set out only from concrete historical material, so the diversity of real processes cannot be disclosed if he then does not return from the abstract to the concrete to create the historical synthesis in which the individual or particular can assume its place.

The Marxist concept of social formations, however, was frequently distorted in Marxist historical practice, where the richness of reality has frequently been squeezed into the Procrustean-bed of the general law, and the individual deprived of his genuine historical role. Too often, Marxist historiography has attributed absolute validity to the 'laws' instead of conceiving them as 'tendencies', and has viewed history crudely in terms of the social formations and their development, while neglecting to note that this concept is an abstraction relating to the whole of human society which was not intended to dictate a programme which every country necessarily followed in all its steps. Marxist historiography often fell into a vulgar form of linear historical development.

The same holds for determinism. A truly scholarly character could not, of course, be achieved without a 'strict' determinism. It is precisely on the basis of its determinism that Marx speaks about the capacity of scientific historiography to explain social phenomena 'with the exactness of the natural sciences'. But this is hardly the determinism which historians claiming to be Marxists frequently represent in their works in a simplified manner. The assertion of laws, the causal determinations cannot mean in scientific historiography the absolute determinism of Hobbes's or Spinoza's social theory, nor are they identical with the historical approach of Fichte, in which the accidental is only appearance and 'Everything that really exists, exists with absolute necessity, and that in a manner as it actually exists.'

The determinism of scientific historiography can arise only from the fact that the actions and choices of human beings are free but, at the same time, they are historically and causally determined, these constituting a unity. It is in this context that Marx's famous lines are frequently quoted, where he considers history to be such a drama in which men are not only actors but also authors. In this concept, freedom and necessity are not antitheses, but categories which transform into each other. 'History', says Marx, 'is nothing else but the sequence of individual generations, each of which exploits the materials, capital, forces of production bequeathed to it by all its predecessors; thus it continues the inherited activity under completely changed conditions on the one hand, while it modifies the old circumstances with quite different activities on the other hand.'[10]

Thus, historical development is realized through the activities of man, who is simultaneously determined and free. Similarly, the random, the individual is not an excluded 'appearance' either, in fact the general and regular breaks its way precisely through the entangled singularity of random events.

There are, however, epochs when society wonders at chance and is inclined to attribute events to its ferocious play. In 1916 the Irish historian J. B. Bury entitled his work on the role of chance in history *Cleopatra's Nose*; after World War II, Friedrich Meinecke interpreted the German catastrophe of the previous forty years by reducing it a series of unfortunate random events.[11] The dates are significant – 1916 in Bury's case, as he witnessed the collapse of his liberal dreams; and 1946 in the case of the aged Meinecke, who had lived through the bloody drama and destruction of his country. The sharp judgment of the great British historian E. H. Carr is justified: 'In a group or a nation which is riding in the trough, not on the crest, of historical events, theories that stress the role of chance or accident in history will be found to prevail.'[12] And let us not forget that in our days the revival of this general approach to history is again not an isolated phenomenon but also a symptom of alienation in the developed world.

Having accepted the dialectical unity of the regular and the random, of the general and the individual as one of the cornerstones of the scientific discipline, we may also add that the mode by which general rules are applied, the extent of determination, and the role of the accidental are not the same in different spheres of history, and may play different roles also within individual branches of historiography. We may agree that the highest degree of theoretical generalization can, in principle, be attained in economic history, while in the field of political and cultural history the play of the individual and the random is greater. Individual events, features, and the particular properties of persons necessarily distinguish these spheres of history from history characterized by less personal processes taking place on a massive scale.

Thus, history may be defined as the order of regular tendencies to be explained from the great disorder of individual phenomena and random events. It is the science of *man*, who, under the manifold pressures of determining forces, acts freely, suffers, falls, achieves recognitions and thus also becomes capable of changing his conditions. As the French historian Fustel de Coulanges once put it, 'History is not a collection of all kinds of events having occurred in the past, but the science of human societies.'[13]

It should be obvious, however, that the historical discipline becomes scientific not simply on the basis of its philosophical assumptions, but mainly through its methodology. The distinction between the general and the individual makes the task of *comparison* the fundamental methodological basis of scientific historiography. Only the recognized law, the particular compared to the general, provides a foundation for historical comparison. Simple analogy – which investigates what distinguishes one country from the other and what is common in the historical process of every country in itself – is insufficient. Comparison becomes scientific only when it also takes into account the facts of *change*. From this point of view Marc Bloch's definition is highly instructive: 'History', he writes, 'is the science of change and – in many respects – of differences.'[14] Difference and change are equally and simultaneously important, since without change – which is the substance of history – difference would at most amount to a matter of time; that is, it would collapse into the determinism expounded by Herder, who once declared that 'the difference between enlightened and backward, civilized and uncivilized nations, is not one of species but only one of degree'.[15] This acceptance of the complete identity of processes fails to take into account the kind of change which produces radically new circumstances and conditions for further change and which makes it impossible, as Heraclitus recognized, to step into the same river twice. The recognition of 'compassion' as a fundamental methodological principle does not in itself provide a solution to the problem of historical explanation. The comparative method frequently stumbles among categories of the national, regional and universal and its proper application still awaits full development.

The perception of regularities in historical processes has made it possible for the discipline of history to develop a scientific methodology of the analysis of long historical periods. And what new worlds and what new interrelations have been disclosed by the analytical concept of the *longue durée*! Although its progress has in practice been uneven, as it grapples with its own evidential and methodological problems, the concept of the *longue durée* has maintained its own compelling relevance in that it has led historians to contemplate the present and to ponder the role and the place of the present in history.

The present of course is not yet history. Every generation has drawn its lines of demarcation, where it closed off the process of scientific historical inquiry and ceded the ground to different researchers of the present. The epoch following World War II is not yet history! The three-quarters of a century after World War I can not yet be subjected to unbiased investigation. How frequently is this heard – even from distinguished scholars. This is an old prejudice, which Bloch challenged almost fifty years ago:

> there are many who would gladly repeat that since 1914, or since 1940, there has been no more history. Yet they would not agree very well in other respects as to the reasons for this ostracism. Some, who consider that the most recent events are unsuitable for all really objective research just because they are recent, wish only to spare Clio's chastity from the profanation of present controversy.[16]

This is the most obvious motive of seclusion from the present – and one which characterizes a considerable number of our own generation of historians in the same manner as it did several of our predecessors. They worry for the scholarly character of the discipline. I do not wish to underestimate the particular difficulties and traps of writing contemporary history. But what must be recognized is that present and past cannot be separated from each other, neither by the plea that 'I am not interested in the present, only in the past,' which is a familiar approach of many historians, nor by the claim that 'I am not engaged in the dead past, only in the present,' which is a frequent profession of non-historians. Present and past, however, are not simply interrelated processes, where the present is merely a point immediately becoming past at the momentary end of the line of the past. Present and past are mutual starting-points for understanding each other.

This concept has a double meaning, only one aspect of which emphasizes contemporary research. Its other, perhaps more important, aspect is the perception of the living present in the past. Invested with the inescapable knowledge of the present, the historian reaches back into the furthest past. It is this inextricable unity of past and present which allows the historian, even while disowning any claims to predict the future, to analyse and explicate historical tendencies of his times.

History, having become scientific, is now equipped to serve the basic Baconian scientific principle: 'We should not know for the sake of knowing, but in order to be able to act.' Or, in a different formulation: 'We have to be able to trace back every science to usefulness and action.' Bacon, of course, was referring to the natural sciences, and he considered history to be – in his time with justification – only an explanation serving cognition. Yet, having surpassed the old Aristotelian ideal of contemplative knowledge, which has inhibited history in the past, and having established the possibility that history is a scientific discipline, the question may now be asked to what extent can historical knowledge, like that of the social sciences, be aimed at action? Can the historian lay claim to social usefulness?

Contemporary social usefulness is a dangerous criterion to be employed by a researcher into the past. And the risks which it entails have frequently deterred historians from intervening in public affairs. Yet even down to our own times other scholars have been equally persuaded to seek out historical proofs of the value of the social and political goals which they considered just. The objection that such historically rooted arguments may also be much against the good of society is not in itself insuperable. For is this not a danger in every discipline? Can the social usefulness of physics, mathematics or chemistry be challenged by the atomic bomb, the remote-controlled missile or chemical weapons?

Admittedly the issue is more ambiguous in the case of historiography. The question arises as to what extent historians can remain intact from the effects of a given era, from the 'Weltanschauung' of some generation, and from the repeated historical revaluations which they have derived from their determined historical experience. Yet revaluation is not necessarily a pejorative term. The enrichment of our knowledge, methods and our historical experiences leads quite naturally to a revision of earlier views. New methods and new recognitions lead in every discipline to revaluations.

Still the question is not simple in the case of historiography, not only because historical revaluations are more frequent but because they are frequently non-scientific. Epochs following upon one another interpret the same historical material in different ways, even without any methodological enrichment. In times of dissatisfaction and change, gradualist reformers may become despised opportunists, while the same people are raised to exemplary status in the eyes of generations living in a period of consolidated evolution. The latter, that is, turn away from examples of revolutionary subversives – sometimes with reverence, but anyway with aversion, perhaps even with contempt. From this point of view it seems more appropriate to invert Cicero's famous statement and say: *Vita est magistra historiae*! Life is the schoolmaster of history!

If then every generation re-creates its picture of history, may a historian seriously aim at social usefulness? Should he not regard his task simply to disclose facts, to present causal interrelations and refrain from judgment, while leaving efforts at usefulness to other disciplines of the social sciences? Yet if historical research does not abandon the claim of being scientific, it cannot renounce social usefulness. What kind of usefulness?

Much could be said about the spiritual and moral usefulness of history. The usefulness of increasing knowledge, of enriching memory – be it that of the individual or of society – is self-evident. A similarly obvious use of history is that it is entertaining. Entertainment is a social gain not to be belittled. As Bloch observed:

even if history were judged incapable of other uses, its entertainment value would remain in its favor. Or, to be more exact (for everyone seeks his own pleasures), it is incontestable that it appears entertaining to a large number of men. As far back as I can remember, it has been for me a constant source of pleasure . . . Its role, both as the germ and, later, as the spur to action, has been and remains paramount. Simple liking precedes the yearning for knowledge . . . Let us guard against stripping our science of its share of poetry. Let us also beware of the inclination, which I have detected in some, to be ashamed of this poetic quality. It would be sheer folly to suppose that history, because it appeals strongly to the emotions, is less capable of satisfying the intellect.[17]

The claim to *scientific* usefulness means, of course, more than that, as Gunnar Myrdal has affirmed: the epoch expects collaboration in the solution of practical tasks. Medical science long ago produced therapy, and natural sciences technology, because such tasks had long ago been formulated for them:

None of the social sciences have gone as far as medicine, or the natural sciences . . . The integrated and planned society of today, and still more of tomorrow, will not only raise the demand for social scientists in engineering functions but will also make the social sciences much better founded upon empirical records of the social processes and will press for more intensive analysis of social relations.[18]

Myrdal was not writing here of history. He had in mind economics, sociology, perhaps social psychology and jurisprudence. But can the discipline of history join the investigation and solution of the practical problems of the present? The question had already been addressed decades ago by Bloch when he spoke about those scientists who 'reserve the examination' of the human present 'for branches of learning quite distinct from that which has the past for its object'. Such observers, he continues:

claim, for example, to understand the contemporary economic system on the basis of observations limited to a few decades. In a word, they consider the epoch in which we live as separated from its predecessors by contrasts so clear as to be self-explanatory. Such is also the instinctive attitude of a great many of the merely curious. The history of the remoter periods attracts them only as an innocuous intellectual luxury. On one hand, a small group of antiquarians taking a ghoulish delight in unwrapping the winding-sheets of the dead gods; on the other, sociologists, economists, and publicists, the only explorers of the living.[19]

Against this view the famous medievalist responded: 'Historical works have to become increasingly aware of their task . . . all of us have to examine our conscience in our professional workshops. Historical studies have to maintain the link with the present, the source of all life.'[20]

In citing Bloch, I have quietly assumed that the social usefulness of historiography is akin to medical therapy or science-based technology; I do so with certain reservations. But my reservations refer not to principle, but to the actual performance of our researches. For in spite of the imperfect character of our achievements and our knowledge, and of the frequency of our revaluations, there remain sufficient grounds for us to claim that we can still make progress on the road to the apprehension of our past and thus of our present, by the scholarly exploration and interpretation of history. History – the collective memory of society – is the means by which the social knowledge which is central in the decision-making process of our times is accumulated. Individual examples, cases when it can directly be demonstrated that having learnt from history we have acted more intelligently, are myriad. But in the present context let me refer to only a few – to the international handling of the present debt crisis, to the fact that, in spite of the grave indebtedness, the world has been capable of avoiding the grave mistakes of the early 1930s and thus the collapse of the international financial-monetary system. We have learnt the lessons of the Great Depression. I may refer also to the more resolute international stand taken against aggression which has not repeated the mistakes of 'appeasement' committed more than half a century ago. There can, however, be no doubt about the fact that an even greater multitude of examples and cases with the opposite sign could be listed. We still have much to learn.

On the whole, it can still be affirmed that a more conscious, more scholarly decision-making is evolving. Historiography, by its analysis of the historical processes reaching right into the present, has joined with the social sciences in providing foundations for the preparation of government policy, and – depending on the depth of and limits to their knowledge – they influence its implementation.

Historiography, together with the other social sciences, undertakes a part in the evaluation of social change and becomes itself a part in the complex process of cognition. Historiography *begins* to become 'magistra vitae' also in the scientific sense of the term.

ELEVEN

POLITE LETTERS AND CLIO'S FASHIONS

John Lukacs

It will be obvious to members of the Royal Irish Academy that the title of my discourse derives, in part, from my reading of the excellent bicentennial history of the academy.[1] 'Polite Literature' was one of the Sections of the Academy at its beginning. Indeed, its charter of incorporation defined the purpose of the Academy as being '[to promote] the study of science, polite literature and antiquities'.[2] Professor W. B. Stanford, in his valuable chapter devoted to the history of that Section, was elegantly apologetic about this. 'Polite', he wrote, 'obviously carried associations with a standard of elegance and refinement suitable for an Academy that was intended to be "a select society of gentlemen". But it would not be long before the era of dilettantism and amateurism in literary and linguistic scholarship would come into disrepute.'[3] To which I would now add that a similar, and perhaps analogous, development had occurred within not only literary but also historical scholarship. I further read that during the nineteenth century 'historical topics became commoner' in the Transactions and Proceedings of the Academy; and then, in 1901, the Academy changed the title of the Section from 'Polite Literature and Antiquities' to 'Archaeology, Linguistics and Literature'. As Stanford wrote, this showed a kind of demotion of 'literature to third place but still, rather curiously, subsuming history under either Literature or Archaeology, despite the pleas of Bury and others that it was essentially a science'.[4]

The purpose of this paper is to propose that there is no longer any reason to be apologetic about Polite Literature or, as I put it in my title, Polite Letters. I chose this title not because of a *captatio benevolentiae*, and not out of the wish to make some kind of sly or arch reference to a phrase sodden with antiquated charm. On the contrary: my argument is that near the end of the twentieth century that phrase may be more timely than Bury and others; that history is essentially a Science; that when, at the end of the eighteenth century, the gentlemen of the Royal Irish Academy inclined to consider Literature and History together they were not altogether wrong. What has happened, after two centuries, is that the relative hierarchy within their alliance has changed. It is not history that is a part of literature but it is literature that shows signs of becoming a part of history, in a newer and broader sense of that word, in the sense that history is more than a discipline, it is – or, more precisely, it has become – a form of thought.

Everything has its history, including history. A distinct historical consciousness – as distinct from historical existence, and then from historical thinking – may be said to have arisen only three or four hundred years ago, in western Europe and England. Consequently during the eighteenth century the appetite of all kinds of readers for all kinds of history rose. So, during the last three centuries we may discern the following large developments. In the eighteenth century history was seen as literature. In the nineteenth century, largely (though not exclusively) because of the solid achievements of German scholarship, history was seen as a science – a development that reached England and Ireland more slowly and more hesitantly than elsewhere (which is why at the end of that century Bury's insistence that history was a science was already outdated). We must consider, too, that the word 'science' in that century had a more spacious meaning than it has acquired since. It was somewhat akin to the German *Wissenschaft*, meaning both science and knowledge (the word 'scientist', in English, appears only in the second half of the nineteenth century). Thus during two centuries history advanced from literature to science.

But for the twentieth century we cannot make such a general statement. It seems, rather, that in our time we have witnessed two essentially conflicting and divergent tendencies. One still dominant tendency is to consider history as a social science. The other is to consider it as a form of thought.

The consideration of history as a social science has sprung from several sources. The main one of these has been the general reluctance of academic historians to relinquish the prestige that the scientific notion of history brought to their professions and thus to themselves. That was partly the result of the general acceptance by 1914 of the Ph. D. degree conferred upon historians throughout the world. It reflected a general belief (a belief that had not existed a century earlier) that the historian was but another scientific specialist, that is, a professionally accredited scientific student of records. That such a narrow concept of the historian has reduced him, in effect, to an archivist (as it reduces, too, the view of the past to merely that of the recorded, and not the remembered, past) has not been fully grasped. Gradually during this century a further, rather inadequate, variant of the older nineteenth-century concept of history as a science began to gain acceptance: the notion that, if history is not quite like a science it is surely a social science of a certain kind. I say 'inadequate', because most historians were reluctant to recognize the essential difference that men such as Dilthey had proposed as early as 1875, that is, the distinction between *Naturewissenschaften* and *Geisteswissenschaften*, issuing from the perception that man's knowledge of man is essentially different from his knowledge of other, less complex, organisms and matters. This is so not only because of the complexity of the human being but because, especially in the case of history, the observer and the observed belong to the same species, in consequence of which not only the subjects of historical knowledge but, indeed, the nature of that knowledge itself differs from the natural sciences. Throughout the twentieth century we may observe evidences of a lamentable confusion among many historians who will accept theoretical criticisms of historical determinism as if they were truisms; and yet they go on writing and teaching history as if history were in some way determined.

Another reason for the acceptance of history as a social science has been more creditable. One hundred years ago J. R. Seeley's simple diction that 'history is past politics and politics present history' was largely taken for granted. This was not very different from the standard nineteenth-century European view as expressed, for example, by Droysen, who said that 'the statesman is the historian in practice', or by Ranke, who saw history as concerned mainly with the life and the relations of states. Yet with the development of universal literacy and mass democracy it became evident that a restriction of historical study to politics resulted in too narrow a scope; that a history of governments and of their relations must consider the history of the governed; that the history of states must, on occasion, be broadened and deepened by contemplating the history of peoples, including the conditions of their everyday lives. The need to explore social, economic and cultural topics had already been recognized throughout Europe before the establishment of the famous *Annales* group at Paris on the eve of the First World War. But the work of the most prominent figures in that group, most notably Lucien Febvre and Marc Bloch, set a standard which continues to demand respect and emulation today. Yet for subsequent generations of social historians pursuit of what seems to be intellectually fashionable and professionally profitable has amounted to a temptation to which many scholars are, alas, not immune. The results are all around us today, ranging from the huge confections of Fernand Braudel to the often unreadable and sometimes even ludicrous publications of specialists. On the one hand we are faced with the boundless pretensions of someone like Braudel to the effect that what he had attempted, and achieved, is the *total* history of a place and of a period. On the other hand we confront a disintegration of the discipline of history, through its implicit disregard of the political thread that, no matter how roughly, had once bound and still binds together the history of nations. This disintegration has created not only specialized 'fields' such as black history and women's history – pursued, alas, by ambitious men and women who seem to be less interested in the history of their people within the academy. The verminous fads of quantification and psychohistory are only extreme examples of the social-scientific attitude, with its wrongheaded practice of thoughtless borrowing and adaptation not only of the methodology and the language of the natural sciences but of the questionable terminology of Freudian psychoanalysis. Thus *corruptio pessimi pessima*; but even for the *optimi* the acceptance of history as a social science has resulted in something that might appear as a more sophisticated and up-to-date way of dealing with history, whereas it is hardly more than a retrospective (and therefore hopelessly shortsighted) kind of sociology.

The alternative to this, I propose, is the recognition of history as a form of thought – indeed, as a dominant form of thought in the twentieth century, consequent to the evolution of our historical consciousness during the last three hundred years; to a gradual revolution of our minds that in the very long run may be more important – and more profound – than the discovery of the scientific method three hundred years ago. The phrase 'history as a form of thought' is essentially epistemological. It suggests an historical philosophy that is the very opposite of a philosophy of history. It recognizes the futility of attempts to define universal laws or patterns for the knowledgeability of history. It issues from the recognition of the historicity of knowledge and of language. Thus it may be said that implicit in the recognition of history as a form of thought lies the perception (i) that 'facts' of history are merely so-called, since they are neither hard, nor distinctly isolatable; (ii) that no fact exists by itself but that its meaning depends on its association with other facts; (iii) that facts are not separable from the words in which they are expressed; (iv) that the statement of every fact depends on its purpose; (v) that history is not only written but spoken and taught and remembered in words that are not those of a scientific terminology but of the common and everyday language; (vi) that words themselves are not merely the symbols of *things* but that they are symbols of *meaning* – that is, they themselves have been formed by history.

Now, unlike the social-scientific school, those who see history in this way do not coalesce into a school of thought. But they have their great forerunners, historians such as Tocqueville, Burckhardt, Huizinga, in whose published works, lectures and letters we find recognitions and elaborations of what I tried to sum up in the previous paragraph. Space does not allow for a detailed account of the pedigree of this alternative view of history. But I shall turn to Jakob Burckhardt briefly for two reasons. The first is the indisputable fact that he was the founder of what we may call cultural history, something that is truer than are any pretensions to 'total history', since what Burckhardt achieved was the historical representation of both the cultural forms and the modes of thinking of a certain place and time, often (though not always) expressed in its art. The second refers to a certain humility of purpose. 'I never dreamed of training scholars and disciples in the narrower sense', he wrote in a letter, 'but only wanted to make every member of the audience feel and know that everyone may and must appropriate those aspects of the past that appeal to him personally, and that there can be happiness in so doing.' And, 'Furthermore we must understand that when we try to immerse ourselves wholly in the reading of a classic, only *we alone* can find what is important *for us*. No reference work in the world with its quotes can replace that chemical bonding that mysteriously occurs when a phrase found by ourselves illuminates something in our mind, crystallizing itself into a real piece of spiritual property that is ours.' And again, 'We are unscientific [*unwissenschaftlich*] and have no particular method, at least not the one professed by others.'[5]

This conception, I once wrote, is something very different from amateurism as well as from subjectivism. For all his stoic contemplation of the world, Burckhardt maintained a high faith in the potentiality of the human spirit: 'The spearhead of all culture is a miracle of mind – namely, speech, whose source, independently of the particular people and the particular language, is in the soul; otherwise no deaf mute could be taught to speak and to understand speech. Such teaching is explicable only if there is in the soul an intimate and responsive urge to clothe thought in words.'[6] To which I should only add: 'to *complete* thought in words', for speech is not only the clothing but also the completion of thought. Thus when speaking about cultural history, we cannot avoid the relationship of history to language. And there are few places in the world such as Ireland where the consideration of that relationship is more appropriate.

It was during my last visit to Ireland that I found F. S. L. Lyons's important and thoughtful book, *Culture and Anarchy in Ireland, 1890-1919*. Lyons's thesis that – contrary to what Matthew Arnold had set forth – culture might be not a unifying but a destructive force, leading to anarchy; that political problems may be the results of cultural problems; that in Ireland, surely since 1916, there was a failure 'to find political solutions for problems which in reality are much more complex', because these problems are cultural, in the broadest sense of the word. Now allow this foreigner to essay a few comments on this important thesis.[7]

What Professor Lyons wrote is applicable not only to Ireland but to most of the world. What he calls 'culture' is something that I might prefer to describe as 'national characteristics' or 'national tendencies', though I am aware that the two things are not quite the same. To put it in simpler and rougher terms: contrary to the lucubration of Marxists and all kinds of social scientists, it is painfully evident that the main historical and political force in this world, even now, has little to do with economics. It is nationalism; and nationalism, a sense of nationality, national characteristics, national consciousness, are cultural and not material factors.

Our problems lie with a definition of 'culture'. I think that Matthew Arnold thought of culture and employed the term in a more narrow and aesthetic sense than we are wont to do. This is what T. S. Eliot implied when he found a certain 'thinness' in Arnold's essay.[8] Lyons duly echoed this: yet I think that he was wrong when he continued that there was 'a prelapsarian innocence' in what Arnold wrote in the 1860s, because at that time 'the social sciences were still in their infancy. There were no social anthropologists or social psychologists to compel him to explain himself more intelligibly.'[9] I think that Lyons, who was a first-class historian and not an academic votary of social science, gave here too much credit to the latter. In my opinion, the shortcoming of Arnold's old-fashioned essay consists in an unwitting philistinism of his own. He thought too much about art and aesthetics, and not enough about language and truth. (It is almost like his American confrère Emerson, who said that 'the corruption of man is followed by the corruption of language', whereas it is arguable that the reverse sequence is true.) To me it seems that while one side – and a very important side – of Lyons's thesis is correct, there is another side, of which he was widely aware but the importance of which he saw differently from this foreign observer: this is the tremendous gain to Ireland (and to Ireland's prestige in the world) that has resulted from the impact of Irish genius on literature in the English language.

Professor Lyons says somewhere that with the spreading of English and the shrinking of Gaelic during the nineteenth century 'the marketplace' was bound to triumph over a remnant in the folk-museum. Yet when Daniel O'Connell admitted that he did not mind the gradual disappearance of Gaelic – 'I am sufficiently utilitarian not to regret its gradual passing'[10] – this was, I would suggest, a utilitarianism entirely different from the contemporary utilitarianism on the other side of the Irish Sea, that of poor Cobden, who wrote around the same time that he 'advocated nothing but what is agreeable to the highest behests of Christianity – to buy in the cheapest market and to sell in the dearest'.[11] To my mind, Professor Lyons's 'marketplace' was not the *mot juste*. The source and driving force of that high mastery of the English language by Irish writers and thinkers and poets has been not utility but attraction, not calculation but affection, the kind of often unconscious affection that a master has not only for his tool but for the scope and purpose of his work. To paraphrase Yeats: how can we tell the painting from the paint?

I should now like briefly to refer to my native country, Hungary, because of the appositeness of a certain chapter of its history to that of Ireland. Between 1867 and 1914 (it is uncanny how the period from Butt to Redmond in Ireland corresponds to the very same years of Hungarian history, from Deák to Tisza) many leading minds in Ireland (especially Griffith) saw in the home rule that had been secured by Hungary from Austria a reasonable and propitious model for Ireland. We also know, in retrospect, that many of these ideas proved to be illusory and outdated. Yet on a cultural –

and not merely political – level (and in terms of a *longue durée* much more meaningful than those enunciated by Braudel) some things happened that proved immensely beneficial in the long run. I have in mind not only the sudden and extraordinary flourishing of literature and of the arts around the turn of the century, in Ireland as well as in Hungary, a flourishing that was not overcast by the pale neuroticism so evident in other cultural capitals of Europe at that time (most notably in Vienna and even in the London of the Yellow Book Nineties). I am thinking of a development that has been insufficiently recognized in Hungary even now. This was the extraordinary assimilation of German-speaking people in Hungary into Hungarian culture. Extraordinary, because, with hardly any exceptions, this was the single such instance in central and eastern Europe at the time. For the German minorities before, say, 1865 their assimilation to what they saw as inferior and peasant-like people was unthinkable and – in more than one sense of the word – unspeakable. And yet in Hungary it did happen: less because of political pressures than because of the Germans' recognition of the increasingly obvious qualities and merits of the native culture of the land where they lived. What I see here is a similarity – though not a parallel – between that Hungarian development and the identification of the Anglo-Irish with Ireland. And this is a process which would not have occurred if, in the early twentieth century, the main demotic language of Ireland had not been English.

It is true, as Professor Lyons wrote, that the tragedy of the Anglo-Irish 'was that, hesitating as they did between two worlds, they could never be fully accepted by either. To the English they came increasingly to seem an anachronism, to the Irish they remain an excrescence.'[11] I am not happy with that word 'excrescence'. Or perhaps I am but not the pejorative sense of it; because excrescence means an outgrowth, an organic function; and I happen to believe that much of the Anglo-Irish and also the Irish-English literature had a function more alive, and more enduring, than the bloodless appearances of Bloomsbury on the once-robust tree of English letters. In this respect I am thinking not only of world-wide celebrated writers of Irish origin such as Joyce or Shaw but of representations such as *The Real Charlotte*, that small masterpiece which not only all lovers of English prose but historians – and not merely historians of the Anglo-Irish – ignore only to their loss. And I think I know that the mastery of that prose is inseparable from the deep-seated Irish loyalties of someone like Edith Somerville, who, born in the Ionian Islands, remained an Irish patriot through the most terrible and tragic years of the Troubles, probably aware of the condition of which Horace once wrote that 'patriae quis exsul se quoque fugit', that an exile flees not only his country but himself. Professor Lyons himself wrote about 'the man or woman in whom love of place transcended divisions based on origins, religion or politics'.[12]

'Love of place' – a phrase and a reality that prompts me toward another, more recent, definition of culture: the celebrated one by Lord Snow.[13] His thesis of the 'Two Cultures' is alarmingly simple. There is a humanistic culture and a scientific one, and the solution is obvious: the humanists should know the second law of thermodynamics and the scientists the *Areopagitica*. That such achievements may result in an aviary of stuffed owls should be obvious. The owl of Minerva, the Greeks told us, flies only at dusk; but Snow's owls will not fly. More important, however, if there are two cultures in our world the division between them is not vertical but horizontal. For the first time in the history of mankind there *is* a global, and therefore international, culture; a culture whose evident examples are airports that all over the world are alike; a culture whose most evident expression is a computerized and bureaucratic business language, a pseudo-scientific jargon artificially glued on something that resembles Anglo-American. Yet next to or, rather, beneath this international language there are the national languages and cultures that are seldom translated and translatable, reflecting not only how people of different nations speak but also how they live: not in their offices, not at their computers, not from nine to five but after five, within their families and in their homes. In this respect we may discern that, as this century proceeds, all great literature, prose as well as poetry, becomes more and more deeply national. There is no such thing as an international poem; and if there is such a thing as an international poet, he ought to be greeted – and kept – inside the waiting-lounges of airports where he truly belongs.

But transcending this appearance of the increasing presence of two cultures in our world, I would suggest that there may be in reality only one culture. The evolution of consciousness, especially in the western world, is now such that every man and woman among us is a walking cultural historian. Or, in other terms: all of us are historians by nature, while we are scientists only by choice. We must admit that history is *not* a science and can never be one: because its very unpredictability issues from the complexity of human nature, whereby the mechanical causality on which all technology and

Newtonian physics depend does not apply to the history of human beings. Thus history cannot be studied scientifically – while (and this is what I mean by history being a form of thought) science can be studied historically. While history is not part of science, it is science that is part of history: because first came nature, then came man, and only then came the science of nature. It is exhilarating, at least to me, to know that this commonsense truth has been confirmed by the recognitions of the greatest physicist of the twentieth century, Werner Heisenberg, who not only stated the fundamental condition of indeterminacy and uncertainty within the existence of the smallest particles of matter, but who also recognized the impossibility of separating the observer from the matter observed – whereby the epistemological recognition of man's own limitations ensues. The true scientific method can no longer assume that it deals with objects or subjects wholly apart from ourselves. On the contrary: it must take into account the process and the purpose of the observation itself – together with the inevitable limitations and suggestions of the human mind and of language. That this provides an escape from Cartesian dualism to a new, chastened, monistic view of the universe has been my conviction for a long time.

In conclusion, I now return to the relationship of polite letters and history. On the one hand we are in the presence of a profound crisis in the study of history that is only partially due to the narrow-minded attraction of many of its practitioners toward something like social science. Another element of the crisis is the inflation of materials, including records, with which the modern historian must deal. In the past the historian was plagued by the incomplete survival of records. When dealing with the history of the last hundred years the problem of the historian has become the very opposite. An overwhelming mass of material threatens to suffocate him. The existence of this new condition calls for a drastic revision of the canons of historical research and scholarship (and of the training of future historians too). That this has not yet happened is a sorry reflection on the professional historians' guild. On the other hand, the fact that we are in the presence of a growing appetite for history, on the part of many people who in the past were hardly interested in it, is a factor of vital importance which few historians have recognized. The evidences of this burgeoning interest in history are so protean that even a superficial sketching of them would require a substantial lecture of its own. Of course appetites can be badly fed, and an interest in history, indeed, the knowledge of history, can be damnably misused. We have had enough evidence of that during the last two hundred years. But that appetite is there: and its very existence proves, at least to me, the continuing evolution of historical consciousness.

Two centuries ago it was historical consciousness and an interest in history that brought about the historical novel. But I think that we must go further than that – especially in this discourse dealing with the relationship of letters with history (or with history as a form of thought). My point is that every novel is a historical novel; and that the appearance of the novel, as a new literary form, was – like professional history – part and parcel of the same development. For a long time the novel was seen as a new prosaic form of the epic. Yet the novel and the epic, as Ortega y Gasset wrote in 1914, 'are precisely poles apart. The epic speaks to us about a world which was and is no longer, of a mythical age whose antiquity is not a past in the same sense as any remote historical time. The epic past is not *our* past. Our past is thinkable as having been the present once, but the epic past eludes identification with any possible present . . .'.[13] It is not a remembered past (history is that) but an *ideal* past.

Consider how, coming out of history, the novel grew with history. Consider, for example, not Walter Scott but the preface with which his contemporary Jane Austen began *Northanger Abbey* in 1816:

> This little work was finished in 1803, and intended for immediate publication. It was disposed of to a bookseller, it was even advertised, and why the business proceeded no further, the author has never been able to learn . . . But with this, neither the author nor the public have any other concern than as some observation is necessary upon parts of the work which thirteen years have made comparatively obsolete. The public are entreated to bear in mind that thirteen years have passed since it was finished, many more since it was begun, and that during that period, places, manners, books and opinions have undergone considerable changes.

Unnecessary to press the point: Jane Austen's concern was decidedly, evidently historical. Now consider what Thomas Hardy wrote eighty years later:

> Conscientious fiction alone it is which can excite a reflecting and abiding interest in the minds of thoughtful readers of mature age, who are weary of puerile inventions and famishing for accuracy; who consider that in representations of the world, the passions ought to be proportioned as in the world itself. This is the interest which was excited in the minds of the Athenians by their immortal tragedies, and in the minds of Londoners at the first performances of the finer plays of three hundred years ago . . .[14]

Another eighty years later it is my conviction that *conscientious history* has come to replace the desideratum which Hardy stated as *conscientious fiction*. It is history which can excite a reflecting and abiding interest in the minds of thoughtful readers of mature age, who are weary (and how weary we are!) of puerile inventions and famishing for truth.

I say 'truth' because I shall venture to go further than Thomas Hardy. In the first place I claim to detect the gradual absorption of the novel (indeed, of perhaps all polite letters) by history, not at all in the form of the historical novel but through something else, indeed, by its opposite. In the second place I venture to see in conscientious history as well as in what Hardy called conscientious fiction more than the far from ignoble attempts to present a mirror of real life; I see in their purpose something not very different from what had once impelled Thucydides to write his first history: the purpose of reducing untruth.

The reduction of untruth cannot be served by an inadequately retrospective and abstract sociologization, no matter how profitable that may be within the airless circles of professional historians straining to impress and write only for professional historians. I shall paraphrase Yeats for the last time: 'Out of our colleges we have come/Small minds, stuffy rooms/Small hatreds, little art.' To which I add Wedgwood's polite little formulation: 'History is an art – like all the other sciences' – because memory is an art, too: truly the mother of all the arts.

This was first delivered as a Royal Irish Academy Discourse on 8 June 1989.

TWELVE

A COMMENTARY ON JOHN LUKACS'S 'POLITE LETTERS'

Aidan Clarke

Historians as a species are not ordinarily much given to reflection and introspection. The widespread currency of Professor Hexter's characterization of the historian's craft, as simply 'doing history', is a witness to a sort of impatient unwillingness to turn aside from the activity itself to thinking about it in the abstract. When historians have turned aside in recent years, it has been most usually to explain rather wearily, even bad-temperedly, what it is that they actually do. Goaded by the expression of philosophical doubts about the validity of the discipline, they have responded by stressing the nature of the evidence they use and the validity of the proof it allows. What historians do, it is insisted, is two things which are quite distinct from one another, and equally prosaic: they examine the evidence of the past, and they write up their results. Most practising historians, I believe, use that dichotomy to resolve in a down-to-earth way the traditional controversy as to whether they are engaged in a science or an art. They take it for granted that when they do their research, they behave as they imagine that scientists behave, *mutatis mutandis*: that is, they scrupulously investigate all the records and seek to establish conclusions that are faithful to the evidence. Most, I believe, would also accept that when they shape their material for presentation they engage in something that approximates to art – in a process that is creative within certain well-understood limits. The most important of these is that the finished product, however polished and felicitously written, remains faithful to the evidence; that the truth as they have found it is never sacrificed, even for the sake of a well-turned phrase, let alone for more ignoble reasons.

Members of this Academy, no doubt, will be quicker than most to observe that the mere maintenance of a scrupulous respect for the evidence involves a rather untutored notion of what scientific method actually entails. But this use of the term has less to do with ignorance than with the disciplinary practice of using language in an everyday manner. Historians refer to scientific method colloquially, to convey a similarity of intent rather than to assert an identity of procedure. Nevertheless, there is a sense in which the test of repeatable results can be met in the reconstruction of past events. Some historical facts are objectively verifiable. Nobody who examines the relevant evidence can doubt that on 24 May 1574 William Talbot of Malahide made his will, leaving a tablecloth valued at £5 to his servant, James Fitzgerald. Though the observer and the observed are of the same species, and though each observer brings his own subjectivity to the inspection of the record, the evidence is unaffected by either consideration. There is, that is to say, a fundamental evidential level at which the Heisenberg principle does not apply and methodological misgivings are out of place. This is, of course, the level inhabited by a still extant subspecies of purveyors of raw information, known as chroniclers. It is also the level at which most historians spend much of their time and at which most monographs originate. And it is, most significantly, the level at which history and the past itself actually meet one another.

The distinction between the two, which is so habitually blurred in ordinary speech, is not as simple as it can be made to appear. Simplistically defined, the past is what actually happened; historical research is the attempt to find out what that was by studying the evidence; the substance of history as a body of knowledge is what has been thus discovered; the writing of history is the presentation of that knowledge in an orderly manner. Of necessity, therefore, history is confined to the knowable past, to that part of the past for which evidence is available. It must follow that historical knowledge is not merely partial but, in important respects, fortuitous and random in kind. John Milton said it best, when he argued that not enough was known about the Church Fathers or what they had written to warrant treating what had survived of their work as authoritative: 'Whatsoever either time or the heedless hand of blind chance has drawn down to this present, in her huge drag-net, whether fish or seaweed, shells or shrubs, unpickt, unchosen, those are the Fathers,' he wrote. Those too are the materials from which history is constructed, and Milton's metaphorical warning is an important one. It sets the limits within which historians must go to work and the operational problems that they must solve in attempting to reconstruct what happened in the past. It also supplies a significant variable in approaches to history, for the problem that all historians are confronted with is that of making up deficiencies in what they know, and the deficiencies may be of very different kinds. Their nature depends upon what the historian is trying to do, but the general rule is simply stated: the further the historian moves away from his sources, the more problematic his activities become.

Those who, prompted by Professor Lukacs, return to *Northanger Abbey* and read beyond the preface will encounter Catherine Morland's reflections on history:

> I read it a little as a duty; but it tells me nothing that does not either vex or weary me. The quarrels of popes and kings, with wars or pestilences, on every page; the men all so good for nothing, and hardly any women at all, it is very tiresome; and yet I often think it odd that it should be so dull, for a great part of it must be invention . . . and invention is what delights me in other books.

Invention may seem too strong a word but, as Professor Lukacs reminds us, the historian is more than a chronicler. It is a professional axiom that the facts of history are meaningless unless and until they are connected with each other, and the essence of the historical activity is the making of those connections. What that involves is most usually thought of as the construction of a narrative, a diachronic account of its subject which not only chronicles the sequence of events but shows how one thing led to another. The sophistication of the demonstration may vary, from simple linear consecution to the consideration of the interactions of multiple sets of facts; the approach may range from the wholly descriptive to the entirely analytical; and the connections established need not be causative in kind. The nub of the matter is that the historian is concerned with using the evidence to make the past intelligible. What that implies is that somewhere between the process of enquiry and the process of composition there is a third thing that historians do, which is to evaluate and interrelate the evidence.

To some amateur historians, history consists only of items of information, consequential or otherwise. They practise a discrete form of total history, the object of which is to find out everything that can be recovered about the abbey of Mellifont, or the battle of Chirbury, or whatever. To most people, history is information about the past; but the stock conversational disclaimer with which most professional historians will be all too familiar – 'I wasn't any good at history because I couldn't remember dates' – is misleading. Most people do not readily distinguish between information and opinion, still less between facts and statements about them: that King John died of eating a surfeit of lamfreys is taken to be a statement of the same order as the judgmental banality that Elizabeth I was a good queen or the conclusion that George III set about regaining political control. Deluded as this may be, there is nonetheless a sense in which the man on the Clapham omnibus is closer to the professional historian than is his amateur colleague. Both take it for granted that history consists of more than the aggregate of past events; both regard history as including what we think about what happened in the past. When we distinguish the historian from the chronicler, or the professional from the amateur, in terms of a concern with the connections between events rather than with the events themselves we are allowing language to blur the issue. What we are actually referring to is explanation. In reconstructing aspects of the past, the historian is seeking to establish not merely what happened but how and why it happened. As a discipline, the concern is with understanding as well as with information. Unfortunately, historians refer slackly to what they do, so that the generic term 'historical knowledge' is used to include what is thought about what is known as well as the basic data which can be objectively verified. The extent of the misunderstandings to which this gives rise is neatly illustrated by the widespread assumption, at least in Ireland, that 'revisionism' is ideologically purposive. This is simultaneously sustained both by the crude belief that what is known about the past is unalterably true and by the sophisticated fallacy that everything about the past is a matter of opinion.

Both forms of confusion are cautionary, and in acknowledging that history deals in more than facts we should be careful not to overstate the case. The connections between events are not simply a matter of judgment. Some of them, indeed, are so self-evident and so long acknowledged that they come to us ready-made and help to confuse the common perception of the nature of historical facts. That civil war broke out in the United States in 1861 is as incontrovertible a fact as the terms of William Talbot's will, but it is also a different order of fact, for it is a disguised generalization, a fact made up of innumerable other facts. Historians use this kind of composite factual statement all the time, and it is not perhaps too much to say that most of what a good many people know about the past consists of propositions of this kind, which, of their nature, are both synthetic and constructive. By that I mean that we neither know, nor can know, all the lesser contributory facts of which they are composed, but we know some of them, can infer many more, and make do without the others. The certainty that civil war broke out in 1861 is not weakened by the uncertainty as to where and by whom the first shot was fired. It is not the case, therefore, that no connections between events are demonstrable; it is the case that historians often conveniently collapse these connections into a summary statement that subsumes them. It is also the case that such statements incorporate the unknown as well as the known. These are not fixed categories, of course: fresh evidence may come to hand to elucidate aspects of the outbreak of the Civil War of which nothing was formerly known. But the process of clarification is a quite separate one: the additional information does not affect the composite fact any more than an enlarged knowledge of molecular structure changes the nature of an apple. For this reason, it is perfectly possible for an active scholar to spend his life working within the confines of a composite fact without affecting its character in the slightest degree.

It seems unlikely that Miss Morland was in the habit of reading the equivalent of research monographs on the outbreak of the American Civil War, and internal evidence suggests that what she did read was David Hume and Dr Robertson. These are very different things, and we perhaps need a more sophisticated terminology to distinguish between 'doing history' and writing about the past. Those who 'do history' are governed in what they may achieve by the nature of the evidence: the authors concerned with the broader sweep are governed in addition both by their unfamiliarity with all of the evidence and by the technical difficulty that many of the connections they need to make are between composite facts. The changing fashions that Professor Lukacs has charted have affected both kinds of historian, of course, but they have much more to do with the difficulties of generalizing historians than with those practitioners who confine themselves to themes where the evidence can be mastered. In a sense, those fashions amount to favouring different ways of making up the deficiencies in the evidence. In Catherine Morland's day, the making-up was literal: words were put in the mouths of the characters in the historical story and it was precisely the poverty of those words that she found so unenchanting and that prompted Voltaire's cynical reflection that history 'is the narrative of events that are supposed to have happened'. Since then, the pendulum has swung: first to a resolution to remain faithful to the evidence, but to find more of it and use it more thoroughly; then to impatience, and it has been to a large extent the determination to extend the limits imposed by the evidence that has been the attraction of approaching history as if it were one of the social sciences.

The proponents of the total history that Professor Lukacs execrates do not hold that everything that ever happened can be known, which would be absurd, but rather that everything that is known can be satisfactorily explained according to synoptic theories that can account also for what is not known, and take their place as a new order of composite fact. That suggests that there must be a final point at which discussion ceases because the problematic has been eliminated. The process of historical enquiry need not cease at that point; the search for fresh evidence may continue, but its evaluation becomes a matter of applying the general formula to each specific case, and the traditional methodology is inverted. The historian becomes a fully-fledged social scientist by dint of proceeding from the general to the particular and deconstructing its particularity. The effect is to go against the grain of the subject as it is commonly understood.

With Professor Lukacs, I believe that the *Annales* school, and Braudel in particular, set themselves an impossible task in writing 'total history', but I suspect that in doing so they probably did no more than reduce to absurdity the pretensions of all of us who engage large themes. I do not know what the compass of a single human mind can span, or how to measure it except in terms of the capacity to master the evidence. The history of a country, or of a century, may be just as elusive an objective as total history. Indeed, the definitive history of anything is commonly thought to be unattainable: whatever their private hopes, the realistic ambition of ordinary journeymen historians extends no further than to write an interim report on their theme. That is not a matter of philosophical doubt, induced by the disabling conviction that what is subjective must necessarily be ephemeral also. It is a matter of recognizing that fresh evidence may come to light, and that the best that can be hoped for is that it will prove confirmatory rather than subversive. The history of the writing of history is a humbling study, and not the least of the valuable ingredients of this evening's discourse is its challenge to historians to recognize that the ubiquity of history, its universal relevance, entitles them to set a correspondingly higher value upon themselves.

Within that context, however, it seems a little odd of Professor Lukacs to acknowledge that everything has its history, to argue that the purpose of historical knowledge is human understanding, and to chart an evolution of historical consciousness of which an important expression is a public appetite for history, while at the same time dismissing certain historical concerns as senseless. One may regret the fragmentation of history and the absence of a unifying theme, but in doing so one is in danger of diminishing the value of the cultivation of the historical approach by making it incapable of functioning. The totality of what is known about the past is, for all practical purposes, an abstract concept since no single person is capable of mastering it, so that when one regrets the fragmentation of history, one regrets the nature of history. When history is offered as a means of advancing human understanding it should not be peddled as an undifferentiated panacea, but rather as an infinitely adaptable tool, capable of tackling the whole variety of different things that different people wish to understand. It would perhaps be intellectually satisfying if the public appetite for history could be fed in a structured way, but what is important is not that history in itself should be consumed as a unified whole but that it should be sampled as an approach which helps to unify the understanding of any of the separate ingredients of which it is composed. That is to say, for instance, that if an interest in cooking encourages an interest in the evolution of diet, what is paramount is the realization that understanding may be enlarged by investigating and explaining how things became what they are. To insist that history employed in that way must have a political thread that binds together the history of nations, or any other all-embracing principle of unity, is to fall into two errors.

The first error is to make an essentially false distinction between history as an intellectual or cultural activity and history as a subject of popular interest. Ideally, no doubt, curiosity about the past ought to be comprehensive, even if the span of a human life is insufficient to satisfy the desire to know vicariously the whole range of human experience: in practice, a soldier may become fascinated by the battles of the English Civil War, a bricklayer by freemasonry, a black American by slavery, or a bank clerk by any of these. Though Trevelyan is out of fashion now, we should not forget his enduring evocation of that poetry of the past which has to do with the peculiar resonances created by the sense of sharing the same space as former generations. Almost anyone may have at least a transient historical interest stimulated by place. The triggers of curiosity are deep and complex and it is all the more difficult to see why we should deny legitimacy to the fragmented interests that arise from accidental conjunctions, when the truth is that those of us who produce history rather than consume it have our own specific areas of interest and competence which, in many instances, are equally adventitious in their origins. Some of us actually investigate and write about the history of freemasons, Civil War battles and slavery. That our interest is professional rather than amateur is beside the point. We may sometimes wonder in what way the psychological puzzle of what draws particular historians to particular subjects affects the way in which they deal with them, but we rarely feel guilty about our failure to devote ourselves to themes of greater significance than the ones that we have chosen, and we leave it to others to fit our work into a larger frame than the one that we have found necessary.

The second error involved in demanding that popular historical consciousness should be schematic is to suppose that the entire body of historical knowledge is capable of integration. Common sense suggests that to note that everything has its own history is effectively to deny the possibility of any universal integration. There may be a rarefied level at which it is possible to relate the history of flags in Ireland to the introduction of the knife and fork in Mexico, but the impression that most people derive from historical study is of the variety of human experience and the particularity of events. If that enlarges understanding by encouraging an attitude of tolerant relativism, it certainly qualifies for inclusion in the Sellar and Yeatman category of good things. As a unifying principle, however, it qualifies at best as a paradox. Although the desire to order knowledge is a constructive one, simple taxonomical principles apply in history as elsewhere: ordering is a matter of sorting things into cognate areas and establishing the relationships between them, if there are any. And when the fish and the shells and the seaweed and the shrubs have been identified, classified and cross-referenced, we remain ignorant of everything that has escaped the huge drag-net of blind chance and conscious that a new trawl may yield a missing link, or disprove an established one. In history, every verdict is unsafe.

If it is true that the growth of historical consciousness is creating a demand which is not being met and an opportunity which is not being taken, part of the reason no doubt lies in the fact that the product does not fit the expectation. The historian is not free of fault in this, but neither is the historian a free agent, and the gulf between the researcher and the lay reader can perhaps be bridged by working with the grain that Professor Lukacs describes and presenting history, not as a body of inert knowledge or a repository of meaningful messages about the human condition, but as a useful and interesting approach to pretty well anything. In supporting his call to historians to rally to history's cause, I would add only the plea that in doing so they should not make unreal claims, that they should admit that history, so far as it aspires to understanding as well as to knowledge, is a speculative discipline, that its motive force is curiosity about the past, but that it refracts the past in multiple and imperfect ways. If it did not, it would indeed be dull.

NOTES

INTRODUCTION

1. Tom Dunne (ed.), *The Writer as Witness: Literature as Historical Evidence* (Cork 1987).
2. Studies like Mandelbaum's *The Problem of Historical Knowledge* (New York 1938), Walsh's *An Introduction to the Philosophy of History* (London 1967) and Danto's *Analytical Philosophy of History* (Cambridge 1965) feature regularly on the recommended reading lists of historiographical courses but there is little evidence of their influence over the writings of undergraduates or their teachers.
3. Fischer, *Historians' Fallacies: Toward a Logic of Historical Thought* (New York 1970); for representative reviews, see Marcus Cunliffe in *American Historical Review*, 77 (1972), pp. 113-15 and G.R. Elton in *History*, 57 (1972), p. 92.
4. The classical texts are Elton, *The Practice of History* (London 1967), Hexter *The History Primer* (New York 1971), and *Doing History* (Bloomington, Indiana 1971).
5. See in particular Roland Barthes, 'Historical Discourse', translated in Michael Lane, *Structuralism: A Reader* (London 1970), pp. 145-55.
6. White, 'The Question of Narrative in Contemporary Historical Theory' in White, *The Content of the Form* (Baltimore 1987), p. 31.
7. For further discussion of these basic characteristics of historical argument see Albert Cook, *History/Writing* (Cambridge 1988), pp. 1-12, 206-20.
8. Everyone will have his own favourite among such interminable brawls; 'the storm over the gentry' which raged in English historiography is discussed by Green below; the rising temperature surrounding the rather broader issue of so-called 'revisionism' in Irish historiography can be traced in Ronan Fanning, 'The Great Enchantment: Uses and Abuses of Modern Irish History' in James Dooge (ed.), *Ireland in the Contemporary World: Essays in Honour of Garret FitzGerald,* pp. 131-47; Steven Ellis, 'Nationalist Historiography and the English and Gaelic Worlds in the Late Middle Ages' in *Irish Historical Studies*, 25 (1988), pp. 1-18, and Brendan Bradshaw, 'Nationalism and Historical Scholarship in Modern Ireland' in *ibid.*, 26 (1989), pp. 329-51; but perhaps the most disturbing dog-fight in recent years has been that surrounding David Abraham's *The Collapse of the Weimar Republic* (Princeton 1981), which illustrated at once the extraordinary bitterness which historical disagreement can generate and the inability of disputants to clinch a case even where a considerable degree of factual error had been established; see the exchange in *Central European History*, 17 (1984), pp. 159-290.
9. The means by which competing searches for 'a usable past' have brought

about a fracturing of debate among professional historians in the United States are discussed in Peter Novick's admirable *That Noble Dream: The 'Objectivity Question' and the American Historical Profession* (Cambridge 1988), pp. 415-629; the connection between the partisan character of historical argument in the public media in Ireland and the decline of history in the schools is the subject of Nicholas Canny's 'Editorial: A Crisis in Irish History', *Irish Economic and Social History Newsletter*, 3 (1991), p. 1.

10. Dunne, 'A Polemical Introduction' in *The Writer as Witness*, pp. 1-9.
11. White's provocative style has sometimes led him to state or to be understood to hold far more radical views on the correspondence of history and fiction than is in fact the case: compare his 'The Fictions of Factual Representation' in *Tropics of Discourse: Essays in Cultural Criticism* (Baltimore 1978) with his sensitive critiques of Michel Foucault, Fredric Jameson and Paul Ricoeur in *The Content of the Form*, pp. 104-84.
12. This would appear to be the principal difficulty of White's own application of his critical theory, *Metahistory: The Historical Imagination in Nineteenth-Century Europe* (Baltimore 1973) and of Said's similar and equally influential *Orientalism* (London 1978); with the partial exception of Cook, *History/Writing*, there has as yet been no sustained analysis of the operations of any contemporary school of historians from a literary critical as distinct from a logical or philosophical perspective.
13. Hexter, 'The Rhetoric of History' in *Doing History*, pp. 3-28; for a perceptive critique of the limitations of Hexter's defence of historical rhetoric, see Louis O. Mink, 'The Theory of Practice: Hexter's Historiography', in Barbara C. Malament (ed.), *After the Reformation: Essays in Honour of J.H. Hexter* (Manchester 1980), pp. 3-21.

CHAPTER 1

1. C.R. Elrington and J.H. Todd (eds), *The Whole Works of . . . James Ussher* (17 vols, Dublin 1847-64), iv.
2 James Ussher, *Veterum Epistolarum Hibernicarum Sylloge* (Dublin 1632).
3. Hugh Trevor-Roper, *Catholics, Anglicans and Puritans: Seventeenth-Century Essays* (London 1989), especially pp. 144-9.
4. Peter Lombard, *De Regno Hiberniae Sanctorum Insula Commentarius* (Louvain 1632), P.F. Moran (ed.) (Dublin 1868); M.J. Byrne (ed.), *The Irish War of Defence, 1598-1600; Extracts from the De Hibernia Insula Commentarius of Peter Lombard* (Cork 1930), p. viii; T.W. Moody, F.X. Martin, F. J. Byrne (eds), *A New History of Ireland, iii* (Oxford 1976), pp. 596-7; J. T. Leerssen, *Mere Irish and Fíor-Ghael: Studies in the Idea of Irish Nationality, its Development and Literary Expression prior to the Nineteenth Century* (Amsterdam 1986), p. 311.
5. Geoffrey Keating, *Foras Feasa ar Éirinn: The History of Ireland*, David Comyn and P.S. Dinneen (eds) (4 vols, London: Irish Texts Society 1902-14).
6. Bernadette Cunningham, 'Seventeenth-Century Interpretations of the Past: The Case of Geoffrey Keating' in *Irish Historical Studies*, xxv, no. 98 (1986), pp. 116-28.
7. John Colgan, *Acta Sanctorum Veteris et Majoris Scotiae, seu Hiberniae Sanctorum Insulae . . .* (Louvain 1645) (Facsimile reprint, Dublin: Irish Manu-

scripts Commission 1948), preface, sig. b1v-b2v.

8. *Ibid.*; John Colgan, *Triadis Thaumaturgae, seu Divorum Patricii, Columbae, et Brigidae . . . Acta* (Louvain 1647); Terence O'Donnell (ed.), *Fr John Colgan, OFM 1592-1658: Essays in Commemoration* (Dublin 1959).
9. For an account of this enterprise see Tomás Ó Cléirigh, *Aodh Mac Aingil agus an Scoil Nua-Ghaeilge i Lobháin* (2nd ed., Dublin 1985); Canice Mooney, 'St Anthony's College, Louvain', in *Donegal Annual* (1969), pp. 18-48; Brendan Jennings, *Michéal Ó Cléirigh, Chief of the Four Masters and his Associates* (Dublin 1936); for the scholarly context see Benignus Millett, 'Irish Literature in Latin, 1550-1700' in *NHI, iii*, pp. 561-86; Cathaldus Giblin, 'The Contribution of Irish Franciscans on the Continent in the Seventeenth Century' in Michael Maher (ed.), *Irish Spirituality* (Dublin 1981), pp. 88-103.
10. Paul Walsh (ed.), *Genealogiae Regum et Sanctorum Hiberniae* (Maynooth: Record Society 1918); J.H. Todd and William Reeves (eds), *The Martyrology of Donegal; A Calendar of the Saints of Ireland* (Dublin: Irish Archaeological and Celtic Society 1864); R.A.S. MacAlister & John MacNeill (eds), *Leabhar Gabhála: The Book of Conquests of Ireland, The Recension of Micheál Ó Cléirigh, part i* (Dublin, undated 1910s); John O'Donovan (ed. and trans.), *Annála Ríoghachta Éireann: Annals of the Kingdom of Ireland by the Four Masters from the Earliest Period to 1616* (7 vols, Dublin 1851, reprint New York 1966).
11. Jennings, *Micheál Ó Cléirigh, and his Associates*, *passim*; Paul Walsh, 'Irish Scholars at Louvain', in Paul Walsh, *Irish Men of Learning* (Dublin 1947), pp. 246-51: Ó Cléirigh, *Aodh Mac Aingil*, pp. 10-14, 27-40.
12. Paul Walsh, 'The Learned Family of Ó Maolchonaire', in Walsh, *Irish Men of Learning*, pp. 34-48; Paul Walsh, *The Ó Cléirigh Family of Tír Conaill* (Dublin 1938); on Ó hEodhasa see James Carney, *The Irish Bardic Poet* (Dublin 1967).
13. On Florence Conry see Jennings, *Micheál Ó Cléirigh and his Associates*, pp. 24-30; Flaithrí Ó Maolchonaire, *Desiderius, otherwise called Sgathán an Chrabhaidh*, T.F. O'Rahilly (ed.) (Dublin 1955), pp. vii-xvii.
14. Jennings, *Micheál Ó Cléirigh and his Associates*, *passim*; on Ward, see also F. O'Brien, 'Irish Franciscan Historians of St Anthony's College, Louvain: Fr Hugh Ward' in *Irish Ecclesiastical Record*, 5th ser., xxxii (1928), pp. 113-29; Ward himself compiled a *Life of St Romuald*, patron of the diocese in which Louvain was situated; the work was published at Louvain in 1662, almost thirty years after Ward's death. On Chamberlain see Felim O'Brien, 'Robert Chamberlain, OFM' in *Irish Eccl. Record*, 5th ser., xl (1932), pp. 264-80.
15. On Hugh MacCaughwell as military chaplain see Brendan Jennings, *Wild Geese in Spanish Flanders* (Dublin: Irish Manuscripts Commission 1964), doc. 182, 23 Dec. 1605; Ann Grainne Henry, 'Wild Geese in Spanish Flanders; The Irish Military Community in Flanders 1586-1610: An Emerging Identity' (MA thesis, St Patrick's College, Maynooth 1986), p. 238.
16. Sir Henry Sidney to Queen Elizabeth, 20 May 1577, PRO SP63/58/29.
17. Brendan Jennings, *The Irish Franciscan College of St Anthony at Louvain* (Dublin 1925); Ó Cléirigh, *Aodh Mac Aingil*; on establishment of Louvain under the archbishop of Malines see Brendan Jennings (ed.), *Louvain Papers, 1606-1827* (Dublin: Irish Manuscripts Commission 1968), docs 5, 6, 7, 50, 57.
18. On income of chaplains see Jennings, *Wild Geese in Spanish Flanders*, docs 306, 349, 1190, 1205, etc.; on building in 1619 *ibid*, docs 656, 657; on numbers of students see Jennings, *Louvain Papers*, doc. 21; S. P. Dom. Charles I, vol.

13, f. 22, printed in Peter Guilday, *The English Catholic Refugees on the Continent, 1558-1795* (London 1914), pp. 28-9; Brendan Jennings, 'Irish Preachers and Confessors in the Archdiocese of Malines, 1607-1794', in *Archivium Hibernicum*, xxiii (1960), pp. 148-64; Cathaldus Giblin, 'The Irish Colleges on the Continent' in Liam Swords (ed.), *The Irish French Connection* (Paris 1978), pp. 9-20.

19. *NHI*, *iii*, p. 624.
20. Myles Dillon et al., *Catalogue of Irish Manuscripts in the Franciscan Library Killiney* (Dublin 1969), pp. ix-xvii; G. Henry, *Wild Geese*, pp. 363-4.
21. O'Donovan (ed.), *Annals of the Kingdom of Ireland*, i, pp. lvi-lvii; compare, for example, *AFM,* s.a. 1602 (pp. 2290-3) with the source text by Lughaidh Ó Cléirigh which was used by the annalists, printed in Paul Walsh (ed.), *The Life of Aodh Ruadh Ó Domhnaill* (2 vols, Dublin 1948), i, pp. 340-1. The annalists have added a reference to the Franciscan Flaithrí Ó Maolchonaire, defining his relationship to O'Donnell, along with a description of O'Donnell as a 'leader and earthly prince in the island of Erin'.
22. The availability of source manuscripts was not an insurmountable problem for the Franciscans; there is ample evidence of co-operation in this matter between the Franciscans and Protestant scholars and manuscript collectors, including James Ware and James Ussher; see J.T. Leerssen, 'Archbishop Ussher and Gaelic Culture' in *Studia Hibernica*, 22/3 (1982/3), pp. 50-8; for Ware's involvement see note 67 below.
23. Cunningham, 'Seventeenth-Century Interpretations of the Past', pp. 121-2; the Four Masters transcribed sections of Ó Cléirigh's recension of the *Leabhar Gabhála* into their annals without alteration, *AFM*, i, p. xxxiii; B. Cunningham and R. Gillespie, 'Englishmen in Sixteenth-Century Irish Annals' in *Irish Economic and Social History*, xvii (1990), pp. 5-21.
24. Cunningham, 'Seventeenth-Century Interpretations of the Past', p. 123; Keating, *Foras Feasa ar Éirinn*, i, pp. 3-7; Ó Cléirigh, *Leabhar Gabhála*, introd.
25. *AFM*, s.a. 1538; A.M. Freeman (ed.), *Annála Connacht: The Annals of Connacht, A.D. 1224-1544* (Dublin 1944), s.a. 1538; W.M. Hennessy (ed.), *The Annals of Loch Cé: A Chronicle of Irish Affairs, 1014-1590* (2 vols, London 1871), s.a. 1538.
26. W.M. Hennessy and B. MacCarthy (eds), *Annála Uladh, Annals of Ulster . . . A Chronicle of Irish affairs* (4 vols, Dublin 1887-1901), s.a. 1538.
27. *AFM*, s.a. 1538.
28. See B. Cunningham and R. Gillespie, '"Persecution" in Seventeenth-Century Irish' in *Éigse*, xxii (1987) pp. 15-20.
29. Breandán Ó Buachalla, 'Annála Ríoghachta Éireann is Foras Feasa ar Éirinn: An Comhthéacs Comhaimseartha' in *Studia Hibernica*, 22/3 (1982-3), pp. 59-105.
30. Breandán Ó Buachalla, 'Na Stiobhartaigh agus an t-Aos Léinn: Cing Seamas', *Proceedings of the Royal Irish Academy, sect. C*, 83, no. 4 (1983) pp. 81-134.
31. *AFM*, s.a. 1582; see also Michelle O'Riordan, 'The Gaelic Mind and the Collapse of the Gaelic World' (Ph.D. thesis, University College Cork 1985), pp. 134-5.
32. *AFM*, s.a. 1582, note.
33. Walsh (ed.), *Geneal. Reg. et Sanct. Hib*., p. 6.
34. See for example Bonaventure Ó hEodhasa, *An Teagasg Críosdaidhe* (Antwerp 1611), Fearghal Mac Raghnaill (ed.) (Dublin 1976) pp. 18, 19.

35. Walsh (ed.), *Geneal. Reg. et Sanct. Hib.*, pp. 7-8, 143
36. Peter Burke, 'How to be a Counter-Reformation Saint', in Kaspar Von Greyerz (ed.), *Religion and Society in Early Modern Europe, 1500-1800* (London 1984), pp. 45-55.
37. Walsh (ed.), *Geneal. Reg. et Sanct. Hib.*, p. 143.
38. A parallel project was the Franciscan-led research on the medieval philosopher John Duns Scotus, who was also claimed as an Irishman; see John J. Silke, 'Irish Scholarship and the Renaissance, 1580-1673' in *Studies in the Renaissance*, xx (1973), pp. 200-1; Leerssen, *Mere Irish and Fíor Ghael*, p. 304.
39. On secular/regular dispute see Aidan Clarke, 'Colonial Identity in Early Seventeenth-Century Ireland' in T.W. Moody (ed.), *Nationality and the Pursuit of National Independence: Historical Studies XI* (Belfast 1978), pp. 57-71.
40. Historical Manuscripts Commission, *Report on Franciscan Manuscripts Preserved at the Convent, Merchant's Quay, Dublin* (Dublin: HMSO 1906), p. 90; for discussion of the uses of hagiography in secular politics see David Rollason, *Saints and Relics in Anglo-Saxon England* (Oxford 1989), *passim*.
41. Walsh (ed.), *Geneal. Reg. et Sanct. Hib.*, p. 144; the Louvain Franciscans were not the first Irish writers to take up the challenge of the Scots; among the Old English contributions to the debate were Henry Fitzsimon's *Catalogus Aliquorum Sanctorum Hiberniae* (Douai 1615, reprinted Liège and Antwerp 1619 and 1621) and David Rothes's *Hibernia Resurgens* (Rouen 1621); see also Edmund Hogan, *Distinguished Irishmen of the Sixteenth Century* (London 1894), pp. 26-8 for Richard Fleming's role.
42. Stephen Wilson, *Saints and their Cults: Studies in Religious Sociology, Folklore and History* (Cambridge 1983), p. 26.
43. Colgan, *Acta Sanctorum*, preface, sig. blv; in contrast, Keating seems to have taken the multiplicity of saints at face value, Keating, *Foras Feasa,* iii, pp. 109-13.
44. Colgan, *Triadis Thaumaturgae*; Ludwig Bieler, 'Trias Thaumaturga' in O'Donnell (ed.), *Fr John Colgan, OFM*, pp. 41-9.
45. Walsh (ed.), *Geneal. Reg. et Sanct. Hib*, p. 138 (my transl.).
46. For example, John Wilson, *The English Martyrologie* (1608).
47. Brian Ó Cuív, 'Flaithrí Ó Maolchonaire's Catechism of Christian Doctrine', in *Celtica*, i (1950) pp. 161-98.
48. Ó hEodhasa, *Teagasg Críosdaidhe*, pp. viii, xii-xiii; the first edition was published by J. Mesius in Antwerp; his Irish type font was later acquired by the Franciscans and used for the second edition, which they themselves printed in 1614; Thomas Wall, 'The Catechism in Irish: Bonaventure O'Hussey OFM', in *Irish Eccl. Record*, 5th ser., lix (1942), pp. 36-48.
49. Aodh Mac Aingil, *Scathán Shacramuinte na hAithridhe*, Cainneach Ó Maonaigh (ed.) (Dublin 1952), ll. 3080-3 (my transl.); on Mac Aingil's Irishness in a European context see Tadhg Ó Dúshlaine, 'Athléamh ar Aodh Mac Aingil' in *Irisleabhar Mhá Nuad* (1975/6), pp. 9-25; Tadhg Ó Dúshlaine, *An Eóraip agus Litríocht na Gaeilge, 1600-1650, Gnéithe den Bharócachas Eorpach i Litríocht na Gaeilge* (Dublin 1987), ch. 3.
50. RIA MSS 23. 0. 41; 23. 1. 19, etc.; see Ó hEodhasa, *Teagasg Críosdaidhe*, p. xi.
51. Ó hEodhasa, *Teagasg Críosdaidhe*, p. 95.
52. See J. O'Donovan (ed.), *Catechism of the Council of Trent* (Dublin 1867), pp. 90-105.
53. Ó hEodhasa, *Teagasg Críosdaidhe*, pp. 18-19.

54. Richard Morres of Templemore to Salisbury [1611], *Calendar of State Papers, Ireland, 1611-14*, pp. 184-5.
55. Mac Aingil, *Scathán*, ll. 67-73 (my transl.); similar sentiments are expressed in ll. 1550-5.
56. *Ibid.*, ll. 4970-99; see also ll. 5351-6; but the expression of such sentiments cannot be interpreted as anti-English; Mac Aingil was loyal to James I, and blamed the King's educators for his Protestantism, ll. 5457-62; 5494-9.
57. Edward Rogan, *Synods and Catechesis in Ireland* c. *445-1962: A Juridico-historical Study . . . with Special Reference to Catechesis* (Rome 1987), pp. 28-43.
58. Ó hEodhasa, *Teagasg Críosdaidhe*, p. 88; see Patrick J. Corish, 'Catholic Marriage under the Penal Code' in Art Cosgrove (ed.), *Marriage in Ireland* (Dublin 1985), pp. 67-70.
59. Margaret MacCurtain, 'Marriage in Tudor Ireland' in Cosgrove (ed.), *Marriage in Ireland*, pp. 63-4; for one example of disregard of Tridentine guidelines see B. Jennings (ed.), *Wadding Papers, 1614-38* (Dublin 1953), pp. 335-8.
60. Antoin Gearnon, *Parrthas an Anma*, Anselm Ó Fachtna (ed.) (Dublin 1953), p. 137. Similar concerns are evident in the tract on the mass written by the secular priest Geoffrey Keating: Geoffrey Keating, *Eochair-sgíath an Aifrinn*, Patrick O'Brien (ed.) (Dublin 1898).
61. Ó Maolchonaire, *Desiderius*, ll. 1511-1613, ll. 3323-35; for an indication that these sections are additions to the text see introd., pp. xvi-xvii.
62. Cunningham and Gillespie, '"Persecution" in Seventeenth-Century Irish'.
63. Theobald Stapleton, *Catechismus, seu Doctrina Christiana Latino-Hibernica . . .* (Brussels 1639, IMC facsimile, Dublin 1945), oráid don léachthóir; see also Bernadette Cunningham, 'Geoffrey Keating's *Eochair-sgíath an Aifrinn* and the Catholic Reformation in Ireland' in W.J. Sheils and D. Wood (eds), *The Churches, Ireland, and the Irish: Studies in Church History, XXV* (Oxford 1989), pp. 138-9.
64. On Gearnon's catechism see Patrick Wallace, 'Irish Catechesis and the Heritage of James Butler II, Archbishop of Cashel, 1774-1791' (Ph. D. thesis, Catholic University of America 1975), pp. 83-4.
65. J. Delumeau, *Catholicism from Luther to Voltaire* (London 1977), p. 186.
66. *AFM*, pp. lv-lviii; Walsh (ed.), *Geneal. Reg. Sanct. Hib.*, pp. 5-6, 142; Colgan, *Acta Sanctorum*, dedication; HMC, *Report 4*, Appendix, p. 604; Colgan, *Triadis Thaumaturgae,* dedication.
67. HMC, *Report on Franciscan Manuscripts*, p. 42.
68. Annie Hutton (trans.), *The Embassy in Ireland of Mons G.B. Rinnuccini . . . 1645-9* . . .(Dublin 1873), pp. 141-7; for example: 'the Regulars . . . accustomed to live out of their convents and acting as chaplains with good stipends to the Barons of the island, not constrained by the discipline of the monastery to wear the religious habit [after celebrating mass] often to our great scandal, on the very table from which the altar cloth has been but just removed, playing cards or glasses of beer together with the food and dinner are at once laid'. I owe this reference to Raymond Gillespie.
69. On the successful aspects of the Irish mission see John Bossy, 'The Counter Reformation and the People of Catholic Ireland', in T.D. Williams (ed.), *Historical Studies VIII* (Dublin 1971), pp. 155-69.
70. Helga Hammerstein, 'Aspects of the Continental Education of Irish Students in the Reign of Elizabeth I' in *Historical Studies VIII* (Dublin 1971), p. 153.
71. G. Henry, *Wild Geese*, p. 327.

72. See J.J. Silke, 'Primate Lombard and James I' in *Irish Theological Quarterly*, xxii (1955), p. 128 for Lombard's expression of this view.

CHAPTER 2

1. See, for example, A. Grafton, 'Protestant versus Prophet: Isaac Casaubon on Hermes Trismegistus', *Journal of the Warburg and Courtauld Institutes*, 46 (1983), pp. 78-93.
2. On the relationship between historical Pyrrhonism and existing theories of history, see A. Momigliano, 'Ancient History and the Antiquarian', *Studies in Historiography* (London 1966), pp. 10-13.
3. On the latter see Gilles Declerq, 'L'Histoire du Calvinisme de Louis Maimbourg et sa réception par la critique protestante', in *De la mort de Colbert à la révocation de l'Edit de Nantes* (Marseilles 1984), pp. 199-212.
4. On the role of the royal historiographers in France, see O. Ranum, *Artisans of Glory: Writers and Historical Thought in Seventeenth-Century France* (Chapel Hill 1980).
5. Jean de Léry, *Histoire d'un voyage faict en la terre du Brésil* (1578, new ed. Paris 1980), p. 109.
6. Erasmus, *A Diatribe or Sermon concerning Free Will*, 1519, E.F. Winter (ed. and trans.) (New York 1967), pp. 3-11. Pierre-Daniel Huet, *Demonstratio Evangelica* (Paris 1678); see also Huet's *Traité de la foiblesse de l'esprit humain* (London 1741, published posthumously but written before 1690).
7. R.H. Popkin, 'Scepticism and the Counter-Reformation in France', *Archiv für Reformationsgeschichte*, 51 (1960), pp. 58-87.
8. On this, see W. Rex, *Essays on Pierre Bayle and Religious Controversy* (The Hague 1965), pp. 96-9.
9. O. Ranum, *op. cit.*, pp. 14-17, 22-4.
10. E. Labrousse, *Pierre Bayle, tome I: Du pays de Foix à la cité d'Erasme* (The Hague 1963), pp. 168-200.
11. Jean Frégeville, *Chronologie . . . contenant la générale durée du monde* (Paris 1582); *Palma Christiana, Sive Speculum Veri Status Ecclesiae* (London 1593).
12. See Vignier, *Théâtre de l'Antichrist* (1610); Du Plessis Mornay, *Mystère de l'iniquité* (1611); George Thomas, *La Chasse de la beste romaine*. In general, see B. Dompnier, 'L'Histoire religieuse chez les controversistes réformés au début du XVIIe siècle', in P. Joutard (ed.), *Historiographie de la Réforme* (Paris 1977), pp. 16-24.
13. E. Labrousse, 'Les Guerres de religion vues par les huguenots du XVIIe siècle', in Joutard, *op. cit.*, pp. 37-44.
14. See Labrousse, *Bayle* (Oxford 1983), p. 36.
15. Ranum, *op.cit.*, pp. 27-54.
16. *Nouvelles de la république des lettres*, April 1684, art. III.
17. Bayle, *Critique Générale*, pp. 23-4. Gilles Declerq, *loc. cit.*, pp. 199-201.
18. *Critique Générale*, p. 114.
19. On this see Gilles Declerq, 'Un Adepte de l'histoire éloquente: le père Maimbourg S.J.', *XVIIe Siècle*, xxxxi, no. 143 (1987), pp. 119-32, and Ruth Whelan, *The Anatomy of Superstition: A Study of the Theory and Practice of Pierre Bayle* (Oxford 1989), pp. 63-71.
20. Quotations are from Bayle's *Oeuvres diverses* (4 vols, The Hague 1727),

Critique Générale, p. 7 (my transl.).
21. *CG*, p. 12.
22. E. Labrousse, *Pierre Bayle, tome II: Héterodoxie et rigorisme* (The Hague 1964), pp. 65-8; Carlo Borghero, *La Certezza e la Storia: Cartesianismo, Pirronismo e Conoscenza Storica* (Milan 1983), pp. 229-37.
23. Bayle, *Dictionnaire historique et critique*, vol. I, p. 490, Art. 'Beaulieu', rem. F.
24. See *CG*, p. 10.
25. René Pintard, *Le Libertinage érudit de la première moitié du XVIIe siècle* (Paris 1943).
26. See, in particular, P.O. Kristeller, 'The Myth of Renaissance Atheism and the French Tradition of Free Thought', *Journal of the History of Philosophy*, vi (1968), pp. 233-43.
27. Sextus Empiricus, *Works* (Loeb ed. 1955), vol. i, p. 81.
28. Montaigne, *Essais*, II, xii in *Oeuvres complètes*, A. Thibaudet and M. Rat (eds) (Paris 1980), p. 430.
29. But see J. Beaude, 'Amplifier le dixième trope, ou la différence culturelle comme argument sceptique', *Récherches sur le XVIIe Siècle*, v (1982), pp. 21-30.
30. See the critical comments on modern accounts of the history of scepticism in R.H. Popkin, 'The Religious Background of Seventeenth-Century Philosophy' in the *Journal of the History of Philosophy,* xxv (1987), pp. 40-1.
31. Montaigne, *Essais*, I, xxi.
32. Both reprinted in La Mothe Le Vayer, *Deux dialogues*, E. Tisserand (ed.) (Paris 1927).
33. See n. 29 above.
34. 'Dialogue sur le sujet de la divinité', *Deux dialogues*, pp. 94-5.
35. See R.H. Popkin, *The History of Scepticism from Erasmus to Spinoza* (London 1971).
36. See in particular 'Introduction à la lecture de Confucius', *Journal des Savants*, XVI, 2 (1688) and *Voyages* (Amsterdam 1711).
37. D.P. Walker, *The Ancient Theology: Studies in Christian Platonism from the Fifteenth to the Eighteenth Century* (London 1972), *passim*. For a discussion of Bayle's position, see Ruth Whelan, 'La religion à l'envers: Bayle et l'histoire du paganism antique', in *Les religions du paganisme antique dans l'Europe Chrétienne* (Paris 1987), pp. 115-28.
38. Rex, *op. cit.*, pp. 30-74, interprets the text primarily as an attack on Catholicism.
39. *Pensées diverses*, p. 10.
40. *Ibid.*, pp. 11, 12.
41. *Ibid.*, p. 22.
42. *Ibid.*, p. 51.
43. *Ibid.*, p. 40.
44. *Ibid.*, p. 84.
45. *Ibid.*, pp. 104, 105.
46. *Ibid.*, p. 110.
47. Gabriel Naudé, *Sciences des princes, ou considérations politiques sur les coups d'état* (Paris 1752).
48. *Suite de la Critique Générale*, p. 274.
49. *Ibid.*, p. 278.
50. See Descartes' *Règles pour la direction de l'esprit, ii: Oeuvres Philosophiques* (3

vols, Paris 1976), vol. i, pp. 80-4.
51. On this see Robin Briggs, 'Church and State' in *Communities of Belief: Cultural and Social Tension in Early Modern France* (Oxford 1989), pp. 216-20.
52. *Pensées Diverses*, pp. 58-9.
53. *Critique Générale*, pp. 86-7.
54. *Commentaire Philosophique*, p. 396.
55. *Ibid.*, p. 408.

CHAPTER 3

1. Josiah Quincy, quoted in Peter Shaw, *American Patriots and the Rituals of Revolution* (Cambridge, Mass.: Harvard University Press 1981), p. 160. See also Philip Davidson, *Propaganda and the American Revolution, 1763-1783* (1941; New York: W.W. Norton 1965), p. 144; Ebenezer Baldwin in *Appendix* to Samuel Sherwood, *A Sermon, Containing, Scriptural Instructions to Civil Rulers, and All Free-Born Subjects* . . . (New Haven, Conn.: T. S. Green 1774), pp. 74-5.
2. Gordon S. Wood, 'Rhetoric and Reality in the American Revolution', *William and Mary Quarterly*, 3d ser., 23 (January 1966), pp. 3-32. The literature on republicanism and its origins includes: Robert E. Shalhope, 'Toward a Republican Synthesis: The Emergence of an Understanding of Republicanism in American Historiography', *William and Mary Quarterly*, 3d ser., 29 (January 1972), pp. 49-80; Joyce Appleby, 'Republicanism in Old and New Contexts', *William and Mary Quarterly*, 3d ser., 43 (January 1986), pp. 20-34; Joyce Appleby, *Capitalism and a New Social Order: The Republican Vision of the 1790s* (New York: New York University Press 1984); Bernard Bailyn, *Ideological Origins of the American Revolution* (Cambridge, Mass.: Harvard University Press 1967); Bernard Bailyn, 'The Central Themes of the American Revolution: An Interpretation', in Stephen G. Kurtz and James H. Hutson (eds), *Essays on the American Revolution* (Chapel Hill: University of North Carolina Press 1973), pp. 3-33. See also Douglass Adair, 'The Tenth Federalist Revisited', *William and Mary Quarterly*, 3d ser., 8 (January 1951), pp. 48-67. J.G.A. Pocock, *The Machiavellian Moment: Florentine Political Thought and the Atlantic Republican Tradition* (Princeton: Princeton University Press 1975); J.G.A. Pocock, *Virtue, Commerce, and History* (Cambridge: Cambridge University Press 1985); Gordon S. Wood, *The Creation of the American Republic* (Chapel Hill: University of North Carolina Press 1969); '*The Creation of the American Republic, 1776-1787*: A Symposium of Views and Reviews', *William and Mary Quarterly*, 3d ser., 44 (July 1987), pp. 549-640.
3. Gordon S. Wood, 'A Note on Mobs in the American Revolution', *William and Mary Quarterly*, 3d ser., 23 (October 1966), pp. 635-42; Richard Hofstadter and Michael Wallace (eds), *American Violence: A Documentary History* (New York: Knopf 1970), pp. 63-79; Richard Maxwell Brown, *Strain of Violence: Historical Studies of American Violence and Vigilantism* (New York: Oxford University Press 1975), pp. 41-66.
4. Bernard Bailyn, *The Ideological Origins of the American Revolution* (Cambridge, Mass.: Harvard University Press 1967), p. ix.
5. Jack P. Greene, 'Slavery and Independence: Some Reflections on the Relationship among Liberty, Black Bondage, and Equality in Revolutionary South

Carolina', *South Carolina Historical Magazine*, 80 (July 1979), p. 197.

6. Bailyn, *Ideological Origins*, pp. ix, 86, 88-9, 119-59.
7. Robert Middlekauff, *The Glorious Cause: The American Revolution, 1763-1789* (New York: Oxford University Press 1982), pp. 126-35, quotation p. 130. On the role of the dissident English Whigs, see Caroline Robbins, 'Algernon Sidney's *Discourses Concerning Government*: Textbook of Revolution', *William and Mary Quarterly,* 3d ser., 4 (July 1947), pp. 267-96; *idem*, *The Eighteenth-Century Commonwealthman: Studies in the Transmission and Circumstances of English Liberal Thought from the Restoration of Charles II until the War with the Thirteen Colonies* (Cambridge, Mass.: Harvard University Press 1959).
8. See Jack P. Greene, 'The Seven Years' War and the American Revolution: The Causal Relationship Reconsidered', in Peter Marshall and Glynn Williams (eds), *The British Atlantic Empire before the American Revolution* (Bournemouth, Eng.: Frank Cass 1980), pp. 85-105.
9. See Jack P. Greene, 'The Role of the Lower Houses of Assembly in Eighteenth-Century Politics', in Jack P. Greene (ed.), *The Reinterpretation of the American Revolution 1763-1789* (New York: Harper and Row 1968), pp. 101, 105; Edmund S. Morgan, 'The American Revolution Considered as an Intellectual Movement', in *ibid*., p. 570.
10. Greene, 'Seven Years' War and the American Revolution', pp. 98-9.
11. See David Doyle, *Ireland, Irishmen and Revolutionary America, 1760-1820* (Dublin and Cork: Mercier Press 1980), pp. 3, 7 (quotation).
12. Wood, *Creation of the American Republic*, p. 4.
13. Thad W. Tate, for instance, notes that, compared with Massachusetts, where royal troops were billeted upon a restive population and punitive measures threatened economic ruin to the port of Boston, Virginia was only lightly affected. Yet throughout the 1760s and 1770s, the Old Dominion seethed with protest, sedition, and treason against the crown. Thad W. Tate, 'The Coming of the Revolution in Virginia: Britain's Challenge to Virginia's Ruling Class, 1763-1776', *William and Mary Quarterly*, 3d ser., 19 (July 1962), pp. 324-5.
14. Pierre Bourdieu, *Outline of a Theory of Practice* (New York: Cambridge University Press 1977), p. 21: 'The constitutive power which is granted ordinary language lies not in the language itself, but in the group which authorizes it and invests it with authority.' This would apply to the American revolutionaries in the language choices they made.
15. Cassius [Aedanus Burke], *An Address to the Freemen of the State of South-Carolina . . .* (Philadelphia: Robert Bell 1783).
16. Thomas Bradford Chandler, *What Think Ye of Congress Now? Or, An Enquiry How Far the Americans Are Bound to Abide by, and Execute the Decisions of, the Late Congress?* (New York: James Rivington 1775), p. 47.
17. Chalmers in Merrill Jensen, *Tracts of the American Revolution 1763-1776* (Indianapolis: Bobbs-Merrill 1967), p. 488.
18. John J. Zubly, 'The Stamp Act Repealed' in Randall M. Miller (ed.), *'A Warm & Zealous Spirit': John J. Zubly and the American Revolution, A Selection of His Writings* (Macon, Ga.: Mercer University Press 1982), p. 44 and *idem*, 'Helvetius' Essays' in *ibid*., p. 185.
19. See ch. 3 of Bertram Wyatt-Brown, *Southern Honor: Ethics and Behavior in the Old South* (New York: Oxford University Press 1982), for further elucidation of the conflicts within the system. See also M. I. Finley, *The World of Odysseus* (New York: Viking Press 1965); Curtis Brown Watson, *Shakespeare and the*

Renaissance Concept of Honor (Princeton: Princeton University Press 1960); Edwin Honig, *Calderon and the Seizures of Honor* (Cambridge, Mass.: Harvard University Press 1972).

20. James T. Kloppenberg, 'The Virtues of Liberalism: Christianity, Republicanism, and Ethics in Early American Political Discourse', *Journal of American History*, 74 (June 1987), pp. 9-33.
21. James Britton et al., *The Development of Writing Abilities (11-18)* (Houndsmills and London: Macmillan Education Ltd 1975), pp. 98-100.
22. *An Address of the Legislature to the Inhabitants of the Commonwealth of Massachusetts* (Boston: Benjamin Edes 1781), p. 21. John McKenzie, *Letters of Freemen*, pp. 23, 61, 64, quoted in Greene, 'Slavery or Independence', p. 198.
23. Thomas Paine, *Common Sense* in *Common Sense and The Crisis* (New York: Freethought Press 1946), pp. 26-7.
24. Thomas Paine, *Letter Addressed to the Abbe Raynal on the Affairs of North-America, in which the Mistakes of the Abbe's Account of the Revolution of America are Corrected and Cleared Up* (Philadelphia: Melchior Steiner 1782), p. 13. Needless to say, the British pamphleteers also worried that national honour would be stained if the Americans were successful. See Anon., *Considerations on the Measures Carrying On with Respect to the British Colonies in North America* (London: R. Baldwin 1774), pp. 48-9, 84-5, 157-8.
25. *Observations on the American Revolution Published According to a Resolution of Congress by their Committee for the Consideration of those who are Desirous of Comparing the Conduct of the Opposed Parties and the Several Consequences which have Flowed from it* (Philadelphia: Styner and Cist 1779), p. 34.
26. *An Address of the Legislature to the Inhabitants of the Commonwealth of Massachusetts* (Boston: Benjamin Edes 1781), p. 21.
27. See J. P. Peristiany (ed.), *Honour and Shame: The Values of Mediterranean Society* (London: Weidenfeld & Nicolson 1965) and Michael Herzfeld, 'Honour and Shame: Problems in Comparative Analyses of Moral Systems', *Man*, n.s. 15 (June 1980), pp. 339-51. On New England and secular honour, see Evarts B. Greene, 'The Code of Honor in Colonial and Revolutionary Times with Special Reference to New England', *Publications of the Colonial Society of Massachusetts,* 26 (Boston: Colonial Society of Massachusetts 1927), pp. 367-88.
28. 'A British Bostonian' [John Allen], *An Oration, Upon the Beauties of Liberty, Or the Essential Rights of the Americans. Delivered at the Second Baptist-Church in Boston. Upon the Last Annual Thanksgiving. Humbly Dedicated to the Right-Honourable the Earl of Dartmouth* (Boston: D. Kneeland and N. Davis 1773), pp. 27-8.
29. Thacher quoted by Harry S. Stout, *The New England Soul: Preaching and Religious Culture in Colonial New England* (New York: Oxford University Press 1986), p. 306.
30. He continued: Reject 'the soft arts of luxury and effeminacy', and sacrifice the pursuit of wealth to the cause of liberty, for those who admire wealth alone 'almost deserve to be enslaved', John Hancock, *An Oration Delivered March 5, 1774, at the Request of the Inhabitants of the Town of Boston: To Commemorate the Bloody Tragedy of the Fifth of March 1770* (Boston: Edes and Gill 1774), p. 18.
31. Warren quoted in Howard Mumford Jones, *O Strange New World, American Culture: The Formative Years* (New York: Viking Press 1964), p. 286.

32. Quotations from Melvin Yazawa, *From Colonies to Commonwealth: Familial Ideology and the Beginnings of the American Republic* (Baltimore: Johns Hopkins University Press 1985), pp. 94, 95.
33. Hutchinson quoted by Shaw, *American Patriots and the Rituals of Revolution*, p. 161.
34. James Otis, *The Rights of the British Colonies Asserted and Proved* (Boston: Edes and Gill 1764) in Bernard Bailyn (ed.), *Pamphlets of the American Revolution vol. I 1750-1765* (Cambridge, Mass.: Harvard University Press 1965), p. 437.
35. Robert R. Palmer, *The Age of the Democratic Revolution: A Political History of Europe and America, 1760-1800* (2 vols, Princeton: Princeton University Press 1959), p. 155. The rates were in 1765: Great Britain, 26s; Ireland 6s 8d; Massachusetts 1s; Connecticut 7d; Virginia 5d. Palmer does not, however, make clear what his figures meant: do they include county, parish and provincial taxes or merely the sums garnered for the central authority? The subject of pre-revolutionary taxation on all levels of government has not received the historical scrutiny the topic warrants.
36. Thomas Jefferson, 'Virginia Resolutions on Lord North's Conciliatory Proposal [June 10, 1775]', in Julian Parks Boyd (ed.), *The Papers of Thomas Jefferson* (21 vols, Princeton: Princeton University Press 1950), 1: pp. 172, 173, 231. The resolution continued: 'we consider ourselves as bound in Honor as well as Interest to share our general Fate with our Sister Colonies . . . and having in vain appealed to the native honour and justice of the British nation, a new course of action is necessary'. For an anthropological approach, see F. G. Bailey, *Gifts and Poison* (Oxford: Blackwell 1971).
37. Niccolo Machiavelli, *The Prince and the Discourses* (New York: Modern Library 1940), 'The Prince', ch. XVII, p. 62; see also ch. 16, pp. 57-8.
38. Bernard Bailyn, *The Ideological Origins of the American Revolution* (Cambridge, Mass.: Harvard University Press 1967), pp. 162 ff.; see also Conrad Russell, *Parliaments and English Politics, 1621-1629* (New York: Oxford University Press 1979), pp. 49-53, 56-7, and 376, on subsidy issues. On Irish taxation, *Four Letters on Interesting Subjects* (Philadelphia 1776), p. 5, quoted by Bernard Bailyn (ed.), *Pamphlets of the American Revolution, vol. 1 1750-1776* (Cambridge, Mass.: Harvard University Press 1965), I, p. 78.
39. James Otis, *The Rights of the British Colonies Asserted and Proved* (Boston 1764), in Bailyn (ed.), *Pamphlets of the American Revolution*, I, p. 452.
40. William Gordon, *The Separation of the Jewish Tribes after the Death of Solomon, Accounted for, and Applied to the Present Day, in a Sermon before the General Court, on Friday, July the 4th, 1777, Being the Anniversary of the Declaration of Independency* (Boston: J. Gill 1777), p.11.
41. Quoted in Davidson, *Propaganda and the American Revolution, 1763-1783*, pp. 140-1. Men of more temperate dispositions also spoke in passionate language.
42. J.G.A. Pocock, *The Ancient Constitution and the Feudal Law: A Study of English Historical Thought in the Seventeenth Century* (1957; Cambridge: Cambridge University Press 1987), pp. 331-2. See also, Lois G. Schwoerer, *'No Standing Armies!' The Antiarmy Ideology in Seventeenth-Century England* (Baltimore: Johns Hopkins University Press 1974); J.G.A. Pocock, 'Machiavelli, Harrington, and English Political Ideologies in the Eighteenth Century', *William and Mary Quarterly*, 3d ser., 22 (October 1965), pp. 549-83, esp. 558-64; Lewis D. Cress, *Citizens in Arms: The Army and the Militia in American Society*

to the War of 1812 (Chapel Hill: University of North Carolina Press 1982), pp. 15-33. Jerrilyn Greene Marston, *King and Congress: The Transfer of Political Legitimacy 1774-1776* (Princeton: Princeton University Press 1987), pp. 134-45.

43. Robbins, *Commonwealthman*, p. 339; Bailyn, introd., in *idem* (ed.), *Pamphlets of the American Revolution*, pp. 41-4, esp. 42, n. 7, in which he points out that J.G.A. Pocock dates the issue only as far back as 1675, but there was a nostalgia in Commonwealthman writings for the old feudal times when 'the "nobility" secured the people against the insults of the prince and the prince against the popularity of the commons'. Robbins, *Commonwealthman,* p. 104.
44. Quoted in Walter H. Conser, Jr, 'The Stamp Act Resistance', in Walter H. Conser, Jr, Ronald M. McCarthy, David J. Toscano and Gene Sharp (eds), *Resistance, Politics, and the American Struggle for Independence, 1765-1775* (Boulder, Col.: Lynne Rienner 1986), p. 26.
45. See Frank W. C. Hersey, 'Tar and Feathers: The Adventures of Captain John Malcolm', in *Publications of the Colonial Society of Massachusetts*, 34 (April 1941), pp. 450-1; Shaw, *American Patriots and the Rituals of Revolution*, *passim*; Jones, *O Strange New World*, pp. 281-93.
46. Paul A. Gilje, *The Road to Mobocracy: Popular Disorder in New York City, 1763-1834* (Chapel Hill: University of North Carolina Press 1987), vii, p. 66.
47. Conser, 'Stamp Act Resistance', p. 42.
48. Blackstone quoted by Marston, *King and Congress*, p. 18.
49. Frederic M. Litto, 'Addison's *Cato* in the Colonies', *William and Mary Quarterly*, 3d ser., 23 (July 1966), pp. 431-49.
50. Louis B. Wright, *The First Gentlemen of Virginia: Intellectual Qualities of the Early Colonial Ruling Class* (San Marino: Huntington Library 1940), esp. p. 283; Moses Coit Tyler, *The Literary History of the American Revolution* (New York 1897), I, pp. 210 and 213 ff. 'Give me liberty or give me death,' Patrick Henry's famous exclamation, bears resemblance to Addison's lines in *Cato*, 'It is not now a time to talk of aught/But chains, or conquest; liberty, or death.' Litto, 'Addison's *Cato*', p. 445.
51. Elliot J. Gorn, '"Gouge, Bite, Pull Hair and Scratch": The Social Significance of Fighting in the Southern Backcountry', *American Historical Review*, 90 (February 1985), pp. 18-43. See also Carl Bridenbaugh, 'Violence and Virtue in Virginia, 1766; Or, the Importance of the Trivial', in *idem*, *Early Americans* (New York: Oxford University Press 1981), pp. 188-212. Court-martial order remanded by General George Washington: General Orders, 18 January 1778, in John C. Fitzpatrick (ed.), *The Writings of George Washington from the Original Manuscript Sources, 1745-1799* (Washington DC: United States Government Printing Office 1933), 10: p. 312; *ibid*., 3 August 1778, 12: pp. 272-3.
52. Constantia Maxwell, *Dublin under the Georges, 1714-1850* (London: George G. Harrap & Co. 1936), p. 88.
53. David Noël Doyle, *Ireland, Irishmen and Revolutionary America, 1760-1820* (Dublin and Cork: Mercier Press 1980), pp. 51-151.
54. We owe much to David Doyle for the recovery of this aspect of eighteenth-century American history. On Irish localism see Doyle, *Ireland, Irishmen and Revolutionary America*, p. 118; on Irish habits see William Edward Hartpole Lecky, *A History of Ireland in the Eighteenth Century* (5 vols; New York: D. Appleton & Co. 1893), I, pp. 286-7. On Irish-American connections see Grady McWhiney, *Cracker Culture: Celtic Ways in the Old South* (University, Ala.:

University of Alabama Press 1988).

55. Hezekiah Hayden to 'Honor'd Father & Mother, July 4, 1776', quoted in Davidson, *Propaganda and the American Revolution 1763-1783*, p. 341.
56. Robert Howe to Henry Laurens, 9 June 1777, quoted in Richard Walsh (ed.), *The Writings of Christopher Gadsden, 1764-1805* (Columbia, SC: University of South Carolina Press 1966), p. xxiv.
57. In fact, concern over status seemed a prime motive for the tide of resignations that afflicted the army during the winter of 1777-8. Charles Royster, *A Revolutionary People at War: The Continental Army and American Character, 1775-1783* (Chapel Hill: University of North Carolina Press 1979), p. 87. Royster points out that to attain the cachet of 'gentleman' was so powerful a motive that many, insecure in the sought-for status, risked appearing boorish and offensive in the process of asserting their gentility. See *ibid.*, pp. 88-95. One disgruntled colonel, who lost a seniority dispute with another, wrote to General Washington: 'It is impossible for a soldier, who is tenacious of his honor (the only jewel worth contending for) to suffer himself to be degraded by being superseded . . .', *ibid.*, p. 199. The congruence of this language in the army with the civilian rhetoric against the crown should be obvious. 'To sink under the command of men whose superior in rank I had been acknowledged . . . tasted indeed too loathsome of degradation,' wrote Adjutant General John Trumbull of Connecticut in 1777, *ibid*, p. 200. See John Trumbull to John Hancock, 22 February 1777, John Trumbull to James Lovell, 30 March 1777, in Trumbull, *Autobiography*, pp. 39, 46. See also Charles P. Whittemore, *A General of the Revolution: John Sullivan of New Hampshire* (New York: Columbia University Press 1961), pp. 24-5, 227-9. When given a staff instead of a line appointment as major-general, Nathanael Greene ruefully remarked, 'I am taken out of the Line of splendor,' Nathanael Greene to Joseph Reed, 9 March 1778, in Richard K. Showman (ed.), *The Papers of General Nathanael Greene, Vol. II, January 1777-October 1778* (4 vols; Chapel Hill: University of North Carolina Press 1980), p. 307, see also Greene to Alexander McDougall, 28 March 1778, *ibid.*, p. 326 and James Thomas Flexner, *The Young Hamilton: A Biography* (Boston: Little, Brown 1978), pp. 262-3.
58. Nathanael Greene to George Washington, 21 May 1776, in Showman (ed.), *The Papers of General Nathanael Greene, Vol. I, December 1775-December 1776*, pp. 216-17.
59. Trevor Colburn (ed.), *Fame and the Founding Fathers: Essays by Douglass Adair* (New York: W. W. Norton 1974), pp. 3-26.
60. Quoted by Trevor Colburn, headnote, before Douglass Adair, 'Fame and the Founding Fathers', p. 3.
61. Israel Evans, *An Oration Delivered at Hackinsack, On the Tenth of September, 1780. At the Interment of the Honorable Brigadier Enoch Poor, General of the New-Hampshire Brigade* (Newburyport, Mass.: J. Mycall 1781), p. 8 (italics mine) . Parenthetically, the distinction he drew between honour as moral principle guiding the conscience and honour as reputation for civic excellence touched upon an inherent ambiguity in the ethic, one recognized since the time of Aristotle.
62. Samuel Sherwood, *A Sermon, Containing, Scriptural Instructions to Civil Rulers, and All Free-Born Subjects . . . Also an Appendix* . . . by the Rev. Ebenezer Baldwin (New Haven, Conn.: T. and S. Green 1774), p. vi.
63. See Plutarch, *The Life of Timeleon*, noted in Douglass Adair, 'Fame and the

Founding Fathers', in Colburn (ed.), *Fame and the Founding Fathers*, p. 13, n. 9. See also Niccolo Machiavelli, *The Discourses*, ch. 10, in *The Prince and the Discourses*, pp. 141-5.

64. Adair, 'Fame and the Founding Fathers', p. 7.
65. Joseph Addison as quoted by Forrest McDonald, *Novus Ordo Secolorum: The Intellectual Origins of the Constitution* (Lawrence, Kansas: University Press of Kansas 1985), p. 198.
66. Although McDonald does not see this formulation as part of a larger concern over gentility and honour as such, I have paraphrased his words here and owe much to his insights: see McDonald, *Novus Ordo Secolorum*, pp. 198-9. See also Robert M. Weir, '"The Harmony We Were Famous For": An Interpretation of Pre-Revolutionary South Carolina Politics', *William and Mary Quarterly*, 3d ser., 26 (October 1969), pp. 473-501, esp. 496.
67. McDonald, *Novus Ordo Secolorum*, p. 192. A graceful horseman, always in command of his mount, and a favourite among women, Washington also fulfilled the parlour graces and the athletic requirements of the country gentleman. See Paul Leicester Ford, *Washington and the Theatre* (New York 1899), p. 50; Forrest McDonald, *The Presidency of George Washington* (Lawrence, Kansas: University Press of Kansas 1974), p. 26.
68. Adams quoted by McDonald, *Novus Ordo Secolorum*, p. 191, n. 10. 'Inspired with public virtue, touched with the wrongs and indignant at the insults offered his country, the high-spirited Cassius exhibits an heroic example:– "Resolved as we are," (replied the hero to his friend) "resolved as we are, let us march against the enemy, for tho' we should not conquer, we have nothing to fear,"' Josiah Quincy, Jr, *Observations on the Act of Parliament Commonly called the Boston Port-Bill; With Thoughts on Civil Society and Standing Armies* (Philadelphia: printed for John Sparhawk 1774), p. 50. Such sentiments were common: they show how the classical past served very immediate circumstances.
69. William Smith, *An Oration in Memory of General Montgomery, and of the Officers and Soldiers Who Fell With Him* . . . (Philadelphia: n.p. 1776), p. 4.
70. Douglass Adair, '"Experience Must Be Our Only Guide": History, Democratic Theory, and the United States Constitution', in Colburn (ed.), *Fame and the Founding Fathers*, pp. 107-23.
71. Wood, *Creation of the American Republic*, pp. 48-53, devotes attention to 'the appeal of antiquity', but does not seem to recognize its connection with the ethics of gentility and honour.
72. Quoted in Phyllis Vine, 'Preparation for Republicanism: Honor and Shame in the Eighteenth-Century College', in Barbara Finkelstein (ed.), *Regulated Children/Liberated Children: Education in Psychohistorical Perspective* (New York: Psychohistory Press 1979), p. 49, from Miller, *Revolutionary College*, p. 180. See also Susan Ford Wiltshire (ed.), *The Usefulness of Classical Learning in the Eighteenth Century: Papers Presented at the 107th Annual Meeting of the American Philological Association* (n.p. 1977).
73. Phyllis Vine, 'The Social Function of Eighteenth-Century Higher Education', *History of Education Quarterly*, 16 (Winter 1976), pp. 409-24.
74. James Emerson, *A Thanksgiving Sermon* . . . (Boston: Edes and Gill 1766), p. 7.
75. Quincy, *Observations on the Act of Parliament*, pp. 69-70.
76. F. Nwabueze Okoye, 'Chattel Slavery as the Nightmare of the American

Revolutionaries', *William and Mary Quarterly*, 3d ser., 37 (January 1980), p. 5. This scholar has accused Bernard Bailyn and other leading historians of revolutionary America with a gross and 'fallacious' misrepresentation of the question when they note that the existence of chattel bondage had no major part in the struggle for American independence. But he himself has misunderstood the problem as explained in the text.

77. Thomas Gordon, letter, 21 April 1722, *Cato's Letters*, 65, quoted in John Philip Reid, *The Concept of Liberty in the Age of the American Revolution* (Chicago: University of Chicago Press 1988), p. 38.
78. Duncan J. McLeod did not put the matter in these terms, but his statement that 'John Dickinson could think of no "idea of slavery more *complete*, more *miserable*, more *disgraceful*, than that of a people, where justice is administered, government exercised, and a *standing army maintained* AT THE EXPENCE OF THE PEOPLE and yet WITHOUT THE LEAST *Dependence* UPON THEM"', makes sense only when the rubrics of honour are considered as the foundation of the protest. See Duncan J. McLeod, *Slavery, Race, and the American Revolution* (New York: Cambridge University Press 1974), p. 16; cf. Okoye, 'Slavery as Nightmare', p. 8.
79. Mayhew quoted in Reid, *Concept of Liberty*, p. 45.
80. Americanus [Timothy Ford], *The Constitutionalist: Or, An Inquiry How Far It is Expedient and Proper to Alter the Constitution of South Carolina* (Charleston: Markland, M'Kiver & Co. 1794), pp. 39-40, quoted in Greene, 'Slavery or Independence', p. 205.
81. Christopher Gadsden to Henry Laurens, 5 June 1774, in Richard Walsh (ed.), *The Writings of Christopher Gadsden, 1746-1805* (Columbia SC: University of South Carolina Press 1966), p. 95. See also Kenneth S. Greenberg, 'Revolutionary Ideology and the Proslavery Argument: The Abolition of Slavery in Antebellum South Carolina', *Journal of Southern History*, 42 (August 1976), pp. 365-84; and Donald L. Robinson, *Slavery in the Structure of American Politics, 1765-1820* (New York: W. W. Norton 1971), pp. 60-1, 463, n. 23; Paul K. Conkin, *Self-Evident Truths* (Bloomington: Indiana University Press 1974), pp. 109-10.
82. George Washington to Bryan Fairfax, 24 August 1774, in FitzPatrick (ed.), *Writings of George Washington*, 3: p. 242.

CHAPTER 4

1. François Furet, *Penser la Révolution* (Paris 1978); transl. by Elborg Forster as *Interpreting the French Revolution* (Cambridge 1981).
2. *Ibid.*, pp. 48-52.
3. K.M. Baker, 'On the Problem of the Ideological Origins of the French Revolution', in D. Lacapra and S.L. Kaplan (eds), *Modern European Intellectual History: Reappraisals and Perspectives* (Ithaca, New York and London 1982), p. 210; a demand also implicit in the classic work, too little contemplated by historians, by Theodor W. Adorno and Max Horkheimer, *Dialektik der Aufklärung* (Amsterdam 1947).
4. D. Outram, 'Le Language mâle de la vertu: Women, Politics and Public Language in the French Revolution', in R.S. Porter and P. Burke (eds), *The Social History of Language* (Cambridge 1987), pp. 120-35. This is also true for ac-

counts dependent on Furet in this respect, e.g. Carol Blum, *Rousseau and the Republic of Virtue: The Language of Politics in the French Revolution* (Ithaca, New York and London 1986) and Lynn A. Hunt, *Politics, Culture and Class in the French Revolution* (Berkeley, Los Angeles and London 1984).

5. Peter Novick, *That Noble Dream: The 'Objectivity Question' and the American Historical Profession* (Cambridge, London and New York 1988).
6. Linda Orr, 'The Romantic Historiography of the Revolution, and French Society', *Consortium on Revolutionary Europe, Proceedings 14* (1984) (Athens, Ga. 1986), pp. 242-8. Those accounts, such as Simon Schama's *Citizens* (Viking, New York 1989), which do dwell on the 'traumatic' history of the Revolution, do so in an anecdotal narrative mode which effectively operates to deprive of meaning the very incidents which are being related.
7. For expansion, see D. Outram, *The Body and the French Revolution: Sex, Class, and Political Culture* (Yale, New Haven and London 1989).
8. E.g. Emil L. Fackenheim, *The Jewish Return into History: Reflections in the Age of Auschwitz and A New Jerusalem* (New York 1978).
9. E.g. Carl Schmitt; see Outram, *The Body and the French Revolution*, pp. 13-15, for more consideration of Schmitt and the idea of a 'Jewish' history of the state.
10. *Surveiller et Punir: Naissance de la Prison* (Paris, Gallimard 1977); Outram, *The Body and the French Revolution*, pp. 16-21.
11. R.R. Palmer, *The Age of the Democratic Revolution* (2 vols, Princeton 1956).
12. K.M. Baker, 'Politique et opinion publique sous l'Ancien Régime', *Annales ESC*, 42 (1987), pp. 41-72; S. Maza, 'Le Tribunal de la nation: les mémoires judiciaires et l'opinion publique à la fin de l'ancien régime', *Annales ESC*, 42 (1987), pp. 73-90.
13. Claude Perroud (ed.), *Les Mémoires de Mme Roland* (2 vols, Paris 1905), II, p. 464.
14. Norbert Elias, *State Formation and Civility* [U.S. title *Power and Civility*]: *The Civilising Process*, E. Jephcott (trans.) (Oxford 1982; New York 1986); *The Court Society*, E. Jephcott (trans.) (Oxford 1983).
15. E.g. the distinguished work by Patrice Higonnet, *Sister Republics* (Harvard 1988).
16. Joan B. Landes, *Women and the Public Sphere in the Age of the French Revolution* (Cornell: Ithaca, New York and London 1988).
17. Ronald Paulson using examples from Spain and Naples has identified this, in Freudian terms, as the 'family drama' of Ancien Régime monarchy; Paulson, *Representations of Revolution 1789-1820* (New Haven and London 1983), pp. 71-9; 301.
18. Adorno and Horkeimer, *Dialektik der Aufklärung.*
19. Geoffrey Best (ed.), *The Permanent Revolution: The French Revolution and its Legacy 1789-1989* (Fontana, London 1988).
20. See the argument in P. Bourdieu, *Distinction: A Social Critique of the Judgement of Taste*, Richard Nice (trans.) (Cambridge, Mass. 1984); 'Le Marché des biens symboliques', *L'Année sociologique*, 3d ser., XXII, 1972, pp. 49-126. The argument in relation to science is expanded in my 'The Politicising of Reason: Science and the Public Realm in the Era of the French Revolution', *Science in Context* (1990), where I establish science as a site for the bourgeoisie of miraculous transformations of power, as well as of its legitimation.
21. We should therefore heed the recent calls of Alisdair McIntyre for a

reintegration of these previously rigidly demarcated intellectual areas: it is only thus that history can demonstrate its public importance by working at the junction of fact and value: Alisdair McIntyre, *After Virtue* (2nd ed., London 1985), pp. 265-72.

CHAPTER 5

1. Marilyn Butler, *Maria Edgeworth: A Literary Biography* (Oxford: Clarendon Press 1972), p. 136.
2. National Library of Ireland MS. 10,166/209.
3. John Robison's scientific publications are listed in the *DNB*. The political work was *Proofs of a Conspiracy against all the Religions and Governments of Europe* . . . This ran to many editions in the first two years, including a '4th ed.' published in Dublin by Watson in 1798. Robison was himself a freemason.
4. Maria Edgeworth, *Tales and Novels* (18 vols, London: Baldwin & Cradock 1832), vol. 6, pp. 174-5. Quotations from Edgeworth's fiction are taken from this collected edition, though it should be noted that the text of *Patronage* underwent extensive revision between the first edition of 1814 and 1832.
5. *Tales and Novels*, vol. 6, p. 1.
6. J. B. Du Bos, *Réflexions critiques sur la poésie et sur la peinture* . . . (Paris: Pissot 1770); see pp. 5-6, 9. Francis X. J. Coleman, *The Aesthetic Thought of the French Enlightenment* (Pittsburgh: University of Pittsburgh Press 1971), pp. 30-1, etc., has a brief discussion of ennui in Du Bos' account of the origins of aesthetic interest.
7. George Berkeley, *Works*, George Sampson (ed.) (London: Bell 1898), vol. 2, p. 223.
8. R. B. McDowell and John A. Woods (eds), *The Correspondence of Edmund Burke: Volume IX May 1796-July 1797* (Cambridge: Cambridge University Press 1970), p. 162.
9. Jonathan Swift, *Irish Tracts 1728-1733*, Herbert Davis (ed.) (Oxford: Blackwell 1971), p. 112.
10. See Butler, p. 60 , n. 1, etc.
11. *Memoirs*, vol. 1, p. 61.
12. *Ibid.*, vol. 2, p. 48.
13. *Tales and Novels*, vol. 1, p. ix.
14. *Ibid.*, vol. 1, p. xiii.
15. *Ibid.*, vol. 18, p. 338.
16. See Marilyn Butler, *Jane Austen and the War of Ideas* (Oxford: Clarendon Press 1975), pp. 219-20, n. 2.
17. *Tales and Novels,* vol. 14, pp. 222-3.
18. *Ibid.*, vol. 14, p. 138.
19. *Ibid.*, vol. 14, p. 145.
20. *Ibid.*, vol. 14, p. 241.
21. *Ibid.*, vol. 14, p. 275.
22. Bodley Library, Oxford, MS. Eng. Misc. e 1463, f. 11.
23. Bodley Library, Oxford, MS. Eng. Misc. c 896, f. 45. A printed text, to which Edgeworth's transcription is very close, may be found in François de Salignac de la Mothe Fénelon, *Oeuvres,* Jacques Le Brun (ed.) (Paris: Gallimard 1983),

vol. 1, pp. 277-510; see esp. 493-4.

24. For the 'Essay on Burke' see Appendix 3 in Maria Edgeworth, *The Absentee*, W.J. Mc Cormack and Kim Walker (eds) (Oxford: World's Classics 1988), pp. 282-4.
25. *Tales and Novels*, vol. 15, pp. 25-6. See *Essays on Practical Education* (London: Johnson 1798), vol. 2, pp. 586-7.
26. *Tales and Novels*, vol. 15, p. 293.
27. *Patronage* involves a plot against Lord Oldborough, and the means of detecting this (by acronym and cipher) is based on the cabal (Clifford, Arlington, Buckingham, Ashley and Lauderdale) of 1672. The reference to Algernon Sidney, irrelevant in the fictional context, makes sense in the light of Sidney's association with political plotting.
28. *Tales and Novels*, vol. 16, p. 126.
29. Temple is twice associated with texts which he reads virtually as a form of self-composition; on the first occasion he reads a life of Lord Chancellor Guildford, and on the second he quotes from a letter written by a secretary to Lord Chancellor West; see *ibid.*, vol. 16, p. 114 and n.
30. *Ibid.*, vol. 14, p. 139.
31. *Ibid.*, vol. 14, p. 86. The 1832 edition diverges from the first, and clarifies to some slight degree its greater obscurity as to how the acronym operates.
32. *Memoirs*, vol. 2, p. 19. The references to Gottlieb Leibnitz (1646-1716) and also to John Wilkins implicate the notion of a universal language (see *Tales and Novels*, vol. 15, p. 84), by means of which the assumed gap between reference and referent, the passage between place and place, might be closed, and the arbitrary aspects of discourse in general brought under a rule.
33. *Tales and Novels*, vol. 16, pp. 175-6.
34. *Ibid.*, vol. 14, p. 148.
35. See the preface to *Castle Rackrent*, n. 13 above. Writing as secrecy, together with the division of readership into quasi-hermetic groups of privileged *illuminati*, is not unconnected with Edgeworth's highly contradictory attitude in *Patronage* towards class, breeding and culture.
36. *Memoirs*, vol. 1, pp. 88-90.
37. See William L. Pressly, *The Life and Art of James Barry* (New Haven, London: Yale University Press 1981) pp. 63-4. Among Barry's other targets was Du Bos's *Réflexions*, see n. 6 above.
38. William Blake, 'The Marriage of Heaven and Hell'.
39. *Tales and Novels*, vol. 14, p. 1.
40. See the republication of the early text in *Patronage*, with an introduction by Eva Figes (London: Pandora 1986), p. 108. I have dealt with this image in connection with the problem of literary origination in 'French Revolution . . . Anglo-Irish Literature . . . Beginnings? The Case of Maria Edgeworth' in Hugh Gough and David Dickson (eds), *Ireland and the French Revolution* (Dublin: Irish Academic Press 1990), pp. 229-43.
41. National Library of Ireland MS. 10,166/865 (Edgeworth to Margaret Ruxton, 20 August 1812).

CHAPTER 6

1. Fredric Jameson, *The Political Unconscious* (London 1981), esp. pp. 65-8.

2. R.B. McDowell, *Ireland in the Age of Imperialism and Revolution, 1760-1801* (Oxford 1979), p. 371.
3. Davis's indebtedness to Wolfe Tone actually took the form of a rudimentary history painting, for in a rough sketch for the frontispiece of his proposed biography of Tone, he depicted a scene in which, as he described it himself, 'Liberty takes down the sword suspended from the ivied wall over Tone's grave and hands it to me!' (National Library of Ireland, MSS. 1791-2). For *The Nation*'s unease with republican sentiments see Kevin McGrath, 'Writers in *The Nation*, 1842-4', *Irish Historical Studies*, vi, no. 23 (March 1949), pp. 195-6.
4. Thomas Davis, 'National Art' in *Literary and Historical Essays* (Dublin 1865), p. 154.
5. 'The History of Ireland' in *ibid.,* pp. 36-7.
6. 'Art Unions', in *ibid*., p. 163.
7. Sir Joshua Reynolds, *Discourses on Art*, Robert R. Wark (ed.) (New Haven and London 1975), p. 69.
8. Dr Johnson's insistence that art and literature address themselves to the universal rather than the particular elevated this doctrine to canonical status in the eighteenth century. In his 'Preface to Shakespeare', he wrote that Shakespeare's 'characters are not modified by the customs of particular places, unpractised by the rest of the world . . . or by the accidents of transient fashions or temporary opinions: they are the genuine progeny of common humanity, such as the world will always supply, and observation will always find' (*Dr Johnson on Shakespeare*, W.K. Wimsatt [ed.] [Harmondsworth 1969], p. 59).
9. Joseph Addison, *The Spectator*, no. 416 (in Joseph Addison and Sir Richard Steele, *The Spectator*, Gregory Smith [ed.], vol. 3 [London 1973], p. 291).
10. G.E. Lessing, *Laokoon*, E.C. Beasley (trans.) (London 1914), chs xiv-xxii.
11. See J.G.A. Pocock, *The Machiavellian Moment: Florentine Republican Thought and the Republican Tradition* (Princeton, NJ 1975), and *Politics, Language and Time* (Chicago and London 1989). For an outstanding discussion of civic humanism in relation to painting, see John Barrell, *The Political Theory of Painting from Reynolds to Hazlitt* (New Haven and London 1986). My account of Reynolds and James Barry in this essay is greatly indebted to Barrell's study.
12. See Barrell, *Political Theory of Painting*, ch. 1.
13. Reynolds, *Discourses*, p. 134.
14. See Norman Bryson, 'Representing the Real: Gros' Paintings of Napoleon' in *History of the Human Sciences*, i, no. 1 (May 1988), pp. 81-2.
15. The 'rectilinear' rationality and 'geometric determination' of David's picture is discussed in Robert Rosenblum, *Transformations in Late Eighteenth-Century Art* (Princeton, NJ 1969), p. 72. The most succinct expression of Burke's critique of the drive towards abstraction in republicanism is in his 'Letter to the Sheriffs of Bristol' (1777) on American affairs: 'Civil freedom, gentlemen, is not . . . a thing that lies hid in the depth of abstruse science. It is a blessing and a benefit, not an abstract speculation . . . Far from any resemblance to those propositions in geometry and metaphysics, which admit no medium, but must be true or false in all their latitude; social and civil freedom, like all other things in common life, are variously mixed and modified, enjoyed in very different degrees, and shaped into an infinite diversity of forms, according to the temper and circumstances of every community' (Edmund Burke, *Works*, Bohn ed., ii [London 1888], p. 30).
16. See Rosenblum, *Transformations*, pp. 50-106. For an analysis of the distinctive

republican concept of the past, with its insistence on a break between the present and classic antiquity, see Lynn Hunt, *Politics, Culture, and Class in the French Revolution* (London 1984), pp. 27 ff.

17. Turnbull's *Treatise on Ancient Painting* was published in 1740 (David Irwin, *English Neoclassical Art* [London 1966], p. 22).
18. Thomas Crow, *Painters and Public Life in Eighteenth-Century Paris* (New Haven and London 1985), pp. 256-7. See ns 74 and 75 below.
19. [Thomas Campbell], *An Essay on Perfecting the Fine Arts in Great Britain and Ireland* (Dublin 1767), p. 34. Though the authorship is uncertain, internal evidence (e.g. the argument that painting is a more difficult art than poetry; the fact that Ireland has no competitors in 'Landskips', and the encomiums to Barret, Fisher, McArdell, Frye and, above all, West) points strongly to common authorship of the essay and Thomas Campbell's anonymous *A Philosophical Survey of the South of Ireland* (London 1777).
20. Sylvester O'Halloran, *An Introduction to the Study of the History and Antiquities of Ireland* (Dublin 1772); Thomas Leland, DD, *The History of Ireland from the Invasion of Henry II* (Dublin 1773).
21. Campbell, *A Philosophical Survey*, pp. 83-4, 239.
22. Campbell's relationship to Dr Johnson's circle is discussed by S.C. Roberts in the introduction to *Dr Campbell's Diary of a Visit to England in 1775*, James L. Clifford (ed.) (Cambridge 1947).
23. Thomas Campbell, *Strictures on the Ecclesiastical and Literary History of Ireland* (London 1790), pp. 13-14. His target is Sylvester O'Halloran's *Insula Sacra* (Limerick 1770).
24. Campbell, *Strictures*, pp. 10, 23, 18.
25. Anthony Pasquin, *Memoirs of the Royal Academicians, being an Attempt to Improve the National Taste* (London 1794), pp. 6-7.
26. Tom Dunne, 'Haunted by History: Irish Romantic Writing 1800-50' in Roy Porter and Mikulas Teich (eds), *Romanticism in National Context* (Cambridge 1988), p. 72.
27. Stanley Ayling, *Edmund Burke: His Life and Opinions* (London 1988), p. 155.
28. Barrell, *Political Theory of Painting*, pp. 158-62.
29. Reynolds, *Discourses*, p. 282.
30. Barrell, *Political Theory of Painting*, p. 151.
31. See, for example, William Preston's spirited poem, *The Contrast or a Comparison between the Characters of the English and Irish in the year 1780: A Poem* (Dublin 1780), written in the heyday of the Volunteer movement, where the author writes of heroic virtue – 'the classic Tome/Th'immortal monuments of Greece and Rome' – that: 'Now, should she come to woo the British train,/ Her brightest beauties were display'd in vain; /Condemn'd, proscrib'd, ah! whither could she fly?/ To what fond bosom? or what kindling eye?' The answer is: Ireland, where 'virtue reigns, sublime supreme, confest;/A nation feels her like a single breast'.
32. James Barry, 'A Letter to the Right Honourable the President, Vice-Presidents and the rest of the Noblemen and Gentlemen of the Society for the Encouragement of Arts, Manufactures, and Commerce' (1793) in *The Works of James Barry, Esq., Historical Painter*, vol. ii (London 1809), p. 445.
33. As the name of an Irish street ballad, 'A New Song called the Beautiful Phoenix' (1776) indicates, the image of the phoenix was also used to express Irish solidarity with the American colonists (R.B. McDowell, *Irish Public*

Opinion 1750-1800 [London 1944], pp. 44-5).

34. James Barry, 'Lectures on Painting Delivered at the Royal Academy' (1784-93) in *Works*, i, pp. 374 ff.
35. Barry, 'A Letter' in *Works*, vol. ii, p. 457 ff.
36. Richard Sennett, *The Fall of Public Man* (Cambridge 1977).
37. Sir Joshua Reynolds, 'Journey to Flanders and Holland' in *The Literary Works of Sir Joshua Reynolds*, ii (London 1852), pp. 188-91.
38. James Barry, 'An Inquiry into the Real and Imaginary Obstructions to the Acquisitions of the Arts in England'(1774), in *Works*, ii, p. 246.
39. 'James Barry' in Richard Ryan, *Biographia Hibernica*, i (London 1819-21), p. 68.
40. Barry, 'Lectures on Painting' in *Works*, i, p. 372.
41. James Barry, 'An Account of a Series of Pictures in the Great Room of the Society of Arts, Manufactures, and Commerce, at the Adelphi' (1783), in *Works*, ii, p. 361.
42. Barry was not the first visually to represent the Irish harp in a republican setting: an elaborate frontispiece to John Toland's edition of James Harrington's *Oceana and Other Works* (Dublin 1737) pays homage to the proto-republican (and ex-Catholic) Irish writer Toland, by surrounding an emblematic Irish harp (in addition to a rose and thistle) with profiles of Solon Lycurgus, Numa, Lucius Junius and Junius Brutus, amongst others.
43. Barry, 'An Account of a Series of Pictures', *Works*, ii, p. 371. Barry accepted that 'the ingenious Mr Macpherson' had contributed greatly to Ossian's reputation by his publications, but he took issue with Macpherson's attempt to deprive Ossian of his Irish ancestry. For the eighteenth-century Irish response to Macpherson, see Clare O'Halloran, 'Irish Re-Creations of the Gaelic Past: The Challenge of Macpherson's Ossian'. *Past and Present,* no. 124 (August 1989), pp. 69-95.
44. The Act has been acknowledged as 'the first decree granting complete religious liberty to emanate from an assembly' ('Religious Freedom' in *Encyclopaedia of Social Sciences*, xiii [New York 1942], cited in Leo Pfeffer, *Church, State and Freedom* [Boston 1953], p. 73).
45. Juan de Mariana (1536-1624) became notorious in Church history for his defence of regicide, which he supported on the grounds that sovereignty rested ultimately in the people, not in monarchs.
46. *The Letters of Charles O'Conor of Belanagare*, Catherine Coogan Ward and Robert Ward (eds)(Ann Arbor, Michigan 1980), i, pp. 283, 284, 286, 294.
47. *The Letters of Charles O'Conor*, ii, p. 264. Barry explained that he chose Pole because he was 'the last English cardinal, and, as far as my knowledge extends, the first writer, who to the new fangled doctrines of the divine right and irresistible power of kings, and the passive obedience of subjects opposed those sacred rights of the people' (Barry, 'A Letter' in *Works*, ii, p. 451). A central feature of Barry's attempt to redefine republicanism within a Catholic frame was his argument that the divine right of kings was instituted by Protestant monarchs such as Henry VIII.
48. William Burke's *An Account of the European Settlements in America*, revised by Edmund Burke, was first published in London (1757). O'Conor refers to the Irish reprint, which would seem to be that published by Peter Wilson in 1762 *(The Letters of Charles O'Conor*, ii, pp. 109-10).
49. George Sigerson, *The Last Independent Parliament of Ireland* (Dublin 1919),

pp. xxv-xxvi.

50. Barry, 'An Account of a Series of Pictures', *Works*, ii, p. 367.
51. James Barry, 'A Letter to the Dilettanti Society' (1793), in *Works*, ii, pp. 574-5.
52. Ryan, *Biographia Hibernica*, pp. 67-8. The most authoritative presentation of this argument was Reynolds's Eighth Discourse (1778), which was greatly influenced by Lessing: see especially Reynolds, *Discourses,* pp. 146-7.
53. Given the tendency in civic humanism to conceive of time in terms of contingency and random details, it followed that the inclusion of too many particulars in a painting was tantamount to exposing the serenity of universal themes to the incursions, indeed the ravages, of time.
54. Joseph Cooper Walker, *Historical Memoirs of the Irish Bards* (2nd ed., Dublin 1818), ii, p. 3.
55. *Portraits by Sir Joshua Reynolds*, Fredrick W. Hilles (ed.) (London 1952), p. 128 (cited in Barrell, *Political Theory of Painting*, p. 159).
56. Campbell, *Strictures*, p. 9.
57. Cooper Walker, *Historical Memoirs*, i, pp. 12, 67.
58. Samuel Weber, 'Capitalizing History: Notes on *The Political Unconscious*' in *Diacritics*, 13, no. 2 (Summer 1983), p. 27.
59. Barry, *Works*, i, p. 264. Burke's authorship of the anonymous letter sent to Barry in 1783 has been questioned by Robert W. Wark, but stylistic turns in the phraseology, as well as the overall arguments, point strongly to Burke's hand in drafting the letter.
60. In contrast to the level of abstraction in David's *The Oath of the Horatii*, which invents a scene that is not in any of the literary sources (Bryson, 'Representing the Real', p. 81), the origins of Barry's *The Baptism of the King of Cashel*, as related by his earliest biographies, attest to a deep immersion in Irish history: Barry was supposed to have found the story not in any artistic source but through his own acquaintance with Irish legends. ('Mr Barry' in *Public Characters of 1800-1801* [London 1801], p. 304; Thomas Campbell, *A Philosophical Survey*, p. 444).
61. William Drennan, 'Intended Defence on a Trial for Sedition, in the Year 1794', in *Fugitive Pieces in Verse and Prose* (Belfast 1815), p. 194.
62. See William Pressly's valuable article, 'James Barry's *The Baptism of the King of Cashel by St Patrick*', in *Burlington Magazine*, cxviii (September 1976), pp. 643-6.
63. Pressly, *art cit.*, p. 644. Barry's work was directly associated with the campaign for legislative independence in Ireland. The first version of his St Patrick painting was actually hung in the Irish House of Parliament, and in the late 1770s his prints 'The Phoenix' and 'Philoctetes' circulated among radical groups in Ireland. In 1780 he was admitted to the Order of Saint Patrick, the leading patriotic society in Dublin, whose name attests to the political resonance of St Patrick for the patriot movement. See William Pressly, *James Barry: The Artist as Hero*, Tate Gallery catalogue (London 1983), pp. 157, 161.
64. See the illuminating remarks by Michael Cohen in *Engaging English Art* (Tuscaloosa and London 1987), p. 31: 'Composition, especially that of a number of figures, can work to signal the passage of time. E.H. Gombrich points out a strategy used in pictures where a crowd of onlookers watches some important event; it is "that dramatic device of bystanders not looking at the scene itself but at each other, which extends the time span. They have seen what is happening and are now exchanging glances or remarks.' (The

Gombrich citation is from E.H. Gombrich, 'Moment and Movement in Art' in *The Image and the Eye* [London 1982], p. 55.)

65. See William Pressly, *The Life and Art of James Barry* (New Haven and London 1981), pp. 181-2.
66. Barry, 'Lectures on Painting', *Works*, p. 494.
67. Barry, *Works*, i, pp. 317, 323.
68. Davis lamented : 'Ireland has had some great painters – Barry and Forde for example . . . But their works were seldom done for Ireland, and are rarely known in it . . . Irish history has supplied no subjects for our greatest Artists; and though, as we repeat, Ireland possessed a Forde and Barry, creative Painters of the highest order, the pictures of the latter are mostly abroad' (Davis, 'National Art', pp. 155-6, 158).
69. [Joseph Cooper Walker], *Outlines of a Plan for Promoting the Art of Painting in Ireland: with a List of Subjects and Painters drawn from the Romantic and Genuine Histories of Ireland* (Dublin 1790), p. 16.
70. *Ibid.*, p. 17. The quotation, we are told, 'is altered from Mr Hayley's admirable Epistle to an eminent painter'.
71. Reynolds, *Discourses*, p. 62.
72. Cooper Walker, *Outlines*, p. 20; Barry, 'Lectures on Painting', *Works*, ii, p. 415.
73. Cooper Walker, *Outlines*, pp. 23, 32 (my italics).
74. See Edgar Wind's classic study, 'The Revolution of History Painting', reprinted in Harold Spencer (ed.), *Readings in Art History* (2nd ed., New York 1976), ii, pp. 233-52. The prohibition on painting contemporary scenes was at one with the civic humanist view that the heroic past was totally sealed off from the present.
75. Albert Boime, *Art in the Age of Revolution 1750-1800* (Chicago and London 1987), pp. 281-4. Wheatley's large-scale homages to the patriot movement, the most famous of which were *A View of College Green with a Meeting of the Volunteers on the 4th of November, 1779* (1780) and *The Irish House of Commons: Henry Grattan urging the Claim of Irish Rights, 8 June 1780*, would appear to be among the first history paintings to dispense with the safety valve of exotic locations, and to anchor historic events in a specific time and place. It was as if, due to the pressure of Irish politics, history painting was finally forced to confront the exigencies of actual history.
76. Cooper Walker, *Outlines*, p. 36.
77. Charles Owen O'Conor Don, *The O'Conors of Connaught* (Dublin 1891), pp. 297-303; *The Life of Theobald Wolfe Tone*, W.T.W. Tone (ed.) (Washington 1826), vol. i, pp. 144-5.
78. T.A. Emmet, 'Part of an Essay towards the History of Ireland' in W.J. MacNevan, *Pieces of Irish History* (New York 1807), pp. 14-15 (my italics).

CHAPTER 7

1. S.T. Coleridge, *Notebooks* (Nonesuch Coleridge), pp. 176-7. I am very grateful to Heather Glen for drawing my attention to this passage.
2. Enoch Powell, *Freedom and Reality: Selected Speeches*, J. Wood (ed.) (London 1969), p. 245; cited in Tom Nairn, *The Break-Up of Britain: Crisis and Neo-Nationalism* (2nd, expanded, ed., London 1981), p. 266.

3. H.M. Chadwick, *The Nationalities of Europe and the Growth of National Ideologies* (Cambridge 1945), p. 3.
4. John Plamenatz, 'Two Types of Nationalism', in Eugene Kamenka (ed.), *Nationalism: The Nature and Evolution of an Idea* (Canberra 1973), p. 27.
5. Cf. the opening sentence of Gerald Newman's recent book, *The Rise of English Nationalism: A Cultural History 1750-1830* (London 1987): 'It is strange to think how greatly English nationalism has eluded our scholarly attention.'
6. Benedict Anderson, *Imagined Communities: Reflections on the Origin and Spread of Nationalism* (London 1983), p. 69.
7. See K.M. Elisabeth Murray, *Caught in the Web of Words: James Murray and the Oxford English Dictionary* (London 1977). One indication of the fierceness of his Liberalism is that in 1910, following the Lords' rejection of the 'People's Budget', he wanted to see an English equivalent of the French Revolution (p. 335).
8. See the discussion of Stubbs in J.W. Burrow, *A Liberal Descent: Victorian Historians and the English Past* (Cambridge 1981), Part II.
9. Some examples of the unsteady definitions of the patria during this period are given in J.H. Grainger, *Patriotisms, Britain: 1900-1939* (London 1986), ch. 1. The more general problem of the changing limits of the British polity is raised in J.G.A. Pocock, 'The Limits and Divisions of British History: In Search of the Unknown Subject', *American Historical Review*, 87 (1982), pp. 311-36.
10. Patrick Wright, *On Living in an Old Country: The National Past in Contemporary Britain* (London 1985); see also Alun Howkins, 'The Discovery of Rural England', in Robert Colls and Philip Dodd (eds), *Englishness: Politics and Culture 1880-1920* (Beckenham 1986).
11. Newman, *Rise of English Nationalism*, esp. ch. 6; Newman seems both to exaggerate the novelty of his enquiry and to press his case about a 'middle-class nationalist movement' a little hard.
12. Herbert Butterfield, *The Englishman and his History* (London 1944), p. 2; cited in Burrow, *Liberal Descent*, p. 295.
13. I am adapting the term from Lewis Campbell, *On the Nationalisation of the Old Universities* (London 1901). Campbell was referring not to the possibility of taking Oxford and Cambridge into public ownership, but rather to those changes in recent decades that had led them to be seen as 'national' rather than 'sectional' institutions (he was primarily concerned with their shedding of their exclusively Anglican character and their subsequent incorporation of the Nonconformists). The more general features of the process in this period are touched upon in T.W. Heyck, *The Transformation of Intellectual Life in Victorian England* (London 1982), esp. chs 6 and 8.
14. This problem is interestingly touched upon with reference to American literature in Russell Reising, *The Unusable Past: The Theory and Study of American Literature* (London 1986), ch. 1.
15. This constellation of attitudes has, of course, persisted well into the twentieth century, perhaps, in some quarters, right up to the present. For a compendium of conventional clichés on the subject, see the semi-official compilation edited by Ernest Barker, *The Character of England* (1947), for example p. 572 for the claim that, although philosophy has proved 'outside the reach of the native genius' (or, in a characteristic and unselfconscious hunting metaphor, 'the English mind has baulked and stumbled at the fence of philosophy'), this has more than been made up for by the glories of English poetry. 'There is a

compensation in things; and the genius which denied England any great philosophy in prose may be said to have atoned for that denial by another and greater gift.' 'Greater': still cultural Top Nation, at least.

16. The passage is quoted in John H. Fisher, 'Nationalism and the Study of Literature', *American Scholar*, 49 (1979-80), p. 10, who misattributes it to 1897, three years after Morley's death. *The First Sketch* sold over 40,000 copies; see John Gross, *The Rise and Fall of the Man of Letters* (London 1969), p. 172. For a rather chatty account of Morley, Professor of English at University College, London 1865-89 (and no relation of John Morley), see Jo McMurty, *English Language, English Literature: The Creation of an Academic Discipline* (Hamden, Conn. 1985), ch. 2.
17. For details see Charles Morgan, *The House of Macmillan (1843-1943)* (London 1943), pp. 62-3. The role of the later *Oxford Book of English Verse* would repay investigation; cf. Paul Fussell's comment that this anthology 'presides over the Great War in a way that has never been sufficiently appreciated'; *The Great War and Modern Memory* (London 1975), p. 159.
18. Details of the unsuccessful wooing of George Eliot are given in Morgan, *House of Macmillan*, pp. 115-18, which reveals that Arnold was another potential contributor who got away.
19. For a perceptive discussion of the series see Gross, *Rise and Fall of the Man of Letters*, pp. 106-8, including the judgment that 'no comparable series has ever come so close to attaining the rank of a traditional British institution'. There is an amusing parody of the somewhat predictable biographical format of the series in Stephen Potter, *The Muse in Chains: A Study in Education* (London 1937), p. 81.
20. For further discussion, see Stefan Collini, '"Manly Fellows": Fawcett, Stephen and the Liberal Temper' in Lawrence Goldman (ed.), *The Blind Victorian: Henry Fawcett and British Liberalism* (Cambridge 1989), pp. 41-59.
21. Edmund Gosse in effect succeeded Stephen as the leading journeyman of letters, contributing several volumes to these series; see Ann Thwaite, *Edmund Gosse: A Literary Landscape* (London 1984).
22. H. S. Solly, *The Life of Henry Morley, LLD* (London 1898), pp. 356-7; quoted in McMurty, *English Language, English Literature*, p. 61.
23. The classic account of this tradition is, of course, Raymond Williams, *Culture and Society 1780-1950* (London 1958).
24. In responding in 1886 to John Churton Collins's circular letter soliciting views in support of his proposal that a course in English Literature should be taught at the universities, Arnold at first replied: 'I should be glad to see at the Universities not a new School established for Modern Literature or Modern Languages, but the great works of English literature taken in conjunction with those of Greek and Latin Literature in the final Examination for honours in Literae Humaniores.' In the subsequently published version of his reply he wrote: 'I should be sorry to see a separate School.' The earlier reply was quoted by Collins in an article in the *Quarterly* in January 1887, and the later one was published in the *Pall Mall Gazette* on 7 January 1887; the latter is reproduced in Appendix I (and the former cited in the editor's notes) in R.H. Super (ed.), *The Complete Prose Works of Matthew Arnold* (11 vols, Michigan 1960-77), XI, pp. 380, 501.
25. 'A Guide to English Literature' (1877), *Complete Prose*, vol. VIII, p. 240.
26. Cf the reminiscence of Sir Arthur Quiller-Couch, lecturing at Cambridge in

1916: 'Few in this room are old enough to remember the shock of awed surmise [*sic*] which fell upon young minds presented, in the late 'seventies or early 'eighties of the last century, with Freeman's *Norman Conquest* or Green's *Short History of the English People*; in which, as through parting clouds of darkness, we beheld our ancestry, literary as well as political, radiantly legitimised.' Sir Arthur Quiller-Couch, *Cambridge Lectures* (London 1943), p. 22 .

27. There is a growing literature on this. For the men of letters, see D.C. Wright, 'The Great War, Government Propaganda, and English "Men of Letters" 1914-18', *Literature and History*, 7 (1978), pp. 70-100; and particularly Peter Buitenhaus, *The Great War of Words: Literature as Propaganda, 1914-18 and After* (London 1988). For the professors see Stuart Wallace, *War and the Image of Germany: British Academics 1914-1918* (Edinburgh 1988).
28. This emerges very clearly from Fussell's marvellous *Great War and Modern Memory,* esp. ch. VII.
29. This would not be strictly incompatible with Buitenhuis's claim that as a result of the willing participation of men of letters in the propaganda war, the prestige of that generation of writers was much diminished; *Great War of Words*, Epilogue.
30. *The Teaching of English in England* (London, HMSO 1921). Among the wealth of quotable passages in this Report the following discussion of Chaucer's debts to Italian and French literature conveys the tone of heated nationalism: 'But he [Chaucer] is himself English of the English; and if we look for earlier appearances of the most permanent, at least of the deepest and most serious characteristics of our race, it is not in any Mediterranean books that we shall find them, but in things written in this island, connected though they be with Chaucer by the slenderest of links, in Beowulf and Alfred and Bede' (p. 213).
31. There is a useful summary of the diverse developments lumped together here in D.L. LeMahieu, *A Culture for Democracy: Mass Communication and the Cultivated Mind in Britain between the Wars* (Oxford 1988). One particularly influential form taken by this anxiety is explored in Francis Mulhern, *The Moment of 'Scrutiny'* (London 1979).
32. See Antoine Compagnon, *La Troisième République des lettres: de Flaubert à Proust* (Paris 1983), pp. 142-3. Compagnon's book is a particularly rich source for suggestive comparisons about the very different relations between politics and literary criticism in France during this period.
33. T.S. Eliot, *After Strange Gods* (London 1934), p. 13.
34. Bernard Crick, *George Orwell: A Life* (London 1980), p. 137.
35. It will be evident even from these very brief remarks that I do not believe that the professionalization of criticism following the so-called 'critical revolution' of the 1920s meant that it was no longer concerned with these large issues of national identity. There seems to me to be some naïvety in claiming that thereafter 'English literature as a discipline in higher education shook off what had previously been its role (as one aspect of its study of the 'national character') and emerged as an autonomous academic domain almost exclusively concerned with the study of its own texts'; Brian Doyle, 'The Hidden History of English Studies', in Peter Widdowson (ed.), *Re-Reading English* (London 1982), p. 28.
36. For example, Geoffrey Hill finds 'an elegiac tinge to the air of this country

since the end of the Great War'; cited in a very perceptive article by David Gervais, '"Something Gone": "England" in Modern English Writing', *English*, 158 (1988), p. 115.

37. T.S. Eliot, 'Milton' (British Academy Lecture 1947), reprinted in *On Poetry and Poets* (London 1957); quotation p. 148.

CHAPTER 8

1. W. C. Sellar and R J. Yeatman, *1066 and All That* (Harmondsworth 1967), p. 71. I am grateful to Stephen Davison and the members of the conference for their comments on this paper.
2. For Clark and Hexter, see pp. 141-2 below; for Stone's recent views, L. Stone, *The Causes of the English Revolution 1529-1642* (2nd ed., London 1986), pp. 165-74.
3. Most assessments of the debate say little about the political dimension after the 1930s, for example M. G. Finlayson, *Historians, Puritanism and the English Revolution* (Toronto 1983); H. Tomlinson, 'The Causes of War: A Historiographical Survey', in *idem* (ed.), *Before the English Civil War* (London 1983), pp. 7-26; and R.C. Richardson, *The Debate on the English Revolution Revisited* (London 1988). Those which do discuss it tend to be from the right, like Jonathan Clark, or the left, like J. Sanderson. 'Reflections upon Marxist Historiography: The Case of the English Civil War', in B. Chapman and A. Potter (eds), *W.J.M.M. Political Questions* (Manchester 1974), pp. 226-51, and H. J. Kaye, *The British Marxist Historians* (Cambridge 1984), pp. 99-130.
4. B. S. Manning, *The English People and the English Revolution* (London 1976) – but see J. S. Morrill, 'Provincial Squires and "Middling Sorts" in the Great Rebellion', *Historical Journal*, 20 (1977), pp. 229-36 – and D. Underdown, *Revel, Riot and Rebellion* (Oxford 1985) – but see reviews by Morrill in *Journal of British Studies*, 26 (1987), pp. 451-67 and M. J. Ingram in *Journal of Historical Geography*, 12 (1986), pp. 432-4, and Anne Hughes's comments in R. Cust and A. Hughes (eds), *Conflict in Early Stuart England*, pp. 240-3.
5. J.P.D. Dunbabin, 'Oliver Cromwell's Popular Image in Nineteenth-Century England' in J.S. Bromley and E.H. Kossmann (eds), *Britain and the Netherlands V* (The Hague 1975), pp. 141-63; B. Bushaway, *By Rite: Custom, Ceremony and Community in England 1700-1880* (London 1982), pp. 74-80. A stronger case for survival of radical ideas after 1660 is made in C. Hill, *Some Intellectual Consequences of the English Revolution* (London 1980), and *idem*, *The Experience of Defeat* (New York 1984).
6. Dunbabin, 'Cromwell', *passim*; R. Ollard, *The Escape of Charles II after the Battle of Worcester* (London 1966).
7. C. Hill, 'The Norman Yoke', *Puritanism and Revolution* (London 1958), pp. 50-122; A. Pallister, *Magna Carta: The Heritage of Liberty* (Oxford 1971), *passim*. Today's 'Sealed Knot' is a 'Society of Royalists and Parliamentarians', unlike the original exclusively Royalist (and socially exalted) group of conspirators.
8. R. Terrill, *R. H. Tawney and his Times* (London 1974), pp. 39-42; J.M. Winter (ed.), *History and Society: Essays by R.H. Tawney* (London 1978), pp. 3-4. C. Hill and E. Dell (eds), *The Good Old Cause* (London 1949), and see pp. 131-5 above.

9. R. Macgillivray, *Restoration Historians and the English Civil War* (The Hague 1974), pp. 18-19, 174; Richardson, *Debate*, chs 2-3, 5.
10. On the aims and value of the work of Clarendon, see H.R. Trevor-Roper, 'Clarendon and the Practice of History', in F.R. Fogle and H. R. Trevor-Roper, *Milton and Clarendon* (Los Angeles 1965); of Hume, V.G. Wexler, *David Hume and the History of England,* American Philosophical Society, Memoirs Series, 131 (Philadelphia 1979); and of Hallam, T. P. Peardon, *The Transition in English Historical Writing 1760-1830* (New York 1933), pp. 207-13, 271-6.
11. H.T. Dickinson, *Liberty and Property: Political Ideology in Eighteenth-Century Britain* (London 1977), pp. 47-9, 164-5; J. C. D. Clark, *English Society 1688-1832* (Cambridge 1985), chs 2-3; Richardson, *Debate*, pp. 48-9.
12. J.W. Burrow, *A Liberal Descent: Victorian Historians and the English Past* (Cambridge 1981), p. 18.
13. Cited by Richardson, *Debate*, pp. 71-2.
14. Burrow, *Liberal Descent*, chs 2-5; and see J. Hamburger, *Macaulay and the Whig Tradition* (Chicago 1976).
15. See the quotation cited on p. 129 above; G. M. Trevelyan, *England under Queen Anne* (3 vols, London 1930-4), lii, pp. 320-1; J.M. Hernon, Jr, 'The Last Whig Historian and Consensus History', *American Historical Review*, 81 (1976), pp. 80-1.
16. Catherine Macaulay, *The History of England from the Accession of James I to the Elevation of the House of Hanover* (8 vols, London 1763-83), iv, pp. 417-18, 421-2, 425-8, 433-6; Richardson, *Debate*, p. 55.
17. Cited by Hernon, 'Last Whig Historian', p. 86.
18. S.R. Gardiner, *History of England from the Accession of James I to the Outbreak of the Civil War* (10 vols, London 1884); *History of the Great Civil War 1642-49* (4 vols, London 1893-4); *History of the Commonwealth to the Protectorate* (3 vols, London 1894-1903).
19. Gardiner, *History of England*, ii, 9; on criticism of Gardiner, see D.M. Fahey, 'Gardiner and Usher in Perspective', *Journal of Historical Studies*, 1 (1968), pp. 137-50; J. P. Kenyon, *The History Men* (London 1983), pp. 214-22; and Finlayson, *Historians*, pp. 17-18, 24-7, 62-7.
20. G. M. Trevelyan, *Clio, A Muse* (London 1913) and *An Autobiography and Other Essays* (London 1949); Hernon, 'Last Whig Historian', pp. 91-2.
21. *Ibid*., p. 91, n. 94.
22. R. Eccleshall, *British Liberalism* (London 1986); F. O'Gorman, *British Conservatism* (London 1986); M. Pugh, *The Making of Modern British Politics* (Oxford 1982), pts 2-4.
23. Trevelyan, *Queen Anne*, iii, pp. 96, 161, 191, 320-1; and see Hernon, 'Last Whig Historian', pp. 81, 87-90.
24. F. Furet, *Interpreting the French Revolution* (Cambridge 1981), esp. pt 1.
25. Eduard Bernstein's *Cromwell and Communism*, published in 1930, was subtitled 'Socialism and Democracy in the Great English Revolution', from the original German title; Christopher Hill's essay on *The English Revolution 1640* was first published in 1940, though the title had been used by Guizot and Engels in the mid-nineteenth century.
26. Terrill, *Tawney*, chs 1-3; Winter, *History and Society,* pp. 7-9.
27. R. H. Tawney, *The Agrarian Problem in the Sixteenth Century* (London 1912); *Religion and the Rise of Capitalism* (London 1926).

28. R. H. Tawney, 'The Rise of the Gentry, 1558-1640', *Economic History Review*, 11 (1941); *idem*, 'Harrington's Interpretation of his Age', *Proceedings of the British Academy*, 27 (1941), pp. 199-223; Winter, *History and Society*, pp. 21-8.
29. *Ibid*., p. 126; Tawney, *Agrarian Problem*, p. 131; Stone, *Causes*, ch. 2.
30. Pugh, *British Politics*, pt 4; P. Addison, *The Road to 1945: British Politics and the Second World War* (London 1977); K. Harris, *Attlee* (London 1982).
31. Kaye, *British Marxist Historians,* pp. 101-2; G. Eley and W. Hunt (eds), *Reviving the English Revolution: Reflections and Elaborations on the Work of Christopher Hill* (London 1988), p. 55; B. Schwarz, '"The People" in History: The Communist Party Historians' Group 1946-56', in R. Johnson, G. McLennan, B. Schwarz and D. Sutton (eds), *Making Histories: Studies in History-Writing and Politics* (London 1982), pp. 44-95.
32. C. Hill, *The Century of Revolution* (Edinburgh 1961), pt 1; *Reformation to Industrial Revolution* (London 1967), pts 1-3; and see Richardson, *Debate*, pp. 110-16. For a full bibliography of Hill's work to 1978 see D. Pennington and K. V. Thomas (eds), *Puritans and Revolutionaries* (Oxford 1978), pp. 382-402.
33. C. Hill, *Change and Continuity in Seventeenth-Century England* (London 1975), pp. 278-82; *idem*, 'A Bourgeois Revolution?', in J.G.A. Pocock (ed.), *Three British Revolutions* (Princeton 1980), pp. 109-39; and see *idem*, 'Parliament and People in Seventeenth-Century England', *Past and Present*, 92 (1981), pp. 101, 103, 115-22; for attacks by Hexter and Clark, see ns 61, 64, 70 below.
34. E. Hobsbawm, 'The Historians' Group of the Communist Party', in M. Cornforth (ed.), *Rebels and their Causes* (London 1978); Schwarz, '"The People" in History', pp. 59, 68-70; and Kaye, *British Marxist Historians*, *passim.*
35. E.g. C. Hill, *Intellectual Origins of the English Revolution* (Oxford 1965) and *Society and Puritanism in Pre-Revolutionary England* (London 1964). M. Heinemann, 'How the Words got on the Page', in Eley and Hunt (eds), *Reviving the English Revolution*, p. 84, and see also pp. 49, 339.
36. *Ibid*., pp. 73-97; C. Hill, *A Turbulent, Seditious and Factious People: John Bunyan and his Church* (Oxford 1988); I. M. Green, 'Bunyan in Context: The Changing Character of Protestantism in Seventeenth-Century England', *VU Studies on Protestant History I* (Amsterdam 1990), pp. 1-27.
37. Schwarz, '"The People" in History', pp. 69-72, 82, 92-5.
38. C. Hill, *The World Turned Upside Down* (London 1972); 'The Religion of Gerrard Winstanley', *Past and Present*, supplement no. 5 (1978); *Milton and the English Revolution* (London 1977); and C. Hill, B. Reay and W. Lamont, *The World of the Muggletonians* (London 1983).
39. J.S. Morrill, 'The Church in England 1642-9', in *idem* (ed.), *Reactions to the English Civil War* (London 1982), pp. 89-114; Keith Thomas, 'The Levellers and the Franchise', in G. Aylmer (ed.), *The Interregnum* (London 1974), pp. 57-78; J.C. Davis, *Fear, Myth and History: The Ranters and the Historians* (Cambridge 1986), chs 1, 6.
40. See the works cited in ns 34-5.
41. L. Stone, 'A Life of Learning', *American Council of Learned Societies Newsletter,* xxxvi (1985), pp. 7-8 (I am grateful to Dr Kevin Sharpe for bringing this article to my attention). Stone is clearly aware of the dangers of moralizing and present-mindedness in his approach but feels they can be kept in check: *ibid*., pp. 16, 21-2.

42. *Ibid.*, pp. 12-19, and see *idem*, *The Past and the Present* (London 1981), ch. 1
43. *Ibid.*, p. 8, and 'Life of Learning', pp. 8, 16, 20 and *passim*.
44. *Ibid.*, pp. 10, 15; *Causes*, pp. 38-40; 'The Bourgeois Revolution of Seventeenth-Century England Revisited', *Past and Present*, 109 (1985), pp. 44-54.
45. 'Life of Learning', p. 19, but see *Causes*, p. 168 for a statement of belief in 'great *as well as* trivial causes' (Stone's emphasis).
46. *Ibid.*, pp. 47-164; and 'Life of Learning', pp. 13-14, 16-19.
47. *Ibid.*, pp. 18-19; 'Second Thoughts', in *Causes*, pp. 165-81; and 'The Results of the English Revolutions of the Seventeenth Century', in Pocock (ed.), *Three British Revolutions*, pp. 23-108. For criticism of Stone's work on the aristocracy, see D.C. Coleman in *History*, 51 (1966). A. Everitt in *Agric. Hist. Rev.*, 16 (1968) and J.H. Hexter, *On Historians* (London 1979), ch. 4.
48. Stone, 'Life of Learning', p. 8. Nevertheless, he seems to be on balance an optimist: *idem*, *Causes*, p. 40.
49. Stone, 'Life of Learning', p. 10; H.R Trevor-Roper, 'The Gentry 1540-1640', *Econ. Hist. Rev. Supplement*, 1 (1953); J.H. Hexter, *Reappraisals in History* (London 1961), chs 2, 5, 6; and *idem*, *On Historians*, chs 4 and 5; see also letters to the editor in *Times Literary Supplement*, 14 November 1975, 12 and 19 December 1975 and 9 January 1976.
50. P. Laslett, *The World We Have Lost* (3rd ed., London 1983).
51. G.R. Elton, 'A High Road to Civil War?', and 'The Unexplained Revolution' are both reprinted in his *Studies in Tudor and Stuart Politics and Government* (3 vols, Cambridge 1974-83), ii, pp. 164-89.
52. D. Brunton and D. Pennington, *Members of the Long Parliament* (London 1954); M.F. Keeler, *The Long Parliament 1640-41: A Biographical Study of the Members*, Amer. Phil. Soc. Memoirs, 36 (Philadelphia 1954).
53. J.P. Kenyon, *The Stuart Constitution* (Cambridge 1966); and see also his *The Stuarts* (London 1958), and *Stuart England* (Harmondsworth 1978).
54. H.R. Trevor-Roper, 'Gentry', and 'The General Crisis of the Seventeenth Century', in T. Aston (ed.), *Crisis in Europe 1569-1660* (London 1965), pp. 59-95; and *idem*, *Catholics, Anglicans and Puritans* (London 1987), chs 2, 4.
55. *Encounter*, vii (6 June 1957), p. 17; H. Lloyd-Jones, V. Pearl and B. Worden (eds), *History and Imagination*, pp. 1-14, 356-69. For Trevor-Roper's reputation as a savage critic, see V. Mehta, *The Fly and the Fly-Bottle* (London 1962), pp. 90-100, 108-14.
56. A. Everitt, *The Community of Kent and the Great Rebellion* (Leicester 1966), *Change in the Provinces* (Leicester 1969), and *The Local Community and the Great Rebellion* (London 1969); J.S. Morrill, *Cheshire 1630-1660* (Oxford 1974) and *The Revolt of the Provinces* (London 1976). See also A. Fletcher, *A County Community in Peace and War: Sussex 1600-1660* (London 1975), and for critiques, C. Holmes, 'The County Community in Stuart Historiography', *Journal of British Studies*, 19 (1980), pp. 54-73, B.S. Manning, 'Parliament, "Party" and "Community" during the English Civil War', *ante*, 14 (1983), pp. 97-119, and A. Hughes, 'Local History and the Origins of the Civil War' in Cust and Hughes (eds), *Conflict*, pp. 193-223.
57. C. Russell, 'Parliamentary History in Perspective 1604-1629', *History*, 61 (1976), pp. 1-27; 'Introduction', in *idem* (ed.), *The Origins of the English Civil War* (London 1973), pp. 12-17, 27-31; *Parliaments and English Politics 1621-1629* (Oxford 1979); and 'The British Problem and the English Civil War', *History*, 72 (1987), pp. 395-415; K. Sharpe, 'Introduction' and '"Revisionism"

Revisited' in *idem* (ed.), *Faction and Parliament: Essays on Early Stuart History* (2nd ed., London 1975), pp. ix-xvii, 1-42; J.S. Morrill, 'Introduction' in *Reactions*, pp. 2-14; J.C.D. Clark, *Revolution and Rebellion: State and Society in England* (Cambridge 1986); see also A. Fletcher, *The Outbreak of the English Civil War* (London 1981).

58. N. Tyacke, 'Puritanism, Arminianism and Counter-Revolution' in Russell (ed.), *Origins*, pp. 119-43 (and see Russell on pp. 17-27), and *idem*, *Anti-Calvinists: The Rise of English Arminianism* (Oxford 1987); C. Russell, *The Causes of the English Civil War* (Oxford 1990), chs 3-4; Morrill, 'The Religious Context of the English Civil War', *R. Hist. Soc. Trans.*, 5th ser., 34 (1984), pp. 155-78; P. White, 'The Rise of Arminianism Reconsidered', *Past and Present*, 101 (1983), pp. 34-54, but see also nos. 114 and 115 (1987); K. Sharpe, 'Archbishop Laud', *History Today*, 36 (August 1986), pp. 26-30.
59. J.H. Hexter, 'Power Struggle, Parliament and Liberty in Early Stuart England', *Jn. Mod. Hist.*, 50 (1978), pp. 1-50; 'Historiographical Perspectives, The Early Stuarts and Parliament: Old Hat and the *Nouvelle Vague*', *Parliamentary History*, I (1982), pp. 181-215; and 'The Birth of Modern Freedom', *Times Literary Supplement* (21 January 1983), pp. 51-4; T. K. Rabb, 'The Role of the Commons', and D. Hirst, 'The Place of Principle', in *Past and Present*, 92 (1981), pp. 55-78 and 79-99; D. Hirst, *The Representative of the People?* (London 1975).
60. W. Hunt, *The Puritan Moment: The Coming of War in an English County* (Harvard 1983); Eley and Hunt, *Reviving the English Revolution*, *passim*; and see K. Wrightson and D. Levine, *Poverty and Piety in an English Village: Terling 1525-1700* (New York 1979), and M. Fulbrook, 'The English Revolution and the Revisionist Revolt', *Social History*, 7 (1982), pp. 249-64.
61. Clark, *Revolution and Rebellion*; and P. Watson, 'The Don Rewriting History', *The Observer* (31 January 1988), p. 21.
62. J. H. Hexter, *The Reign of King Pym* (Cambridge, Mass. 1941).
63. E.g. Hexter, *Reappraisals* and *On History*; B.C. Malament (ed.), *After the Reformation: Essays in Honour of J.H. Hexter* (Manchester 1980), p. ix.
64. Hexter, *On Historians*, p. 244, n. 10.
65. As ns 59 and 63 above, plus Louis O. Mink, 'The Theory of Practice: Hexter's Historiography' in Malament (ed.), *After the Reformation*, pp. 3-21; Rabb, 'Role of the Commons', pp. 74-8.
66. W.H. Dray, 'J.H. Hexter, Neo-Whiggism and Early Stuart Historiography', *History and Theory*, 26 (1987), pp. 133-49.
67. Hexter, 'The Birth of Modern Freedom', pp. 51-4; and 'Power Struggle', pp. 47-50.
68. J.H. Hexter, 'The Not-so-New Men', *New York Review of Books* (18 January 1980), p. 60; see also 'The Making of Modern Freedom', *Times Literary Supplement* (2 September 1983), p. 932; J.K. Galbraith, 'The Death of Liberalism', *The Observer* (26 March 1989), pp. 33-4. I am grateful to Prof. Nicholas Canny for reminding me of the role of Yale University in developing and protecting the history of the English Parliament.
69. Watson, 'Don', pp. 21-2; *New York Review of Books* (13 January 1986), p. 7.
70. E.g. *The Sunday Times*, 12 November 1987, 1 May 1988 and 30 April 1989; Watson, 'Don', pp. 21-2. Though indicating some reservations about Thatcherism, Clark could not resist some provocative sallies: the emergence of modern democracy was not inevitable, or the achievement of high-minded

men, but was 'almost fortuitous', the result of a number of compromises. There was nothing to prevent a return to the more hierarchical, deferential society of the past, which, he believes, is as natural as any other form of political organization; there could, indeed, be a move to one-party government in England. The ideas of his 'rogues' gallery' of historians, which includes not only Hill and Stone, but also J.H. Plumb, Eric Hobsbawm and E.P. Thompson, should continue to be taught in schools and universities, if only in the manner in which Nazi biology is taught, as an example of grievous error.

71. Clark, *Revolution and Rebellion*, *passim*; see ns 57-8 above; Clarke does stress the need to set English events in a wider context but so have Trevor-Roper (see n. 54), Russell ('British Problem' and *The Fall of the British Monarchies 1637-1642* [Oxford 1991]) and A. Clarke, 'Ireland and the General Crisis', *Past and Present*, 48 (1970).
72. For a recent general survey, see E. Breisach, *Historiography Ancient, Medieval and Modern* (Chicago 1983).
73. Furet, *Interpreting the French Revolution*, and Comninel, *Rethinking the French Revolution* (London 1987), *passim*.
74. Eccleshall, *Liberalism*, pp. 52-5; Watson, 'Don', p. 22.
75. See pp. 141-2 above and ns 66-7.
76. G. Aylmer, *Rebellion or Revolution? England 1640-1660* (Oxford 1986); *idem*, 'Collective Mentalities in Mid Seventeenth-Century England: "1. The Puritan Outlook", "2. Royalist Attitudes" and "3. Varieties of Radicalism"', *R. Hist. Soc. Trans.*, 5th ser., pp. 36-8 (1986-8); Fletcher, *Outbreak*.
77. A. Marwick, *The Nature of History* (London 1970), pp. 103-7, 180-7. G. R. Elton, *The Practice of History* (Sydney 1967); R. W. Fogel and G.R. Elton, *Which Road to the Past? Two Views of History* (New Haven 1983).
78. See pp. 136, 139, 141 above.
79. At the time of writing the Ph. D. thesis is under attack both in the United States and the United Kingdom, though less on academic grounds than for the length it takes the average student to complete one.
80. Stone, *Causes*, p. 29; *idem*, ' Life of Learning', pp. 14-15.
81. It also owes a good deal to the greater variety of approach and sophistication of the questions posed and techniques of enquiry applied; but what we are concerned with here is the sharpness of the tone of the debate.
82. G. Hill, 'The Lost Ranters? A Critique of J.C. Davis', *History Workshop Journal*, 24 (1987), pp. 134-40 at 140.
83. See pp. 136-8, 140-2 above.
84. Rabb, 'Role of the Commons'; D. Hirst, *Authority and Conflict: England 1603-1658* (London 1986); J.P. Sommerville, *Politics and Ideology in England 1603-1640* (London 1986); Cust and Hughes (eds), *Conflict in Early Stuart England*, chs 2, 4-6.
85. P. Lake, 'Anti-Popery: The Structure of a Prejudice', in Cust and Hughes (eds), *Conflict in Early Stuart England*, pp. 72-106 and the works cited on pp. 255-6; I.M. Green, '"England's Wars of Religion"? Religious Conflict and the English Civil Wars' in *Church, Change and Revolution* (Publications of the Sir Thomas Browne Institute, New Series, 12, London 1991), pp. 100-21.
86. D. Pennington, 'The Making of the War', in Pennington and Thomas (eds), *Puritans and Revolutionaries*, pp. 161-85; Russell, 'British Problem', and 'The First Army Plot of 1641', *R. Hist. Soc. Trans.*, 5th ser., 38 (1988), pp. 85-106.
87. Hill, 'Parliament and People'; Underdown, *Revel, Riot and Rebellion*, and

Russell's introduction to *Origins of the English Civil War*.

88. I. Roots, 'Interest – Public, Private and Communal' in R.H. Parry (ed.), *The English Civil War and After* (London 1970), pp. 111-22: Morrill (ed.), *Reactions to the English Civil War*, *passim*; Underdown, '"Honest" Radicals in the Counties 1642-49', in Pennington and Thomas (eds), *Puritans and Revolutionaries*, pp. 186-205, and *idem*, 'Settlement in the Counties' in Aylmer (ed.), *Interregnum,* pp. 165-82; B. Worden, *The Rump Parliament* (Cambridge 1974); A. Woolrych, *Commonwealth to Protectorate* (Oxford 1982).
89. Aylmer, *The Levellers in the English Revolution* (London 1975) and 'Collective Mentalities: "3. Varieties of Radicalism"'; W. Lamont, 'The Left and its Past: Revisiting the 1650s', *History Workshop Journal*, 23 (1987), pp. 141-53.
90. See ns 54, 56 and 71 above.
91. J.R. Jones, *Charles II, Royal Politician* (London 1987); J. Miller, *James II, A Study in Kingship* (Hove 1977); Mark Kishlansky, *Parliamentary Selection* (Cambridge 1986); A. Fletcher, *Reform in the Provinces* (London 1986); J. Childs, '1688', *History*, 73 (1988), pp. 338-424.
92. *Times Higher Education Supplement* (28 April 1989), p. 9.
93. Academic historians are not totally innocent of the charge that their concern for technique has led to a growing rift between them and the broader readership of previous generations; they have also failed to make clear to non-academics how difficult it has been over the last fifty years to improve techniques of research and methods of teaching inside the universities at the same time as trying to produce attractively written and approachable studies for a wider audience.

CHAPTER 9

1. W.J.M. Starkie, address 'to the students of Mr Bevis's class on the new system of national education', October 1900 (TCD, Starkie papers, MS. 9210).
2. W.H. Webb, 'History, Patriotism and the Child' in *History*, ii, no. 1 (1913), p. 54.
3. *Times Educational Supplement*, 4 July 1916, p. 87.
4. J.W. Headlam and Paul Mantoux, 'The Effect of the War on the Teaching of History' in *History*, iii, no. 9 (1918), pp. 10-19.
5. Thomas W. Allies to the Powis Commission, 18 February 1869: *Royal Commission of Inquiry into Primary Education (Ireland), Minutes of Evidence*, Q 25402, HC 1870 [C. 6-III], xxviii, pt iv. The same volume contains a rare plea from Stephen de Vere, the Catholic convert, for the teaching of non-partisan history: 'There would be very little difficulty in constructing elementary historical lessons which would confine themselves to facts, and which would avoid all inferential reasoning from those facts' (Q 20236).
6. The Christian Brothers, *Irish History Reader* (Dublin and London 1905), pp. 309, vii.
7. The Christian Brothers, *Historical Class-Book* (Dublin, 1873 ed.), p. 590; Cullen to Powis Commission, *loc. cit.*, Q 27403 (refuting Master Brooke's suggestion that such works provided training in Fenianism). See also John Shelly, *Edmond Ignatius Rice and the Christian Brothers: A Compilation* (Kilkenny 1863), pp. 80-5; Patrick Callan, 'Irish History in Irish National

Schools, 1900-1908' (UCD, MA dissertation, 1975), pp. 7-9; Barry M. Coldrey, *Faith and Fatherland: The Christian Brothers and the Development of Irish Nationalism 1838-1921* (Dublin 1988), chs 3, 6.

8. Shelly, *Edmond Ignatius Rice*, pp. 80, 85 (quoting *The Nation* and Adolphe Perraud).
9. J. Pope Hennessy, 'What Do the Irish Read?' in *The Nineteenth Century*, xv (1884) pp. 926-30; Sinn Féin, *How to Form Sinn Féin Clubs* (n.p., 1917 copy in NLI); Sinn Féin, *Instructions to Sinn Féin Cumainn* (n.p., 1920, copy in NLI); Michael MacDonagh, 'Books in Boyhood: Reminiscences of the Christian Schools Library in Limerick' in *Our Boys*, ii, no. 1 (September 1915), pp. 1-2; *Our Boys*, iii, no. 6 (February 1917), p. 170; Thomas O'Donnell, *The Priest of To-Day: his Ideals and his Duties* (Dublin 1910), pp. 242, 324-5. For the Gaelic League's educational programme of January 1919, see John M. Coolahan, 'A Study of Curricular Policy for the Primary and Secondary Schools of Ireland, 1900-1935, with Special Reference to the Irish Language and Irish History' (TCD, Ph. D dissertation, 1973), pp. 174-5.
10. Callan, 'Irish History in Irish National Schools', p. 10.
11. Joseph Robins, *The Lost Children: A Study of Charity Children in Ireland, 1700-1900* (Dublin 1980), p. 90.
12. P.J. Dowling, *The Hedge Schools of Ireland* (Dublin 1935), p. 111; William Carleton, *Traits and Stories of the Irish Peasantry* (London, 1877 ed.), i, p. 233. According to Benedict Kiely in *Poor Scholar* (Dublin, 1972 ed.), p. 19, the model for Carleton's Mat Kavanagh in 'The Hedge School' was his own teacher, Pat Frayne, who taught at Towney, Co. Tyrone, in about 1800.
13. John Mitchel, *The History of Ireland, from the Treaty of Limerick to the Present Time* (Glasgow, 1876 ed.).
14. Christian Brothers, *Irish History Reader*, p. 310.
15. Commissioners of National Education, *Supplement to the Fourth Book of Lessons* (Dublin 1862), pp. 389-410; *Fifth Book of Lessons* (Dublin 1835), pp. 96 et seq. Scraps of history also appeared in the manuals of geography and history as well as the lower readers. Some of those in the latter were pirated by Whately from a London publisher, who eventually forced the commissioners to apologize and pay legal costs. See extracts from minutes of the commissioners, 26 March, 31 March, 9 April and 10 September 1858, in *Return [of Certain] Minutes of the Board of National Education*, HC 1864 (509), xlvi, pp. 419-20. See also Donald H. Akenson, *The Irish Education Experiment* (London 1970), pp. 227-40.
16. Minutes of commissioners, 10 December 1885, 19 November 1858; commissioners to clerk of Ballinasloe board of guardians, 3 February 1959, in *Return* (1864), pp. 421, 433-4.
17. *Return 'Relating to Books Applied for from Time to Time Other than Those Published by the Commissioners . . .'*, HC 1894 (137), p. lvi; John Coakley, 'The Nationality Problem in Irish Primary Education: Political Socialization and the Teaching of History, 1831-1971' (UCD, MA dissertation, 1974), pp. 88-91.
18. Valerie E. Chancellor, *History for their Masters; Opinion in the English History Textbook: 1800-1914* (Bath 1970), p. 11; Gordon R. Batho, 'Sources for the History of History Teaching in Elementary Schools 1833-1914' in T.G. Cook (ed.), *Local Studies and the History of Education* (London 1972), pp. 137-52; G.M.D. Howat, 'The Nineteenth-Century History Text-Book' in *British*

Journal of Educational Studies, xiii (1965), pp. 147-59; J.M. Goldstrom, *The Social Content of Education, 1808-1870: A Study of the Working Class School Reader in England and Ireland* (Shannon 1972). Chancellor shows that the treatment of Irish history in English text-books, taken as a group, was surprisingly balanced (pp. 64, 109-10, 120-1).

20. Powis Commission, *Report*, p. 163, HC 1870 [C. 6], xxviii, pt i. See also Shelly, *Edmond Ignatius Rice*, pp. 87-9; Coakley, 'The Nationality Problem', p. 69. Coakley detects a long-term reversal of Catholic and Protestant attitudes towards history teaching with Protestants becoming more mistrustful: 'each side advocated the teaching of history only insofar as it felt capable of influencing the content of the course'.
21. Powis Commission, *Minutes of Evidence*, Q 15641, HC 1870 {C. 6-11], xxviii , pt iii; Q 27048, HC 1870 [C. 6-III], xxviii, pt iv. Cullen's evidence included useful epitomes of inspectors' views on history teaching and of the historical content of the commissioners' readers. In the same volume (Q 21914), the Revd John McMenamin of Stranorlar, Co. Donegal, protested that children 'grow up ignorant of history, until they begin reading newspapers, and periodicals, and very often violent articles, and they adopt those isolated one-sided views without due reflection, and I think it drives them very often into evil associations, and combinations, and fits them to become the dupes of designing and evil companions'.
22. Revd James Porter, Kilkenny, to Powis Commission, *Minutes of Evidence*, Q 1864-5, HC 1870 [C. 6-III], xxviii, pt iv; *Reports of Assistant Commissioners*, pp. 859-60, 301, HC 1870 [C. 6-1], xxviii, pt ii. The teaching of history backwards was also urged by the senior inspector for Armagh in 1914: *80th Report of the Commissioners for National Education in Ireland, appendix section I*, p. 38, HC 1914-16 {Ce. 7966], xx. See also Sir Roland K. Wilson, 'Should History be Taught Backwards?' in *Contemporary Review*, lxx (1986), pp. 391-407.
23. W.J.M. Starkie at prize distribution, Albert Model Farm, Glasnevin, 19 February 1900 (TCD, Starkie papers, MS. 9210); see also W.J.M. Starkie, *Recent Reforms in Irish Education* (Dublin 1902).
24. The revised programmes of instruction for each year were reproduced in *Appendix section II* of the 67th, 71st and 74th *CNE Reports*. The introduction of history, English, geography and arithmetic as 'ordinary school subjects' on 7 April 1908 was approved without recorded debate: commissioners of national education, *Minutes of the Proceedings* (1908), p. 135 (copies in NLI and TCD). Modified programmes were applied to smaller schools.
25. Chancellor, *History for their Masters*, pp. 28-9; Coolahan, 'A Study of Curricular Policy', p. 201, quoting Mahaffy's remark to the commissioners of intermediate education on 25 October 1911. Between 1878 and 1903 history was examined at intermediate level only as a minor adjunct to English and other language studies; but in 1903, at Starkie's instigation, history and geography became a separate option. By 1920 it was taken by 11,476 students of all grades, far more than the number taking Irish and almost as many as that taking English. See Coolahan, 'A Study of Curricular Policy', pp. 184-5, 195; Daniel V. Kelleher, *James Dominic Burke: A Pioneer of Irish Education* (Dublin 1988), p. 97.
26. Commissioners of national education, *Notes for Teachers in Connection with the Programmes of Instruction for National Schools* (Dublin 1913 ed., reprinted in 1920), pp. 14-20 (copy in Department of Education Library, Dublin, 1908

ed. unavailable); A.N. Bonaparte Wyse to *Vice-Regal Committee of Inquiry in to Primary Education (Ireland), 1913, First Report, Evidence*, Q 2412, HC 1913 [Cd. 6829], p. xxii. For Starkie's adherence to 'the ideal of Aristotle and Rousseau', see Starkie (1900), cited in note 1; for discussion of the reintroduction of 'Aristotelian' concepts after 1958, see A.T. Atkinson, 'A Review of the Main Principles of History Teaching applied in British and Irish Schools' (TCD, M. Ed. dissertation, 1973).

27. The current manual published by An Roinn Oideachais, *Primary School Curriculum: Teacher's Handbook Part 2* (Dublin 1971), pp. 87-111, incorporates many of Starkie's liberal principles in combination with references to the subject's fostering of 'important civic virtues' as well as 'patriotism, courage, self-sacrifice and devotion to noble ideals' (p. 87).
28. W.J.M. Starkie, *The History of Irish Primary and Secondary Education During the Last Decade* (Dublin 1911), p. 2.
29. Callan, 'Irish History in Irish National Schools', pp. 41-2; Revd P.S. Dinneen, *Native History in National Schools* (Dublin 1905); Henry Mangan, 'Scientific Study of Irish History' in *Freeman's Journal*, 24 March 1908 (in the valuable series of indexed newspaper extracts in PRO, Dublin, ED 7/21), pp. 22-3; [Henry Mangan], 'Clio in Ireland' in the Christian Brothers, *O'Connell School Centenary Record* (Dublin 1928), pp. 58-68.
30. *The Irish Times* (19 June 1911); *Freeman's Journal* (20 June 1911); with further correspondence from John MacNeill and others, *Irish Independent*, 21, 22 and 24 June 1911 (PRO, Dublin, ED 7/22), pp. 85-92. MacNeill claimed that the provision for teaching either Irish or British history affirmed the 'extraordinary principle of the division of the Irish people into two irreconcilable factions'. In *The Murder Machine* (1912), which sketches an educational philosophy uncannily similar to Starkie's, Patrick Pearse shows no awareness of the recent reform of the primary curriculum; but elsewhere he demonstrates closer knowledge of the intermediate syllabus. See Padraic H. Pearse, *Collected Works: Political Writings and Speeches* (Dublin n.d.), pp. 5-50; Seamas Ó Buachalla (ed.), *A Significant Irish Educationalist: The Educational Writings of P.H. Pearse* (Dublin and Cork 1980), pp. 230-1.
31. Coolahan, 'A Study of Curricular Policy', p. 168.
32. 'A.M.' [Revd Andrew Murphy], 'History in the National Schools' in *Irish Educational Review*, ii (1908), pp. 97-8.
33. *Times Educational Supplement*, 6 June 1916, p. 68; O'Brien to Dáil Éireann, 23 February 1972, *Parliamentary Debates*, cclix, col. 246; Mahaffy to *New York Sun*, in *Daily Express* (Dublin), 28 December 1916 (PRO, Dublin ED 7/24), p. 203. O'Brien's expostulation caused Garret FitzGerald to exclaim 'Hear, hear'; but John A. Murphy dissented in 'Little IRA Men' in *Secondary Teacher*, i, no. 3 (Summer 1972), pp. 10-11.
34. *Times Educational Supplement*, 4 July 1916, p. 88; 1 March 1917, p. 74; 5 April 1917, p. 114; *Irish School Weekly*, lxi (15 July 1916), p. 702; lxii (July-August 1916), pp. 21, 44-5, 92, 140.
35. *Irish Independent*, 18 March 1920, (PRO, Dublin ED 7/25), p. 167; see also O'Connell's letter in *Freeman's Journal*, 29 January 1920 (*ibid.*, p. 132).
36. Michael Tierney, *Education in a Free Ireland* (Dublin 1919), p. 45. Tierney also thought it 'desirable' to teach non-Irish history, and preferred the current secondary curriculum to the primary.
37. Roy Foster, 'History and the Irish Question' in *Transactions of the Royal*

Historical Society, 33 (1983), p. 187. For background to the control of education after partition, see Donald Harman Akenson, *A Mirror to Kathleen's Face: Education in Independent Ireland 1922-1960* (Montreal and London 1975) and *Education and Enmity: The Control of Schooling in Northern Ireland 1920-50* (Newton Abbot and New York 1973); E. Brian Titley, *Church, State, and the Control of Schooling in Ireland 1900-1944* (Kingston and Montreal 1983).

38. NI ministry of education, *Final Report of the Departmental Committee on the Educational Services in Northern Ireland*, NI, HC 1923 [Cmd. 15]; Coolahan, 'A Study of Curricular Policy', pp. 445-55.

39. NI ministry of education, *Programme of Instruction for Public Elementary Schools* (Belfast 1924, 1928, 1932, reprinted in 1945); *Programme for Primary Schools* (Belfast 1956); *Primary Education: Teachers' Guide* (Belfast 1974); *Rules and Schedule Containing the Programme of Intermediate Examinations*, NI, HC 1922 (18); Coolahan, 'A Study of Curricular Policy', pp. 455-64; Norman Atkinson, *Irish Education: A History of Educational Institutions* (Dublin 1969), pp. 182-4. The annual *Reports* of the NI ministry of education show that the percentage of senior certificate candidates (or equivalent category) taking the history examination dropped from 86.4 in 1922 to 47.9 in 1926 and 37.1 in 1931, before recovering to 44.9 in 1936. A much higher proportion took history and geography (or history from 1928) for the junior certificate, the subject being part of the standard course up to 1927.

40. For confusion among the children of (London)derry as to their nationality, see A.T. Atkinson, 'A Review of the Main Principles of History Teaching', pp. 185-9; Hon. M. Gibson to 6th All-Ireland Industrial Conference in Cork, *Daily Express* (Dublin), 6 October 1910 (PRO, Dublin ED 7/22), p. 8.

41. Anthony Motherway, 'Developing the History Curriculum in the Primary School 1922-1986' in *Irish Educational Studies*, vii, no. 2 (1988), pp. 35-46; Anthony M. Motherway, 'Curriculum Development: The History Curriculum of the Primary School 1922-1982' (TCD, M. Ed. dissertation 1982). Though history was part of the regular programme, only about a quarter of pupils taking the primary school certificate examination (1929-43) took the optional history paper, which was dropped from the examination thereafter (1943-67). See Motherway (1988), pp. 39-40; James Gilligan, 'The Teaching of History in Senior Standards in the Curriculum of Irish National Schools 1961-1981' (UCD, M. Ed. dissertation, 1982), p. 35.

42. These proportions refer to pupils on the rolls in standards at which history was taught, figures given in the annual *Reports* of the appropriate bodies. The proportion of pupils *ever* at risk of taking history was of course far greater.

43. Coolahan, 'A Study of Curricular Policy', pp. 290, 326; An Roinn Oideachais, *Programme of Primary Instruction* (Dublin 1926, reprinted in 1944) and *Revised Programme for History in National Schools* (Dublin 1962), which slightly modified the 1926 syllabus. A 'note' to the *Report of Second National Programme Conference* (Dublin 1926), pp. 53-5, indicates that Thomas O'Connell and the INTO Executive had unsuccessfully proposed that history be reduced from compulsory to optional status (newspaper cuttings book, Church of Ireland training college, Rathmines).

44. An Roinn Oideachais, *Notes for Teachers: History* (Dublin July 1933, reprinted in 1956). See also n. 27 above; and Kenneth Milne, *New Approaches to the Teaching of Irish History* (London 1979).

45. Patrick O'Farrell, 'History in Ireland – Some Comments and Questions' in

Quest, i (1974), pp. 4-11.

46. Yeats to Seanad Éireann, 24 March 1926, in *Parliamentary Debates*, vi, col. 525; James Johnston Auchmuty, *The Teaching of History* (Dublin and Cork 1940), p. 8. Other attacks on the practice and ideology of history teaching were made by James Dillon and Oliver Flanagan in Dáil Éireann on 8 April 1959: *Parliamentary Debates*, clxxiv, cols 150, 160; G.A. Hayes McCoy, 'A Defect in Irish Education' in *University Review*, iii, no. 4 (1963), pp. 15-22; 'Bias in School History' in *Hibernia*, xxvi, no. 4 (1962), p. 8; John Magee, 'The Teaching of Irish History in Irish Schools' in *Northern Teacher*, x, no. 1 (1970), unpaginated. The patriotic functions of history teaching were reaffirmed by An Roinn Oideachais, *Report of the Council of Education* (Dublin 1954), pp. 98, 180-4; and the report of a Fianna Fáil study group including Martin O'Donoghue and T.D. Williams, published as 'The Teaching of History in Irish Schools' in *Administration*, xv, no. 4 (1967), pp. 268-85.
47. Thomas Joseph Durcan, *A History of Irish Education from 1800* (Bola 1972), p. 58; NI ministry of education, *Questions Set at the Summer Examinations 1937* (Belfast 1937). St Mary's catered for Roman Catholic students.
48. An Roinn Oideachais, *Questions Set at the Examination for Entrance to Preparatory Colleges 1927* (Dublin 1927); 64th *CNE Report, Appendix Section III*, HC [C. 9040], xxvii. The quoted question for 1897 was asked of the least qualified male candidates under the new programme; papers following the old programme had negligible Irish content, while women were asked rather more Irish questions than men.
49. See Callan, 'Irish History in Irish National Schools', especially pp. 120-3 and 131-2. The rules concerning sanction of text-books were several times changed, but the use of works not published in the commissioners' lists was prohibited except with respect to surplus stock of certain books from which sanction had been withdrawn.
50. Foley to Starkie, 21 September 1908 (TCD, Starkie papers, MS. 9209, f. 193). The bishop's magnanimity was rewarded next month when the board sanctioned Browne and Nolan's *Advanced National Reader* after rejecting it in July: see *CNE Minutes* (1908), pp. 298-9, 333-4, 407-8; R. Barry O'Brien, *Dublin Castle and the Irish People* (Dublin 1912 ed.), pp. 247-53.
51. *CNE Minutes* (1916), pp. 323-5 (1917), pp. 67-8, 145, 156-8, 402.
52. *CNE Minutes* (1918), pp. 53, 281 (1919), pp. 116, 138-9 (1920), pp. 72, 105-6 (1912, duplicated minutes in NLI, LO), pp. 110-12. The effect of the change of procedure in 1919 was to remove the invitation to managers to propose new text-books, while placing all existing works under scrutiny of the divisional inspectors followed by reconsideration in the board. For the Maxwell case, see n. 65 below.
53. Interview in *Irish Independent*, 27 February 1917 (PRO, Dublin ED 7/24, p. 214). Starkie claimed misleadingly that 'books are not allowed if objected to by even one member of the Board', a statement contradicted by the divisions and vote recorded in *CNE Minutes* (see note 50 above).
54. Starkie's diary, 4 April 1918 (TCD, Starkie papers, MS. 9211, p. 44).
55. *Ibid.*, 31 May 1918, pp. 228-9.
56. *Ibid.*, 18 June 1918, p. 276.
57. Letters transcribed in Starkie's diary, 31 October 1918 (TCD, Starkie papers, MS. 9212, pp. 169-72). O'Brien won support from the *Freeman's Journal*, 9 May 1917 (PRO, Dublin ED 7/24, p. 238), following the commissioners'

insistence that offensive passages be modified or lose their sanction. See *CNE Minutes* (1917), pp. 67-8.

58. Memorial from R.J. Lynd, for committee on elementary education of the general assembly, to commissioners of national education, 12 August 1902 (TCD, Starkie papers, MS. 9210, p. 468).
59. Revd J.P. Barnes to bishop of Kilmore, 20 November 1901 (Kingsmill Moore papers, Church of Ireland training college, Rathmines).
60. *Journal of the Session of the General Synod of the Church of Ireland* (Dublin 1914), p. 250; leader in *Daily Express* (Dublin), 22 September 1913, with associated correspondence (PRO, Dublin ED 7/24, pp. 33-5). See also Coakley, 'The Nationality Problem', p. 68; Seamas Ó Buachalla, *Education Policy in Twentieth-Century Ireland* (Dublin 1988), p. 239.
61. *Impartial Reporter*, 2 January 1908, reporting meeting of 24 December 1907.
62. *CNE Minutes* (1918), p. 231; *The Irish Times*, 9 June 1917 (PRO, Dublin ED 7/24), p. 245.
63. Revd William Corkey, *The Church of Rome and Irish Unrest: How Hatred of Britain is Taught in Irish Schools* (Edinburgh 1918, reprinted from *The Witness*, Belfast), pp. 36-42. Corkey, brother to a future minister of education in Northern Ireland, was convenor of primary and university education on the general assembly's board of education (1917-45): see William Corkey, *Gladly Did I Live* (Belfast 1963 ed.), p. 244.
64. *Journal of the Session of the General Synod* (Dublin 1918), p. 219. See also 'The Epistles of Shebna the Scribe, History in National Schools' in *Church of Ireland Gazette*, 22 December 1916 (cutting in SPO, RP 24693/1916 in RP 25821/1920) R. Kyle Knox to *Morning Post*, quoted in *Irish Independent*, 30 September 1916 (PRO, Dublin ED 7/24), p. 184.
65. M.J. O'Mullane to *Irish Independent*, 9 July 1921 (PRO, Dublin ED 7/25), p. 220. Maxwell's work was denounced by 'a Catholic teacher' and 'a Catholic manager' (both anonymous) in *Freeman's Journal*, 19 and 22 March 1917; its receipt of a Presbyterian prize and sanction by the commissioners are reported in *The Irish Times*, 19 January 1914, and *Irish Independent*, 12 June 1915 (PRO, Dublin ED 7/24), pp. 19, 78, 140.
66. May C. Starkie, *What is Patriotism? The Teaching of Patriotism* (Dublin 1916), pp. 7, 8, 12, 15; Starkie's diary, 19 May 1918 (TCD, Starkie papers, MS. 9211), p. 208; Coolahan, 'A Study of Curricular Policy', pp. 169-70.
67. Starkie's diary, 19 June 1918 (TCD, Starkie papers, MS. 9211), p. 280, also revealing that William had 'sent May's essay on Patriotism to [Viscount] French, with a note that I don't admit the teaching of disloyalty in general'; *Times Educational Supplement*, 7 September 1916, p. 120, Lord Dunleath to the chief secretary [Duke], enclosing cutting cited in note 64 above ('Epistles').
68. Provisional government, *Minutes of Meetings*, i, 28 January 1922 (State Paper Office, Dublin, G 1/1); *CNE Minutes*, 24 and 31 January 1922 (duplicated minutes in NLI, LO).
69. NI ministry of education, *List of Books in Reading, History . . . Approved for Use in Public Elementary Schools* (Belfast 1926 and 1932 ed.).
70. A.N. Bonaparte Wyse to Mrs A. Stopford Green, 7 April 1927 (NLI, Green papers, MS. 15126/2); Starkie's diary (TCD, Starkie papers, MS. 9211), pp. 177-8; D.A. Chart, *A History of Northern Ireland* (Belfast 1927), p. 24.
71. An Roinn Oideachais, *National Education, Programme for Students in Training*

(Dublin 1974), pp. 38-9; *List of Books Approved for Use in National Schools* (Dublin 1926, 1933, 1959 and 1962 ed.); *Notes for Teachers: History* (Dublin 1933, reprinted in 1956), pp. 29-30. See note 9 above for text-books recommended by Sinn Féin and other organizations.

72. Revd H. Kingsmill Moore, *Irish History for Young Readers* (London 1914); Revd E.C. Hodges (principal of Church of Ireland training college), draft letter to press, 10 February 1938 (newspaper cuttings book, Rathmines).
73. D. Casserley, *History of Ireland* (Dublin 1941); Milne, *New Approaches*, p. 33; Coakley, 'The Nationality Problem', p. 85. Casserley also denounced government policy during the famine and after the Easter Rising, adding that '"Partition" still remains a problem beset with difficulties of more than one kind' (pp. 108, 133, 140 of pt II).
74. An Roinn Oideachais, *Report of the Department of Education for the School Years 1925-26-27* (Dublin 1928), p. 37.
75. Systematic analysis of the contents of 42 text-books in Irish history is provided by Coakley, 'The Nationality Problem', pp. 98 et seq., appendix III. See also the more capricious survey in Callan, 'Irish History in Irish National Schools', pp. 82-110. In order to elucidate and classify bias it would be necessary also to analyse the sequence in which topics are treated, and to detect significant omissions.
76. Starkie's diary, 27 April 1918 (TCD. Starkie papers, MS. 9211), p. 154, developing complaints made three days earlier (p. 146).
77. For each year between 1902 and 1913-14, half or more of the senior inspectors' circuit reports were published in the 69th to 80th *CNE Reports, Appendix Section I.* For the periods 1925-27 to 1929-30, lengthy extracts from the divisional inspectors' reports appeared in An Roinn Oideachais, *Reports.* The contents of all reports that address the teaching of history have been analysed in the appendix.
78. Report of J.P. Dalton (Portarlington circuit) for 1911-12, in 78th *CNE Report, Appendix Section I*, p. 83: complaint to INTO executive concerning an unnamed senior inspector, in *Freeman's Journal*, 22 September 1915 (PRO, Dublin ED 7/24), p. 147. See also *Times Educational Supplement*, 2 May 1916, p. 56, for a letter from a former senior inspector, H.M. Beatty, hoping that history would teach the Irishman 'that this country is not the peerless Niobe of nations, nor Englishmen the unique villains of history'; and Seamus Fenton, *It All Happened: Reminiscences* (Dublin 1948), pp. 222, 232, 244-5, for the contrasting political views of various inspectors, including himself.
79. Starkie's diary, 6 and 14 June 1918 (TCD, Starkie papers, MS. 9211), pp. 245, 259. For other references to Starkie's history inspections, see pp. 332 and 337-8 of the diary just cited; *Leitrim Observer*, 10 November 1917; Fenton, *It All Happened*, pp. 244-5.
80. Report of W.J. McClintock (Enniskillen circuit) for 1913-14, in 80th *CNE Report, Appendix Section I*, p. 26.
81. See appendix. The religious denomination of senior inspectors has been ascertained from a confidential official analysis of the inspection staff in 1901, reproduced in Aine Hyland, 'Educational Innovation – A Case History' (TCD. M. Ed. dissertation, 1975), pp. 343-4. Reports are analysed according to the senior inspector's denomination, though in some cases the comments are attributed to a subordinate. One attribution is conjectural.
82. An Roinn Oideachais, *Report . . . 1930-31* (Dublin 1932), p. 21.

83. An Roinn Oideachais, *Report . . . 1929-30* (Dublin 1931), p. 217.
84. NI ministry of education, *Report . . . 1927-28*, NI, HC 1928 (154), p. 16. See also report of P.J. Kelly (Belfast no. 2 circuit) for 1913-14, in 80th *CNE Report, Appendix Section I*, p. 70: '*History* is probably the worst taught subject in the curriculum.'

CHAPTER 10

1. Aristotle, *The Poetics; Demetrius, On Style*, etc., W.H. Fyfe and W.R. Roberts (transs) (Loeb Classical Library, London 1927), p. 35.
2. Artur Schopenhauer, *Werke* (Berlin 1892), vol. II, p. 516.
3. O. Spengler, *Der Untergang des Abendlandes* (Munich 1923), vol. I, p. 129, 'Natur soll man wissenschaftlich behandeln, über Geschichte soll man dichten.'
4. See in particular Wilhelm Windleband, *Geschichte und Naturwissenschaft* (Heidelberg 1894); Heinrich Rickert, *System der Philosophie* (Heidelberg 1921).
5. K. Popper, *The Open Society and its Enemies* (3rd ed., London 1957), vol. II, p. 251.
6. M. Bloch, *Mélanges historiques* (Paris 1963), vol. I, pp. 6-7 (my transl.).
7. M. Bloch, *The Historian's Craft*, P. Putnam (trans.) (Manchester 1954), p. 13.
8. G.W.F. Hegel, *Vorlesungen über die Philosophie der Weltgeschichte* (Berlin 1970), vol. I, p. 88 (my transl.).
9. Friedrich Engels to Joseph Bloch, 21 September 1890, in Marx and Engels, *Selected Writings* (London 1970), pp. 682-3.
10. K. Marx, F. Engels, *Werke* (Berlin 1958), vol. 3, p. 45 (my transl.).
11. J.B. Bury, *Cleopatra's Nose* (Annual of the Rationalist Press Association, London 1916). Friedrich Meinecke, *Die Deutsche Katastrophe* (Zurich 1946), translated as *The German Catastrophe* by S.B. Fay (London 1950).
12. E.H. Carr, *What is History?* (London 1962), p. 95.
13. Fustel de Coulanges, 'The Ethos of a Scientific Historian' in Fritz Stern (ed.), *The Varieties of History* (2nd ed., London 1970), pp. 179-88.
14. M. Bloch, *Mélanges historiques*, vol. I, p. 8.
15. J.G. Herder, *Ideen zur Philosophie der Geschichte der Menscheit* (Karlsruhe 1970), vol. II, p. 259.
16. M. Bloch, *The Historian's Craft*, p. 37.
17. *Ibid*., pp. 37-8.
18. G. Myrdal, 'The Relation between Social Theory and Social Policy' in *The British Journal of Sociology*, vol. 3 (1953), pp. 215, 231-2.
19. M. Bloch, *The Historian's Craft*, p. 38.
20. M. Bloch, *Mélanges historiques*, vol. I, p. 15 (my transl.).

CHAPTER 11

1. T. O'Raifeartaigh (ed.), *The Royal Irish Academy: A Bicentennial History 1785-1985* (Dublin 1985).

2. *Ibid.*, p. 9.
3. *Ibid.*, pp. 188-99, quotation p. 188.
4. *Ibid.*, p. 195. Nietzsche quoted in John Lukacs, *Historical Consciousness* (2nd ed., New York 1985), p. 235.
5. Burckhardt, *Breife*, Max Burckhardt (ed.), vol. 4, pp. 125, 169, 260; for further discussion see Lukacs, *Historical Consciousness*, pp. 37, 98, 227-36.
6. For elaboration of this point see Lukacs, *op. cit.*, pp. 108-14.
7. Lyons, *Culture and Anarchy in Ireland* (Oxford 1982), p. 1.
8. T.S. Eliot, *Notes towards the Definition of Culture* (London 1948), p. 22.
9. Lyons, *op. cit.*, p. 3.
10. Angus McIntyre, *The Liberator* (London 1965), pp. 127-8.
11. Lyons, *op. cit.*, p. 22.
12. *Ibid.*, p. 72.
13. *The Two Cultures and the Scientific Revolution*, Rede Lecture, Cambridge University (Cambridge 1959).
14. 'Candour in English Fiction' in H. Orel (ed.), *Thomas Hardy: Personal Writings* (London 1967), p. 127.

INDEX

I. GENERAL

Acta Sanctorum Hiberniae, 24, 28
Acton, Lord, 150
Adair, Douglass, 61
Adams, John, 58, 62
Adams, Samuel, 55
Addison, Joseph, 59, 61, 102
Adrian (pope), 114
Alembert, Jean Le Rond d', 81
Allen, John, 54-5
Allenby (E.H.H., lord), 181
American Revolution, 3, 49-65 *passim*, 100, 117
Andrewes, Lancelot, 130-1
Annales, 5, 156, 202, 216
Annals of Connacht, 18
Annals of Loch Cé, 18-19
Annals of the Four Masters, 17-18, 19, 20, 21, 25, 28
Annals of the Kingdom of Ireland, 14, 20-1, 24
Annals of Ulster, 19
Aongus (king of Munster), 122
Apelles, 105, 114
apodictic/apophatic distinction, 164-5
Aristotle, 187, 195
Arnold, Matthew, 129, 139, 204, 205
Arrian, Flavius, 86-7, 92
Asser's *Life of King Alfred*, 129
Attlee, Clement Richard, 153
Auchmuty, J.J., 177
Austen, Jane, 84, 96, 209, 213
Bacon, Francis, 92, 128
Bailey, John, 141
Baldwin, Stanley, 151
Baltimore (George Calvert, lord), 114, 117, 127
Bariere, Mme de, 88
Barry, James, 3-4, 95-6, 108-27 *passim*
Bartas, G. de Salluste du, 34
Baudelaire, Charles, 79
Bayle, Pierre, 2-3, 32, 34, 35-48 *passim*
Beaufort, Daniel Augustus, 77
Beaufort, Frances Anne, 77
Bede, the Venerable, 130
Bergerac, Cyrano de, 41
Berkeley, George, 80, 114, 117
Bernier, François, 41
Blake, William, 96, 155
Bolingbroke (Henry St John, lord), 59
Book of Invasions, 14, 17
Bossuet, Jacques, 41, 45
Brontë sisters, 90
Brooke, Stopford A., 140
Brutus, Junius, 114
Brutus, Lucius Junius, 103-4, 114
Bryant, Sir Arthur, 150
Bunyan, John, 131, 154
Burckhardt, Jakob, 203-4
Burke, Aedanus, 52
Burke, Edmund, 80-1, 89, 105, 108, 109, 110, 117, 119, 120,

123, 130, 149
Burke, William, 117
Burns, Robert, 130
Butt, Isaac, 205

Caesar, Julius, 63
Calderón de la Barca, Pedro, 53
Calvin, John (and Calvinism), 2, 25, 33, 34, 35, 36, 159
Camden, William, 17, 130
Campbell, Thomas (poet), 137
Campbell, Thomas (topographical writer), 105-8, 119
Canisius, Peter, 26
Carleton, William, 170
Carlyle, Thomas, 130
Casaubon, Isaac, 31
Casserley, Dora, 181
Catholic Reformation, 21
Cato the Younger, 114
Chalmers, James, 52
Chamberlain, Robert, 15
Chandler, Thomas, 52
Charles I (of England), 20, 56, 147, 149, 152, 161
Charles II (of England), 147
Chart, D., 181
Chaucer, Geoffrey, 30
Christian Brothers, 169, 170, 171, 180, 181
Churchill, Sir Winston, 150
Cicero, 33, 62, 189, 196
Clare, John, 131
Clarendon (Edward Hyde, earl of), 131, 148
Claude, *see* Lorrain
Clement VIII (pope), 12
Cobden, Richard, 205
Coleridge, Samuel Taylor, 128
Colgan, John, 13, 14, 23, 24, 28
Communist Party Historians' Group, 148, 153, 154
Concannon, Mrs Helena, 178
Condillac, Etienne, 84
Conry, Florence, 15, 27
Copernicus, Nicholas, 46
Corkey, William, 180, 181
Corneille, Pierre, 129
Corry, Isaac, 60
Counter Reformation, 2, 11-30 *passim*, 32-3, 35
Crabbe, George, 131
Cranmer, Thomas, 130
Critique générale (Bayle), 32, 36, 45
Croker, Thomas Crofton, 170
Cromwell, Oliver, 131, 147, 154, 177, 178
Cullen, Paul, 169
Cusack, 171

Danto, Arthur, 5
Darwin, Charles, 128
Daunt, W. O'N., 171
David, Jacques Louis, 103-5, 118-19, 125
Davidson, Robert, 63
Davis, Thomas Osborne, 100, 101, 124, 170
Deák, Ferenc, 205
deconstruction, 6
Defoe, Daniel, 131
Dempster, Thomas, 22, 23
Descartes, René, 46, 208
determinism, 192
Dickens, Charles, 90, 129, 130, 131
Donne, John, 137
Drennan, William, 120
Droysen, Johann Gustav, 201
Dryden, John, 129, 130
Du Bos, J.B.(abbé), 79-80
Dundas, Henry, 128
Dunleath (earl of), 181

Echard, Laurence, 148
Edgeworth, Maria, 4, 77-98 *passim*
Edgeworth, R.L., 77, 81-2, 88, 93, 95, 170
Elgar, Frederick, 129

Eliot, George, 137
Eliot, T.S., 132, 142, 143, 144, 204
Elizabeth I (of England), 12, 16
Emerson, James, 63
Emmet, Robert, 101
Emmet, Thomas Addis, 126-7
Engels, Friedrich, 151, 191
English Civil War, 146-67 *passim*
English Revolution, 151, 154
Enlightenment, 3-4, 67, 71, 75, 77, 78, 79, 81, 84, 90, 92, 93, 97-8, 100, 108, 156
Erasmus, Desiderius, 33
Evans, Israel, 61

fascism, 70, 76, 151
Fénelon, François de Salignac de la Mothe, 88
Féraud, L., 69
Filmer, Sir Robert, 91-2
Fischer, David Hackett, 5
Fitzgerald, James, 212
Fitzsimon, W., 23
Fleming, Thomas, 23, 28
Florimond de Raemond, 35
Foley (bishop), 178
Ford, Timothy, 64
Forde, Samuel, 101
Francis I (of Spain), 114
Franklin, Benjamin, 114
Frederick II (of Prussia), 79, 90
Frégeville, Jean de, 34
French Revolution, 3, 66-76, 100, 151, 162
Fryer, Edward, 123
Fustel de Coulanges, N.D., 193

Gadsden, Christopher, 64
Gardiner, Samuel , 150, 157
Garibaldi, Giuseppe, 134
Gassendi, Pierre, 41
Gearnon, Anthony, 28
gender, 67-8, 75
Genealogies of Saints and Kings, 20, 28
George III (of England), 59, 130, 214
George V (of England), 149-50
Gibbon, Edward, 130, 181
Goldsmith, Oliver, 130
Gordon, Thomas, 50, 59, 64
Gordon, William, 57-8
Grandchamp, Sophie, 72
Grattan, Henry, 60, 82, 83, 169
Great War, 169, 194
Green, J.R., 146
Greene, Nathanael, 60-1
Griffith, Arthur, 183
Gwynn, Mrs Stephen, 179

Hallam, Henry, 148
Hamilton, Alexander, 61
Hancock, John, 55
Hardy, Thomas, 131, 209-10
Harrington, James, 58, 128, 152
Hegel, G.F.W., 6, 66, 190, 191
Heisenberg, Werner, 208, 212
Henry VIII (of England), 12, 114, 179
Heraclitus, 194
Herbert, George, 137
Herder, Johann Gottfried, 194
historians of 20th century, 271
historical painting, 100-27 *passim*
history, localist, 159
history, total, 5, 120, 202, 216
Hoadley, Benjamin (bishop), 50, 59
Homer, 53, 114
Hooker, Richard, 130
Horace, 62, 207
Horatius (and sons), 103
Howe, Robert, 60
Huet, Pierre-Daniel, 33
Huguenots, 34, 35, 36
Hume, David, 71, 78, 106, 109, 128, 130, 148, 188, 215
Hungerford, Mrs, 95
Huntingdon, Enoch, 58
Hutchinson, Thomas, 56

Hyde, Douglas, 174

Ireland, kingdom of (concept), 2, 14, 20-1
Ireton, Henry, 154
Irish language, 168-9, 172, 205
Isabella (of Spain), 16

Jacobinism, 67, 81, 84
James I (of England), 20
James II (of England), 117
Jansenism, 35, 36, 37
Jefferson, Thomas, 57
John (of England), 214
Johnson, Samuel, 102, 106-7, 128, 130, 137
Joyce, James, 206
Joyce, P.W., 173, 177, 178, 179-80, 181

Kant, Immanuel, 71
Keating, Geoffrey, 12, 13, 17, 18, 119, 121
Keogh, John, 101
Kierkegaard, Søren, 165
Kipling, Rudyard, 131
Kossuth, Lajos, 134

La Mothe Le Vayer, François, 31, 39, 40-1, 45
Landgon, Samuel, 55-6
Langland, William, 130
Lanson, Gustave, 142-3
Laud, William, 161
Laurens, Henry, 60
Lawrence, D. Herbert, 131
Le Fanu, Joseph Sheridan, 90-1
Leavis, F.R., 143
Leibnitz, Gottlieb, 92
Leland, Thomas, 106
Leninism, 68
Lessing, G.E., 102
literary history, 2
Lives of the Saints (Colgan), 23, 24
Locke, John, 107, 110, 128
Lombard, Peter, 12, 23
longue durée, 194
Lorrain, Claude Gelée *dit* Le, 100
Louis XIV (of France), 34, 35, 36, 46
Louis XV (of France), 83
Luther, Martin, 25, 35, 170
Lycurgus, 114

Macaulay, Catherine, 149
Macaulay, T.B., 148-9
Mac Caughwell, Hugh (Aodh Mac Aingil), 15, 25, 26
MacCoghlan, Turlough, 28
MacDonagh, Michael, 170
MacDonald, Ramsay, 151
Machiavelli, Niccolo, 44, 57, 61
Maclise, Daniel, 101
Macmillan, Harold, 161
MacNessa, Concovar, 107
Macpherson, James, 106, 107, 114
Maguire family (of Fermanagh), 15
Mahaffy, J P., 173, 174-5, 178, 179, 183
Maimbourg, Louis, 2-3, 32, 34, 36-8, 41, 42, 47
Mariana, Juan de, 114
Marvell, Andrew, 110, 131
Marx, Karl (and Marxism), 3, 6, 66-7, 68, 72, 151-4, 156, 157, 160, 165, 191, 192, 204
Mather, Moses, 55
May, Tom, 148
Mayhew, Jonathan, 64
Mazarin, G. (cardinal), 35, 88, 92
McCarthy, Justin, 179-80
McCarthy, Michael J.F., 179
McKenzie, John, 54
methodology, historical, 3, 4, 212
Michelangelo, 112, 114
Milton, John, 110, 114, 128, 129, 154, 155, 207, 212-13
Mitchel, John, 170, 171, 172, 181, 182

modernism, 142
Moira, Lady, 117
Molyneux, William, 101, 114, 117
Montaigne, Michel de, 39, 40
Montesquieu, Charles, 111
Montgomery, Richard (general), 62
Moore, Kingsmill, 181
Morley, Henry, 137, 139
Morley, John, 137
Morris, William, 131, 140, 155
Murray, James, 134

Napoleon I (of France), 85, 86, 171
National Education, Commissioners of, 171, 172, 173-4, 175, 178
nationalism, 3-4
nationalism, English, 128-45 *passim*
nationalism, romantic, 99-127 *passim*
Naudé, Gabriel, 45
neo-positivism, 187
New Right, 161, 162
North, Francis (lord chancellor), 92
North, Frederick (Lord North), 56-7
Numa, 114

Ó Buachalla, Breandán, 20
Ó Cléirigh, Micheál, 15, 17-18, 20, 21, 22, 24
Ó Gadhra, Feargal, 20, 28
Ó hEodhasa, Bonaventure, 15, 24, 25, 26
Ó Maolchonaire, Fearfeasa, 24
O'Brien, R. Barry, 179
O'Carolan, Turlough, 125
O'Connell, Daniel, 169, 205
O'Connell, J.J., 175
O'Conor, Charles (jnr), 125-6
O'Conor, Charles, 107, 117, 119, 121, 125, 126
O'Donnell, lordship, 15
O'Donnell, Frank Hugh, 179
O'Donnell, Red Hugh, 15
O'Donnell, Thomas, 170
O'Donovan, John, 20
O'Dwyer (bishop), 181
O'Grady, Standish James, 181
O'Halloran, Sylvester, 106, 107, 119, 121
O'Neill, lordship, 15
O'Neill, Hugh, 14
O'Reilly, Hugh, 28
Oldenberg, Henry, 87
Oldmixon, John, 148
Ortega y Gasset, José, 209
Orwell, George, 143
Otis, James, 56, 57

Paine, Thomas, 52, 54, 55, 131
Paley, William, 128
Palgrave, Edward, 137
Pamphilius, 124
Pasquin, Anthony, 108
Pearse, Patrick, 176
Penn, William, 114, 127
Percy, Thomas, 87
Perrin, Jean, 34-5
Philip II (of Spain), 16
Pico della Mirandola, Gianfrancesco, 33
Pitt, William, 128
place of interpretation (vs setting), 4, 90-3, 95
Plato, 173, 180
Plunkett, William Conyngham, 99
Plutarch, 61, 189
Pole, Reginald, 114, 117
political unconscious, the, 4
Poor, Enoch (general), 61
Pope, Alexander, 128, 129, 137
Poussin, Nicholas, 100
Powell, J. Enoch, 128
Priestley, Joseph, 128

provenance (vs setting), 90-1
public opinion (concept), 71-2
Pym, John, 160

Quincy, Joseph, 49, 50, 55, 63

Racine, Jean, 129, 136
Ranke, Leopold von, 46, 150, 201
Raphael, 114
Ray, Nicholas, 56
Reagan, Ronald, 147
Redmond, John, 205
Reformation, 11, 12, 20, 32-3, 34, 37, 38, 111-12, 171
republicanism, 3-4, 49-65 *passim*, 74, 99-100, 104, 110, 111, 122, 126, 129, 131
revisionism, 159-61, 162
Reynolds, Sir Joshua, 96, 100, 101-2, 103, 108-9, 112, 119, 122, 124
Richelieu (Armand-Jean du Plessis, cardinal), 88
Rinuccini (cardinal), 29
Robertson, Joseph, 215
Robespierre, François-Maximilien-Joseph de, 78-9, 90
Robinson, Mrs, 88
Robison, John, 78, 81
Roland, Jean-Marie, 72
Roland, Marie-Jeanne, 72
Rousseau, Jean-Jacques, 67, 72, 173
Russell, Thomas, 126
Russian Revolution, 67
Ryan, Richard, 118

Scaliger, Joseph, 31
Scathán Shacramuinte na hAithridhe (Mac Caughwell), 26
Schopenhauer, Artur, 187
Scott, Walter, 90, 130, 137, 209
Seeley, J.R., 201
setting, fictional. *See* place of interpretation *and* provenance
Sellar and Yeatman (*1066 and All That*), 146
Sextus Empiricus, 33, 39
Shakespeare, William, 53, 61, 114, 128, 129, 130, 131, 136, 137, 138, 182
Shaw, G.B., 206
Shelley, P.B., 131
Sheridan, R.B., 130
Sherwood, Samuel, 61
Sidney, Algernon, 91-2, 93, 110
Sidney, Sir Henry, 15-16
Sidney, Sir Philip, 91, 92, 93, 128
Sigerson, George, 117
Solon, 114
Somerville, Edith, 206-7
Southey, Robert, 130
Spenser, Edmund, 119, 122, 130
Spinoza, Baruch, 192
St Augustine, 43, 46
St Brendan, 23
St Brigid, 14, 19, 23, 24, 25, 169
St Catherine, 19
St Celsius, 13
St Ciaran, 25
St Colman, 23
St Columbanus, 169
St Columcille, 14, 19, 23, 24, 25, 178
St Francis, 25
St Lawrence, 13
St Malachy, 12, 13
St Patrick, 14, 19, 23, 24, 25, 101, 119, 120-2, 125, 169
Stapleton, Theobald, 28
Starkie, May, 180
Starkie, William, 168, 173, 176, 178, 179, 180, 181, 182
Stephen, Leslie, 138
Strange, Thomas, 28-9
Stuart, William, 87
Stubbs, William, 134
Sullivan, A.M., 171
Swift, Jonathan, 80, 81, 87, 89, 128, 130

Tacitus, 189
Taine, Hippolyte, 69
Talbot, William, 212, 214
Tarquinius Superbus, 104
Thacher, Peter, 55
Thatcher, Margaret, 147, 162
Thiebauld, Dieudonné, 79
Thiers, A., 69
Thou, J.A. de, 35
Tisza, István (count), 205
Tocqueville, Alexis de, 203
Toland, John, 91
Tone, Theobald Wolfe, 99, 101, 126, 170, 176
Trenchard, John, 50, 58
Trevelyan, G.M., 146, 148, 149, 150, 151, 157
Triadis Thaumaturgae (Colgan), 24, 28
Trollope, Anthony, 131
Turnbull, George, 105

United Irishmen, 99, 126
Ussher, James, 11, 12

Virgil, 42
Voltaire, 129, 215-16
Vossius, Isaac, 42

Wadding, Luke, 28
Walker, Joseph Cooper, 117, 119, 120, 122, 124, 125
Walpole, Horace, 130
Walpole, Robert, 87
Walsh, William, 5
Ward, Hugh, 14, 15
Ware, Sir James, 29
Warren, Joseph, 55
Warton, Joseph, 135
Washington, George, 60, 62, 64
Wells, Richard, 55
West, Benjamin, 112, 125
Whately, Richard, 172, 174
Wheatley, Francis, 125
Whitaker, 107
Wieland, Christoph Martin, 78
William, Prince (of Prussia), 79
Wilson, Sir Harold, 161
Wolfe, James, 125
Wordsworth, William, 78, 128, 129, 130, 131, 137
Wyse, A.N. Bonaparte, 174, 181

Yeats, W.B., 177, 210

Zubly, John J., 52-3

II. 20TH-CENTURY HISTORIANS AND OTHER SCHOLARS

Alymer, Gerald, 162
Anderson, Benedict, 133-4

Bailyn, Bernard, 50
Baker, Keith, 67
Baker, Kenneth, 145
Barrell, John, 109
Barthes, Roland, 73
Beaude, Joseph, 41
Best, Geoffrey, 75
Bloch, Marc, 189-90, 194-5, 197-8, 202
Braudel, Fernand, 202, 206, 216
Brown, Peter, 75
Burrow, John, 135
Bury, J.B., 193, 200
Butler, Marilyn, 84
Butterfield, Herbert, 150

Carr, E.H., 193
Clark, Jonathan, 146, 159, 160 161, 162, 165, 166
Cobb, Richard, 70
Cobban, Alfred, 162
Cole, G.D.H., 152
Crick, Bernard, 143

Davis, J.C., 165
Dilthey, Wilhelm, 201
Dunne, Thomas, 7, 108

Eley, Geoff, 160
Elias, Norbert, 72
Elton, Geoffrey, 5, 6, 158
Everett, Alan, 159

Febvre, Lucien, 202
Fletcher, Anthony, 162
Foster, Roy, 175
Foucault, Michel, 67, 70
Freud, Sigmund, 84, 99, 202
Fulbrook, Mary, 160
Furet, François, 67, 68, 73, 162
Fussell, Paul, 141

Gilje, Paul, 58-9
Gramsci, Antonio, 154
Green, Alice Stopford, 170, 181
Greene, Jack, 50

Habermas, Jurgen, 70, 74
Hexter, John, 5, 6, 8, 146-7, 150, 156, 158, 160-1, 163, 165, 211
Hill, Christopher, 151, 153-5, 156, 157, 158, 160, 162, 165
Hirst, Derek, 160
Huizinga, Jan, 203
Hunt, Liam, 160

Jameson, Fredric, 99
Jaurès, Jean, 151
Judson, Margaret, 161

Kenyon, John, 158
Kuhn, T.S., 66

Labrousse, Elizabeth, 35
Ladurie, Emmanuel Leroy, 156
Landes, Joan, 74
Laski, Harold, 152
Laslett, Peter, 158
Lefebvre, Henri, 151

Lyons, F.S.L., 204, 205, 206, 207

McIlwain, C.H., 161
Mandelbaum, Maurice, 5
Maxwell, Constantia, 178, 179, 180, 181
McDonald, Forrest, 59, 61
McDowell, Robert Brendan, 99
Meinecke, Friedrich, 193
Middlekauff, Robert, 50
Morrill, John, 159, 161, 162, 165
Murray, K.M. Elisabeth, 134
Myrdal, Gunnar, 197

Namier, Sir Lewis, 158
Newman, Gerald, 135
Notestein, Wallace, 150, 161

O'Brien, Conor Cruise, 175, 183
O'Farrell, Patrick, 177
Orr, Linda, 69

Palmer, Robert, 71
Patterson, Orlando, 63
Pintard, René, 39
Pitt-Rivers, Julian, 51-2
Pocock, J.G.A., 102
Popkin, Richard, 33
Popper, Sir Karl, 188, 190
Pressly, William, 122

Rabb, Theodore, 159
Ranum, O., 35
Richet, Denis, 162
Ricoeur, Paul, 7
Russell, Conrad, 159, 161, 162

Saussure, Ferdinand de, 68
Sharpe, Kevin, 159, 161
Snow, C.P., 207
Soboul, Albert, 67, 151
Spengler, Oswald, 187, 188
Stanford, W.B., 199
Stone, Lawrence, 146-7, 151, 153, 155-8, 160, 163

Tawney, R.H., 148, 151-2, 155, 156, 157, 158, 162, 165
Trevor-Roper, Hugh, 152, 156, 158, 163, 169
Tyacke, N., 159, 162

Weber, Max, 152, 156, 188
Weber, Samuel, 120
Wedgewood, C.V., 150
White, Hayden, 6, 7, 8
Williams, Raymond, 143
Wood, Gordon, 49, 51
Wright, Patrick, 135

Yazawa, Melvin, 56

Zagorin, Perez, 156